The Political Economy of Environmental Taxes

NEW HORIZONS IN ENVIRONMENTAL ECONOMICS

General Editors: Wallace E. Oates, *Professor of Economics, University of Maryland, USA* and Henk Folmer, *Professor of Economics, Wageningen Agricultural University, The Netherlands and Professor of Environmental Economics, Tilburg University, The Netherlands*

This important series is designed to make a significant contribution to the development of the principles and practices of environmental economics. It includes both theoretical and empirical work. International in scope, it addresses issues of current and future concern in both East and West and in developed and developing countries.

The main purpose of the series is to create a forum for the publication of high quality work and to show how economic analysis can make a contribution to understanding and resolving the environmental problems confronting the world in the twenty-first century.

Recent titles in the series include:

Making the Environment Count
Selected Essays of Alan Randall
Alan Randall

Controlling Air Pollution in China
Risk Valuation and the Definition of Environmental Policy
Therese Feng

Sustainable Agriculture in Brazil
Economic Development and Deforestation
Jill L. Caviglia

The Political Economy of Environmental Taxes
Nicolas Wallart

Trade and the Environment
Selected Essays of Alistair M. Ulph
Alistair M. Ulph

Water Management in the 21st Century
The Allocation Imperative
Terence Richard Lee

Institutions, Transaction Costs and Environmental Policy
Institutional Reform for Water Resources
Ray Challen

Valuing Nature with Travel Cost Models
A Manual
Frank Ward and Diana Beal

The Political Economy of Environmental Protectionism
Achim Körber

The Political Economy of Environmental Taxes

Nicolas Wallart

University of Geneva, Switzerland

NEW HORIZONS IN ENVIRONMENTAL ECONOMICS

Edward Elgar
Cheltenham, UK • Northampton, MA, USA

336.2
WI9p
c.2

© Nicolas Wallart, 1999

Published by
Edward Elgar Publishing Limited
Glensanda House
Montpellier Parade
Cheltenham
Glos GL50 1UA
UK

Edward Elgar Publishing, Inc.
136 West Street
Suite 202
Northampton
Massachusetts 01060
USA

A catalogue record for this book
is available from the British Library

Library of Congress Cataloguing in Publication Data
Wallart, Nicolas.
    The political economy of environmental taxes / Nicolas Wallart.
    (New horizons in environmental economics)
    1. Environmental impact charges. I. Title. II. Series.
HJ5316.W35 1999
336.2—dc21   99–15585
                                          CIP

ISBN 1 84064 185 1

Printed and bound in Great Britain by Bookcraft (Bath) Ltd.

Contents

List of figures   *vii*

List of tables   *viii*

Acknowledgements   *ix*

Introduction   1

PART ONE: WHY ENVIRONMENTAL TAXES?

1. Solutions to environmental problems   9

2. Comparison of instruments   25

PART TWO: MODELS OF ENVIRONMENTAL TAXES

3. Pigouvian taxes and the internalization of external costs   45

4. The twofold rationale of the charges and standards approach   57

5. Other environmental taxes   73

PART THREE: THE ACCEPTABILITY OF ENVIRONMENTAL TAXES

6. Two categories of opposition   93

7. Voting for environmental taxes   109

8. Industry opposition   123

PART FOUR: USING THE TAX REVENUES

9. The possible uses of the tax revenues   137

10. Distributional impact   155

11. Comparison between the different uses   171

Conclusion   189

References   *195*
Index   *207*

List of Figures

2.1   Marginal abatement costs (MAC) and the instrument choice   26

3.1   The optimal production of a polluting good   48

3.2   The optimal level of pollution with an abatement technology   50

5.1   Optimality of a particular type of user charge   82

7.1   Environmental tax and direct voting   112

8.1   Cost of environmental protection instruments for firms   124

9.1   Environmental taxes and the government budget   138

10.1 The choice of the polluters' subgroup   163

List of Tables

2.1   Emission tax   32

2.2   Distribution of free permits   33

2.3   Tax with refund of the tax revenue   34

2.4   Comparison between grandfathered permits and covenant with compensation   37

4.1   Sustainable development and the charges and standards approach   68

7.1   The government does not refund revenues   113

7.2   Lump sum refund to all citizens   115

7.3   Refund to the motorists only   116

8.1   Cost of environmental protection instruments for firms   125

9.1   Main public revenues as percentage of GDP, OECD countries, 1995   148

10.1 Factor intensity and pollution in Swiss economic sectors   169

11.1 Macroeconomic impact and the use of tax revenues   177

Acknowledgements

This book is the result of work that has extended over several years. It would never have come to fruition without the help of many different people. Let me first thank my long time advisor and friend, Professor Beat Bürgenmeier, who has always believed in the author and his research. My thanks also go to Professor Gardner Brown, from University of Washington in Seattle, and Professors Bernard Dafflon, Guy Gilbert, and Alain Haurie. The financing of this research was made possible by the Swiss National Science Foundation, University of Geneva and University of Washington. William C. Christ corrected the style with enthusiasm during long days in Seattle. Last but not least, thanks to Ingrid for her love and constant support.

Introduction

Our economic system attributes a fundamental importance to the price of goods and services. Nowadays prices are the most important reference in production and consumption decisions. If prices are such an essential factor, might they reflect, at least partially, the environmental impact of a product? For example, why is it generally less expensive to replace an object than to repair it, when repair is much more favourable from an ecological point of view? Or why isn't energy more expensive, as this would provide an incentive to conserve it?

In a market economy prices reflect supply and demand. However, except in some particular cases, neither supply nor demand takes into account the environmental impact of a product. If prices on the market did have to reflect the environmental impact, this could only result from an intervention by government, through its environmental policy. This immediately raises two basic issues. The first is the kind of environmental policy the government should implement. The second is the process by which environmental policies could be adopted and implemented.

An environmental policy can take the form of regulations, economic instruments, or a combination of the two. An approach based on regulations, also called a 'command-and-control' approach, has been predominant for a long time in industrialized countries. The objective of this approach is mainly to control existing environmental problems. However, the potential of command-and-control instruments for future improvements is increasingly limited nowadays, because of rising compliance costs, a lack of flexibility, and a shortage of incentives for the development of new environmental technologies.

Given the limits of command-and-control instruments, governments are increasingly turning towards economic instruments, which have been advocated by economists for a long time. The basic appeal of economic instruments is their ability, at least in theory, to achieve an environmental objective in a cost-effective manner, which the traditional command-and-control approach is not able to do. The main economic instruments for environmental protection are taxes and emission permits. Both instruments have been the subject of extensive theoretical literature, as well as some policy experiments. In theory, each instrument is able to achieve a given environmental objective in a cost-effective manner. However, in a policy setting, the two instruments raise totally different problems.

This book deals with environmental taxes. By internalizing the environmental costs associated with the production or consumption of goods, environmental taxes force prices to reflect the environmental impact, which is also compatible with a damage prevention approach. Their basic idea – changing prices according to the environmental scarcity – corresponds to the fundamental mechanism of a market economy. Not only are the advantages of environmental taxes widely recognized among economic theorists, but several experiments have been successful in achieving environmental objectives.

However, when trying to implement environmental taxes, obstacles appear to be numerous. Politicians are often reluctant to propose new environmental taxes that might threaten their popularity. When such proposals are put forward, the political process necessary to adopt and implement the taxes seldom develops without difficulties. As a result, existing taxes hardly ever correspond to the standard textbook model. Indeed, the issue of adopting and implementing a specific environmental tax involves not only complex relationships between the politics and economics of environmental regulation, but also scientific, legal, cultural, and ethical aspects.

When confronting a specific environmental problem, the first issue is the choice of the instrument. What is the best environmental policy in a given situation? To answer this question, we have to compare environmental protection instruments with each other. From an economic perspective, the best instrument will be the one that achieves a given environmental objective at a minimal cost. However, under some conditions, different instruments, particularly emission taxes and tradable emission permits, have the same economic impact. If different instruments can be used effectively in a given situation, in the end the choice of the instrument may have more to do with political, legal, or cultural factors, than with economic aspects.

Once the 'environmental tax' instrument is chosen, the next issue is its definition and objective. What exactly is an environmental tax? In a strict sense, this term refers to the standard textbook tax, which internalizes the external environmental costs (i.e. the Pigouvian Tax, referring to Pigou, 1918). This term may be extended to include the charges and standards approach, as advocated by Baumol and Oates (1988), with which the government sets an environmental standard and then implements a charge in order to achieve it. The term may also be extended to include any tax with a positive environmental impact, such as a water charge covering the cost of waste water treatment, or a deposit-refund system for beverage containers. Finally, as more governments are putting the sustainable development concept on their agendas, the environmental tax may also have the objective of paving the way towards sustainable development.

The issue of the definition and objective of the tax is one of the frequent problems facing practitioners. Much of the theoretical work in the field of environmental taxation is done from the point of view of achieving the greatest possible economic efficiency. On the other hand, practitioners have to take various criteria into account when designing a tax, efficiency being only one of them. Yet, when practitioners try to integrate other aspects into a tax project, this is often done at the expense of efficiency. There is a great need for feasible taxes that do not compromise economic efficiency.

Another problem is that environmental taxes are politically difficult to implement. For example, which presidential candidate would put a gasoline tax hike into his program, even if it were an efficient measure to address pollution or global warming problems? Often, when governments propose an environmental tax, this gives rise to significant protest from affected industries, political parties and even from some ecologists, and the project is ruled out. In order to avoid this, it is necessary to understand the political process by which environmental taxes are actually adopted. Why should people vote for an environmental tax, which they will have to pay since they have voted for it?

Furthermore, for ecologists as well as for many citizens, one important concern is related to the ethical problems of putting a price on the environment, commonly referred to as the 'license to pollute' argument. According to this argument, paying the environmental tax gives the right and the freedom to pollute the environment. This is one of the main obstacles for the adoption of any project: there is hardly ever a discussion about an environmental tax without this argument appearing. However, this problem has not been widely addressed in the literature.

As we will see, in addition to the definition of the tax itself, a contested use of the tax revenues is one of the major causes of rejection. Depending on how the revenues are used, there will be many consequences, not only for the quality of the environment, but also for the income distribution, the allocative efficiency, the size of government, the business cycle, political acceptability, etc. However, this question has not been studied in detail. Most analyses found in the literature are based on simple assumptions concerning the use of tax revenues. One example is the CO_2 tax, the revenues of which are redistributed in a lump sum to the population: this scheme would almost certainly trigger fierce opposition from some industries or household groups that would be heavily affected by the tax.

Without being exhaustive, this sample of problems shows that trying to implement an environmental tax is not an easy task. On the one hand, there seems to be a great potential for environmental taxes in all countries. On the other, governments so often wrestle with the assurances of economists, the opposition from industry and ecologists, the political process, and a lack of clarity regarding what environmental taxes are all about. Nevertheless, many theoretical and practical solutions have already been found, and there are more and more examples of environmental taxes, especially in the northern European countries, which have been successful.

This book may be considered from several perspectives. First, our objective is to present, from an implementation perspective, the underlying arguments of the whole environmental tax issue. In order to do that, the book makes a detailed presentation of the instrument; it clarifies points such as the objective of environmental taxes, their expected distributional effects, and the consequences of possible uses of the tax revenues. In this sense, it provides some guidelines for politicians, civil servants, and people working in the environmental field.

The reader may next consider this book as an integration endeavour: integration of the economic theories relevant for the environmental tax issue, integration of the theory and the practice in industrialized countries, as well as integration of insights from other disciplines. Indeed, because the above-mentioned problems are complex and related, a presentation of environmental taxes cannot be limited to efficiency considerations, but has to include various other aspects, among which distributive and acceptability ones are not the least important. With complex problems an interdisciplinary approach is increasingly necessary. Indeed, the environment is interdisciplinary by definition. As a result of this integration endeavour, this book may also be viewed as a dialogue between academics and professionals.

Finally, the last objective of this book is to present, explain, and provide solutions to some of the problems raised by environmental taxes. In order to do that, the book analyses the possible alternatives and their implications; it takes lessons from existing taxes that have been successful; and it proposes new solutions to some existing problems. One of the most important problems for implementation is political acceptability. Consequently, the book provides a detailed analysis of this issue, in the context of direct and representative democracy. It grapples with questions such as: how do you induce people to vote for environmental taxes? How can opposition from industry be reduced? How do you design instruments that are at the same time economically efficient and politically acceptable?

This book is divided into four parts. *Part one* presents the economic analysis of the environment, and reviews the main existing environmental protection instruments (Chapter 1). It then compares the instruments with each other, and shows under which conditions the different instruments are equivalent, based on the analysis of efficiency and distributive aspects (Chapter 2).

In *Part two,* we present the different types of environmental taxes. We start with Pigouvian taxes, which enable the internalization of external environmental costs (Chapter 3). We show that, more often than not, these taxes cannot be applied in a straightforward manner, and have to be replaced with a charges and standards approach, especially when considering sustainable development (Chapter 4). We also present other types of taxes which play an important role in practice, such as user fees, product charges, and the combination of taxes and subsidies (Chapter 5).

One major difficulty when putting theory into practice is the political acceptability of environmental taxes. *Part three* is devoted to this subject. We argue that acceptability problems arise for two main reasons: on the one hand, for reasons related to a rejection of the market as a means to protect the environment, and on the other, because the environmental protection generates losers (Chapter 6). Next, we adopt a public choice approach and consider the losers, who may oppose a tax project in a democracy. In order to do that, we study the functioning both of direct and representative democracies, and the issue of voting for environmental taxes (Chapter 7). As industry is the main opponent to any environmental tax project, a special chapter is devoted to its problems (Chapter 8). We present some conditions that affect the acceptability of an environmental tax. One of the best ways to increase acceptability is through a judicious use of the tax revenues.

For this reason, the question of the use of the revenues from environmental taxes is addressed in *Part four.* We take a public finance approach, presenting the possible uses, and their implications on economic efficiency (Chapter 9). As they are determining factors for the acceptance of a project, we then analyse the distributional aspects (Chapter 10). In the last chapter, we compare the possible uses, showing how they affect factors such as the size of government, administrative cost, international trade, and economic activity (Chapter 11).

PART ONE

Why Environmental Taxes?

1. Solutions to Environmental Problems

This chapter presents the economic approach to environmental problems, as well as the instruments available to correct economic inefficiencies caused by the presence of environmental externalities. The next chapter will compare these instruments, and will show that, in some cases, they can be defined in such a way that they are equivalent from the point of view of both efficiency and equity.

In economics, different approaches may be applied to the environment. The usual approach is based on the externalities theory, but the environment may also be considered through the property rights or the public goods approach. Here we describe these various approaches, and see how they can be used to solve environmental problems.

1.1 ENVIRONMENTAL PROBLEMS VIEWED AS EXTERNALITIES

Marshall (1890) was the first to introduce the concept of external economies, applying it to the influence that technical knowledge and production volume of small firms have on other similar firms. The existence of external effects explained the concentration of businesses in a certain place. Later, Pigou (1918) formulated this concept more precisely, as a divergence between private and social costs. He was the first to observe that external effects could be positive as well as negative, and to propose means to correct this divergence. He was again the first to choose environmental examples to illustrate the divergence between private and social cost (Faucheux and Noël, 1995, p. 77). The name of Pigou is today associated with the concept of external effects, and their correction by means of a tax.

There is an externality (or external effect) when an action by an individual producer or consumer directly affects the satisfaction or the profit of other parties, without the market evaluating and charging or paying them for this interaction. It is the absence of payment that gives rise to an externality. All economic activities, such as the exchange of goods and services, modify the satisfaction or the profit of other agents. Most of these activities are accompanied by a payment as a counterpart (price, salary, interest, etc.); however, in the case of externalities, no monetary transfer follows this modification. For Pigou, an external effect can also be considered as the difference between private and social cost. Indeed, every economic activity leads to a cost, which he calls the 'social cost'. Part of the social cost (the private cost) leads to a compensating payment; the other part (the external cost) does not lead to a compensation.

Nowadays, the existence of externalities is of increasing importance in many areas. For example, the positive externalities of education, public health (vaccination) and research and development, are widely recognized today. Externalities can also be found in the medical area, where the use of some medicines leads to negative externalities through an increase in the resistance of bacteria or viruses (antibiotics, and also malaria medicines give rise to negative externalities). They can also be found in the social area, where the declining social responsibility of firms often leads to a privatization of benefits and a socialization of costs (examples include dismissals, casualisation, insufficient protection against accidents, etc.). Also, the recent literature mentions the increasing importance of 'network externalities'. These appear when a member of a system benefits when other users join and widen the system (Katz and Shapiro, 1994). They can be found in the area of computers, where the ownership of a computer of a certain type increases the value for others through increased possibilities for data or program exchanges. Network externalities also appear with telephones, credit cards, photography, television, etc. Finally, we have 'environmental externalities', such as pollution.

Why are externalities of increasing importance? One reason is probably technological progress that continuously develops and introduces new products and processes, with uncertain technological and social consequences. Moreover, our societies are characterized by growing complexity, and an increasing number of interrelationships. The market favours anonymous decisions; the fragmentation of competencies makes a global approach increasingly difficult. The tendency of businesses to concentrate increasingly on the net income (the 'bottom line') forces them to set aside all other factors, be they environmental, social, political, medical, or moral, because they only mean higher costs and lower profits. Finally, an analytic approach, in order to remain operational, has to concentrate on the core of the problems, in order to bring the most important mechanisms to the fore. Therefore, one may wonder if externalities are not the consequence of a tendency towards a simplified representation of the world, a representation that sets aside the complexity of the problems.

Environmental externalities are numerous. To a certain degree, they are present in all activities and all economic sectors. Even non-polluting sectors use energy and transportation, and produce waste, which indirectly leads to some pollution. In fact, as has been shown first by Ayres and Kneese (1969), environmental externalities are not an anomaly, but a natural process, which is derived from the law of the conservation of material and energy (the first. law of thermodynamics). Indeed, because of this law, all production processes which use energy or transform materials are responsible for a change in the natural environment, in the form of transformed energy or waste production. Environmental externalities are inherent in economic activities. However, only since the rapid post-war economic growth have these externalities become more apparent and more numerous; and finally they have exceeded the assimilative capacity of the environment in many places. Today, negative environmental externalities amount to several percentage points of GNP in industrialized countries.

Given the external cost of pollution, the private cost is less than the social cost. Therefore, the competitive outcome is not optimal: the production and the consumption of the 'polluting good' will be too large (a polluting good is defined as a good, the production, consumption, or disposal of which is associated with polluting emissions). To attain efficiency, a government intervention[1] may be justified; we will see later how this can be done.

Note that the existence of minor externalities does not necessarily require an intervention, because the intervention itself may be a source of inefficiency: there are not only market failures, there are also government failures. When determining whether the market can solve a problem or the government has to step in, it is not a choice between a perfect market and an imperfect government; neither is it a choice between an imperfect market and a perfect government. Instead, it is a choice between an imperfect market and an imperfect government, and an imperfect combination of the two (Wolf, 1988). Small externalities may be tolerated without government intervention, and only substantial externalities will have to be corrected. In many cases, environmental externalities are substantial, and such an intervention will be necessary.

1.2 ENVIRONMENTAL PROBLEMS VIEWED AS AN ABSENCE OF PROPERTY RIGHTS

In order for an externality to be present, it is necessary for the activity of an economic agent to influence the well-being or the production of other agents, without there being a payment in return. However, in an exchange economy, anything may be exchanged if it is the property of someone. As shown by Coase (1960), in the presence of property rights, and under some hypotheses, there always exists a means by which the parties may negotiate so as to ensure economic efficiency. For Coase, if there is an externality problem, i.e. if economic efficiency is not attained, it is because property rights are not defined. The absence of property rights prevents the trade of goods. For example, if a factory emits large amounts of pollution into a river, it is because the river does not belong to anybody, and nobody is able to protect its rights. Therefore, it is the absence of property rights which is the reason for the externality problem.

The Vittel case is an example of this phenomenon. Various agricultural activities and a source of mineral water exist in the same region. Some of the nitrate fertilizers used by farmers filter through the ground to the spring, which substantially reduces the quality of the water. Therefore, one can wonder whether it is the farmers polluting the source of the mineral water, or the existence of the water producer, which is causing the problem (see Le Moigne and Orillard, 1994). To solve this problem, it is sufficient to assign property rights, either to farmers, or to the mineral water producer.

If the absence of property rights is the source of the environmental problem, the government can assign those rights. Once property rights are assigned, individuals can agree on a reduction in the polluting emissions. If property rights concern a piece of land or a forest, they can be assigned to a private individual. However, in most cases of pollution (air, water, etc.) the environment is a public good. The public nature of the environment raises some difficulties for the applicability of the Coase solution. Indeed, if the environment is public, a negotiation between polluter and polluted leads to large transaction costs, and also to a problem of non-revelation of preferences (free rider). Thus, in the case of clean air, even if property rights are assigned, the number of parties involved makes it impossible to reach an agreement on the level of pollution. The public nature of most environmental goods therefore raises the problem of government intervention again.

Government intervention may also be justified if property rights exist, but have been assigned in a way that society believes is unfair. Indeed, until now environmental resources were generally considered to be in unlimited supply; in the past polluters often appropriated *de facto* environmental property rights. Therefore, today it is often the case that polluters have the right to pollute the environment (even if this right is limited). In this case, with the Coase solution, negotiation will result in the polluted paying the polluter. If such a situation is not viewed as being acceptable to society, the government will have to intervene and define a new allocation of property rights.

1.3   THE ENVIRONMENT VIEWED AS A PUBLIC GOOD

In economics, the non-rivalry of consumption and the impossibility of exclusion define public goods and services.

- Non-rivalry of consumption means that, if one individual consumes a certain good, another person can consume the same good at no extra cost (for example, street lighting or national defence are non-rival).
- Impossibility (or difficulty) of exclusion means that it is not possible (or too expensive) to prevent someone who does not pay from consuming this good.

The environment can have characteristics of public goods or of private goods. There can be excludability: a garden, a lake or a natural park can be enclosed, and become private. There can also be rivalry of consumption, for example, where the interest in a site is due to its pristine nature. However, most often, the environment is a public good. The air, the groundwater, the lakes, and the ozone layer, which protects us from ultraviolet rays, are public goods. For instance, with air, one person who breathes the air will not prevent another from breathing it also, hence there is non-rivalry. There is also impossibility of exclusion, to the extent that nobody can charge a price for the consumption of air. Consequently, if the quality of the air deteriorates, a public good is affected.

The public goods theory mainly concentrates on the conditions of an optimal supply of public goods, as well as on their pricing. Facing the impossibility of excluding someone who does not pay the price, a private firm that wants to provide a public good would be confronted with the 'free rider problem'. This refers to the fact that individuals have no interest in paying for a public good, since they cannot be excluded from its consumption. Consequently, the market alone does not provide a sufficient quantity of public goods. In order to have an optimal supply, the government has to step in, ask citizens for their preferences, and then force them to pay for the provision of public goods.

If the environment is a public good, the problem can be dealt with in a similar way. Here, the public good 'environment' is freely provided by nature; consequently, the concern is not the production of an optimal quantity of this good, but rather the limitation of its degradation in an optimal way, or the restoration of its quality to an optimal level. The protection of the public good 'environment' can be provided by government, as is the case with wastewater treatment plants. However, in the majority of cases (road traffic, emissions from chimneys into the atmosphere, etc.), the polluters themselves are in a better position to reduce polluting emissions and assure a given level of environmental quality; polluters, and not government, are able to prevent the degradation of the public good with clean-up equipment. However, as the environment is a public good, polluters will not have sufficient interest in bearing supplementary costs in order to preserve this public good. The market solution will not be optimal, and the government will have to intervene in order to force polluters to protect the environment.

As we observe, the issue of the environment can be analysed both from the viewpoint of the externalities theory and that of the public goods theory. However, mainstream economic theory treats the environment as an externalities problem. Most textbooks in the area of environmental economics hardly mention the term public good. Two reasons explain this preference for the externalities theory. The first is that public goods can be considered as a particular case of externalities. When the entire society is affected, the external effect becomes a public good (Rosen, 1992, p. 94). For this reason, the externalities theory is more inclusive than the public goods theory. The second reason is the fact that, in the absence of a private solution, implications for policy measures are the same in the case of a public or a private good (Baumol and Oates, 1988, p. 21).

For these different reasons, as an economist it is easy to forget that the environment is a public good, and thus only analyse the issue with the externalities theory. However, the fact that the environment is a public good increases the justification for an intervention by the government. Indeed, if externalities diminish the quality of a public good, the nature of the public good prevents a private solution to the problem. In the environmental area, when externalities involve a public good, only the government is able to correct them.

In addition, choosing a public good approach has important implications for the political process as well as for the design of the instrument. With the usual externalities approach, economists estimate the external costs to humans and the environment, and from that data estimate the level of a corrective tax. On the other hand, the public good approach requires that the political process results in an agreement on a certain level of environmental quality, and from there economists estimate the level of a corrective tax. The process of internalizing externalities is one of a technical nature, whereas the process of deciding the level of a public good is one of a political nature. As a result, the choice of a public goods approach changes the perspective on the environmental issue.

For the time being, let us begin by examining the different solutions to deal with the environmental problems. We first examine to what extent the market may solve the externalities problems (private solutions), then we present the instruments government has at its disposal.

1.4   PRIVATE SOLUTIONS?

In some cases, individual decisions can lead to an optimal solution to the externalities problem, without any government intervention. This is the case with altruism, social pressure, and negotiated solutions.

Altruism and Social Pressure

An altruistic polluter takes into account the well-being of the victims of his emissions. That is, his utility depends on the utility of the victims. With U_1 the utility of individual 1, and U_2 the utility of individual 2, individual 1 is defined as altruistic if:

$$U_1 = f(U_2), \text{ with } dU_1/dU_2 > 0.$$

Environmental policy measures aim to include the utility of the polluted in the utility function of polluters. However, when the polluter is already altruistic, the need for such measures decreases or disappears, since U_1 is already a function of U_2. For example, an altruistic smoker may refrain from smoking when considering his office colleagues; likewise, a business may voluntarily refrain from producing a very polluting good, considering the surrounding population. The group of colleagues may also persuade the smoker to stop smoking for his own health, or promise him compensation in return for his (complete or partial) renunciation of smoking.

   If the polluter is not altruistic, the social group can use the carrot and the stick to try to convince him. Thus, the social pressure of a group of colleagues may prevent a smoker from continuing to smoke. If he persists, he faces the risk of acquiring a bad reputation, i.e. the group will implement social sanctions against the producer of the externalities. Social pressure can also be a threat to businesses. The recent boycott of the Shell Company to prevent the sinking of an oil platform is such an example. Similarly, publishing a list of the biggest polluters of a country may be a sufficient threat to push those at the top of the list to take pollution reduction measures, without any legal action.

   As a result of altruism and social pressure, the utility or profit function of the polluter takes into account the utility or the profit of the polluted. However, these threats are more effective in small groups or small communities. It is easier to be altruistic towards someone we know than towards an anonymous crowd. Therefore, these processes are not easily applied to the complex mechanisms of an economy in which many of the production and consumption decisions are accompanied by external effects. The socialization process is not very effective in solving the many types of externalities that exist in a modern society (Stiglitz, 1988, p. 219). In what follows, we will take the usual economic approach, and suppose that everybody pursues an individual objective of utility maximization, in the absence of altruism and social pressure.

The Coase Theorem and the Negotiated Solution

With externalities, if altruism or social pressure are ineffective, the next step is to know if property rights on the environment exist, and if they can be transferred (bought and sold) between polluters and polluted. In the presence of transferable property rights, Coase (1960) shows that through negotiation, an efficient solution to the externalities problem can be reached, whatever the initial distribution of those rights. This is known as the 'Coase theorem'. The existence of transferable property rights allows polluters to bargain with the polluted so that the optimal outcome is reached. Taking again the example of a factory which pollutes a river, if someone has the right to a clean river, this person will be able to negotiate with the polluter so that he reduces his pollution in return for a payment.

Polluters and polluted will negotiate by themselves if the initial distribution is not optimal; indeed, the gain of a group (polluters or polluted) from the negotiation is greater than the loss of the other.[2] In order for the Coase theorem to be applicable, four conditions have to be fulfilled: (1) the market for the good must be characterized by pure competition; (2) each party in the negotiation should be perfectly informed; (3) there should be no public goods and (4) no transaction costs.

The Coase solution can be applied in different ways that include monetary transfers and compensations, the definition of sharing rules (of a natural resource), as well as the allocation of quotas. The negotiation may even lead to a merger between the producer and the receiver of the externality; this can happen without government intervention if the sum of the two agents' welfare is higher with the merger than without. This merger eliminates the existence of externalities.

The Coase theorem has important implications from an equity viewpoint: the initial assignment of property rights will determine which group will have to pay the other. For example, if the factory pollutes a river where a fisherman earns his living, it will be in the interest of both to negotiate in order to agree on a pollution reduction. This negotiation may end with one of the two following results: either the polluted (the fisherman) pays the polluter to reduce its emissions, or the polluter (the factory) pays the polluted so that he will let the factory conduct its polluting business. The determination of who is going to pay the other will depend upon whether the factory has the right to pollute, or the fisherman has the right to fish. In both cases, the allocation of resources will be optimal. However, the fact that the polluted not only has to tolerate the pollution, but also has to pay the polluter, may be viewed as unfair. We will see in Chapter 5 that the polluter-pays principle is one answer to this equity concern.

With practical environmental problems, the scope of the Coase theorem in solving these problems is strongly limited by the following factors:

- Public goods and imperfect information. As a rule, the environment is a public good; its protection through the market will be insufficient, because of 'free rider' behaviour. For example, in the case of diffuse air pollution, if the factory has the right to pollute, no single inhabitant will want to pay the factory in order for it to reduce or stop its emissions. Furthermore, in order to have a Coase solution, the identification of parties in the negotiation, as well as information on marginal cost and benefit functions, is necessary. More often than not, individuals do not have access to this information. As the government is better organized and has access to better information than individuals, it will be able to act on their behalf.

- Transaction costs. If a polluting factory has to negotiate with many persons, this negotiation will be very expensive, leading to a loss of efficiency. Also, if there are too many agreements, the entry of new producers into this market may be limited by high transaction costs, which limit possibilities of competition. In both cases, the government can increase efficiency by dealing directly with the factory.

- With a Coase negotiation, the historical allocation of property rights has important consequences for income distribution. Often, as environmental goods were free, they were hoarded by polluters. When they were no longer available in unlimited quantities, polluters had *de facto* property rights on the environment. As a result, today, a negotiation to reduce pollution leads to a situation in which the victims have to pay the polluters to have the right to a reduction in the pollution level. This situation may be viewed as unfair, especially because even after the payment, the polluted will still have to endure some pollution.

Furthermore, a negotiation process inevitably entails some power play. Tactics may then play a dominant role. As a result, the outcome of the negotiation is no longer optimal, but depends on the relative power of the parties in the negotiation. If the power is unequally distributed, the negotiated solution will not be optimal, even when conditions would otherwise be ideal (few parties in the negotiation, sufficient information, equitably defined property rights). For all these reasons, negotiated solutions are rarely applicable to the environment.

Faced with significant environmental problems, if altruism or social pressure do not work, if property rights are not defined, if negotiation does not lead to an optimal solution or if the optimum attained is unfair, the government has to intervene. Among the instruments available for environmental protection, economists distinguish between the 'command-and-control approach' (standards, regulations, norms, prohibitions, and prescriptions) and 'economic instruments' (mainly taxes, subsidies, assignment of property rights and emission permits). Let us now present these instruments.

1.5   THE USUAL COMMAND-AND-CONTROL APPROACH

Command-and-control regulations are the main instrument for environmental protection in all countries (OECD, 1989). Regulations aim to obtain a modification of the behaviour of the economic agent with regard to the environment. Regulations can take the form of 'performance standards', consisting either of emission limits for each source, or of concentration limits which request emissions-related measures if the concentration is too high. There are also 'technology-based standards', that specify the technology to be used in the production or the treatment of emissions. For example, the obligation to recycle or incinerate, or the requirement to use the best available technology, are technology-based standards. As a rule, performance standards should be preferred to technology-based standards (Oates, 1985).

When the potential damage to human health or life is serious, regulations totally ban a product or activity. For example, asbestos is now banned in many countries, and the same is likely to happen with chlorofluorocarbons (CFC). However, most command-and-control regulations aim only to reduce emissions by a certain amount, in which case this approach competes with the economic one.

Basically, command-and-control regulations force each polluter to achieve the environmental quality standard, independent of the implied costs. For this reason, there is now plenty of evidence that regulations are not the most cost-effective way to achieve a given environmental objective. In addition, and contrary to economic instruments, the command-and-control approach is fundamentally static: once polluters conform to the existing standard, they are no longer encouraged to achieve a further reduction in emissions (unless they expect stricter regulations in the near future). Today, with rising abatement costs and ever more complex regulations, the potential of the command-and-control approach for future improvements is increasingly limited.

1.6   ECONOMIC INSTRUMENTS

Contrary to command-and-control regulations, economic instruments have the potential to minimize the cost of achieving an environmental objective. In practice, however, there is no clear and satisfactory distinction between command-and-control and economic instruments; most instruments share some characteristics of both. Thus, the OECD (1989) has adopted an enumerating approach. The main economic instruments are: the assignment of property rights, marketable emission permits, taxes (also called charges or fees), and subsidies. Agreements between businesses and the government may also be added to this list.

The Assignment of Property Rights

For Coase, the source of the externality problem is the fact that property rights are not assigned, preventing the pollution from being exchanged like an ordinary good in a market. The government can step in, assigning these rights to push economic players to negotiate according to the Coase theorem. By doing this, the assignment of property rights becomes an environmental protection instrument. Taking the example of the individual who fishes in a river polluted by a factory, the government can either assign to the fisherman the right to a clean river, or assign to the factory the right of polluting the river. As soon as the rights are assigned, the fisherman and the factory can agree on an optimal level of pollution.

As we saw before, many problems greatly limit the potential applications of the Coase theorem for the environment. The assignment of property rights is therefore limited to particular cases. However, it deserves to be considered; indeed, if rights can be assigned once and for all, in a satisfactory manner, the government will never again have to intervene in this problem.

Marketable Emission Permits

The next step is to split the emission rights, and to create an artificial market for them. This is the principle of marketable emission permits.[3] With a permit scheme, the government determines the quantity of emissions for a country, or a region. Then, it distributes the corresponding number of permits to the polluters. Each permit grants the right to emit one unit of pollution during a certain period of time. In order to maximize the efficiency of the system, these permits can be exchanged between the different participants. For example, if the government wants to limit total emissions to 50,000 tons of nitrogen oxides (NO_x) per year, it will distribute 50,000 permits to the firms, each one granting the right to emit 1 ton of NO_x during one year. Businesses can sell permits if reducing their emissions is cheaper than the price of the corresponding permits; conversely, they can buy additional permits if this is the cheaper solution. Provided the market for permits works well, the overall abatement costs are minimized.

In addition to its cost-effectiveness, the main advantage of a system of emission permits is that the regulatory authority can directly control the overall quantity of emissions, instead of trying to control it indirectly through related parameters (such as an emission tax). However, emission permits are not always efficient. Indeed, if the instrument is to be efficient, many conditions have to be fulfilled, with regard to the number and size of participants in the permit market, the risk of pollution concentration, and the costs of administration and control of the system.

Initially, permits can either be sold to existing businesses by means of an auction, or be distributed to them without charge. The way in which permits are initially distributed does not affect economic efficiency, but has distributive implications. It also influences the way in which the environmental policy is perceived, since permits distributed to the polluters without charge can be perceived as society's endorsement of polluting emissions. The following chapter will say more about emission permits.

Taxes, Charges or Fees

Unlike permits that directly limit the quantity of pollution emitted, taxes increase the price of emissions, which will indirectly reduce the quantity emitted. This is a simple application of the law of demand, according to which the higher the price of a good, the smaller its consumption. The same mechanism applies to the pollution: the higher the tax, the smaller the polluting emissions. With a tax, the government has to estimate the level of the tax that will attain the desired emission reduction.

Like the other economic instruments, environmental taxes have the potential to be cost-effective in achieving the environmental objective. They provide flexibility in achieving it: with the tax, each polluter has to choose between reducing its polluting emissions, and paying the tax. Therefore, firms with the lowest abatement costs will take abatement measures, whereas others which have higher abatement costs will choose to pay the tax. In this way, the total abatement cost is minimized (see Chapter 2).

In addition, environmental taxes raise revenues for the government, which can be a significant advantage over the other instruments. (Note that emission permits can also provide revenue if they are auctioned off, but this never happens in practice). Furthermore, environmental taxes raise revenues and, at the same time, correct the economic distortions that arise from not taking the environmental costs into account. On the contrary, ordinary taxes (such as the personal income tax) raise revenues but, by doing so, they generate distortions in the economy. Therefore, environmental taxes have the potential to improve the environment and the tax system at the same time (see Chapter 9). The remainder of the book is devoted to this instrument.

Subsidies

Another instrument at the disposal of the government is a subsidy for polluters who reduce their polluting emissions. For an individual firm, a subsidy brings about the same situation as a tax. Indeed, for the firm, the incentive characteristic of a subsidy is identical to that of a tax: in both cases, the firm incurs a financial loss for each unit of pollution emitted. It is therefore in its interest to decrease its polluting emissions.

However, there are major differences between a tax and a subsidy. One of them is related to equity: in the case of a tax, firms pay an amount to the government, and in the case of a subsidy, they receive a transfer. To many, subsidizing polluters is unfair. Because of this equity concern, subsidies have rarely been adopted. Another difference from a tax is related to the government budget: while a tax provides revenues to the public sector, a subsidy has to be financed. In Chapter 2, we will make a more detailed comparison between taxes and subsidies.

Negotiation between Businesses and Government

If there are few polluting firms, or if they are well organized (for example through a consortium of businesses active in the same sector), the government can negotiate with them, and agree on an emission reduction. Sometimes, fearing an unfavourable new environmental regulation, businesses themselves approach the government and negotiate with it.

Negotiation with the government is not traditionally included in the list of economic instruments, nor is it strictly considered as a command-and-control approach. It is rather an improved version of a regulatory approach (OECD, 1989). However, its great flexibility makes it more closely related to an economic instrument. The negotiation can take two forms:

- It can be a preliminary step towards the elaboration of a regulation, in which case it improves its flexibility and possibilities of application.
- It can also take the form of a voluntary agreement between public authorities and polluters on a reduction of the pollution. In this case, negotiations are made official and can be assimilated to an

environmental protection instrument. These voluntary agreements are called 'covenants'.

In both cases, in order for the negotiation to yield good results, information has to be symmetric and not easily manipulated. Indeed, if asymmetric information exists, the government is often at a disadvantage, having typically less information than the businesses. Those with the best information will obtain a negotiated agreement which results in the lowest costs for them. This means a loss of efficiency which is avoided by other instruments. It is also necessary for businesses to be well organized, to be able to agree on an objective, and to be able to achieve it.

Negotiated solutions are interesting mainly because of the flexibility and the absence of constraints that characterize them. However, because of these very characteristics, some people have serious doubts about their effectiveness and the possibility of measuring their effects (Solsbery and Wiederkehr, 1995).

1.7   OTHER INSTRUMENTS

The last category of environmental policy instruments is neither of the command-and-control type, nor of the economic type. These instruments focus on product information and the modification of behaviour.

Product Information

When a lack of information worsens environmental problems, the government can implement a policy to improve the availability of product information. Indeed, the optimal functioning of a market requires the most complete information on all characteristics of the products exchanged. A lack of information is a cause of market failure. Facing this market failure, the government can intervene to improve the availability of information, and therefore the functioning of the economy.

Sometimes poorly functioning markets have a negative impact on the environment. This is the case with equipment goods (such as automobiles or domestic appliances), which consume energy. With these goods, a lack of information on the energy consumption is a cause of market failure. The government can force manufacturers and retailers of these products to indicate the energy consumption so that the consumer can make his choice with full knowledge of the future implications of his purchase. For example, in the United States, large stickers on new cars and refrigerators indicate their energy consumption, relative to comparable models. The choice of energy-saving products benefits the buyer, and at the same time has a favourable impact on the environment.

Ecological Labelling

Ecological labelling is information on the ecological consequences of the consumption of a product. As the environment is a public good, the choice of more ecological products does not directly benefit the buyer. On the contrary, products with a favourable ecological impact are often more expensive than comparable, less clean products (if this were not the case, firms themselves would market ecological products and there would be no need for government intervention). For this reason, eco-labelling relies on strong environmental ethics. Eco-labelling entails a control cost, as well as complex analysis procedures if the whole life cycle of a product has to be taken into account (Delache and Gastaldo, 1992).

Influencing Moral Attitudes

Besides improving information, the government can attempt to influence moral attitudes by persuading individuals to adopt a favourable behaviour towards the environment (this is also called 'moral suasion'). The point is to push economic agents to think from a social point of view instead of from an individual one. From this perspective, environmental education, from primary school onwards, allows future adults to have a better knowledge and comprehension of the mechanisms according to which nature works. Children who have been environmentally educated at school sometimes persuade their parents to behave in an ecological manner.

Education and persuasion are not without cost. As to their effectiveness, it seems to depend on different factors, such as the environmental problem considered, the urgency of the situation, or social and cultural influences. Thogersen (1994) shows that despite individual costs exceeding individual benefits, Danish people sort their waste because of a sense of moral duty. In other areas, information and persuasion seem to be less efficient than regulations or economic instruments. For example, Diekmann and Preisendörfer (1991) show that environmental information and ecological morale do not influence the heating behaviour of Swiss households.

NOTES

1. How is a 'government intervention' justified in economics? In a democracy, the existence of a government may be explained by the pursuit of a higher individual welfare by its

members. Indeed, in the presence of market failures, the maximization of individual welfare requires a collective intervention in order to produce public goods and internalize externalities. The existence of a government is justified because individuals freely accept a constraint in order to attain a higher welfare. However, individual interest is often in conflict with collective interest. For example, individuals want some production of public goods, even if it is in their individual interest to avoid the payment of taxes, which will enable this production. Therefore, the government has to constrain individuals, so that welfare increases (see for example Van den Doel and Van Velthoven, 1993, p. 77). This explanation is consistent with a microeconomic approach, based on individual preferences.

2. We will see later that if the property rights are not assigned, the government may assign those rights to one group or the other. Once property rights are assigned, the two groups will be able to negotiate in order to attain the optimal level of pollution.

3. The following terms are synonymous: emission (or pollution) rights, permits, certificates.

2. Comparison of Instruments

In this chapter, we compare the main instruments for environmental protection, which we presented in the previous chapter. We first compare the broad category of economic instruments with the command-and-control approach. Then, within the category of economic instruments, we compare taxes with subsidies, taxes with emission permits, and covenants with other instruments. Finally, we present arguments showing that economic instruments and regulations can complement one other, instead of replacing each other.

2.1 ECONOMIC INSTRUMENTS VERSUS COMMAND-AND-CONTROL APPROACH

In order to compare economic instruments with regulations, we take two firms, A and B, each one emitting an equal quantity of a pollutant (for example, each firm emits 1,000 kilos of NO_x per year). Each firm has a marginal abatement cost function; this function represents the additional cost incurred to reduce the polluting emission by one unit (for example, the cost of reducing the NO_x emission by 1 kilo per year).

As usual, marginal abatement cost functions have a positive slope. This means that, if it is relatively inexpensive to reduce emissions at the beginning, the more emissions are reduced, the more costly it becomes to abate additional units of pollution. For example, at the beginning, emissions can be reduced for a cost of \$1 per kilo of NO_x reduced; later, as the least costly options have been exhausted, the cost may increase to \$5 per kilo of NO_x reduced.

Let us suppose that the marginal abatement cost (MAC) functions are different for the two firms. Indeed, there is no reason for them to be identical. Here, the MAC is smaller for firm A than for B (see Figure 2.1). In the figure, the polluting emission (e) is measured from left to right, and the emission abatement from right to left. The total abatement cost is represented by the area situated under the marginal cost curve (it is equal to the sum of the costs for each unit of pollution reduced).

Let us suppose that the goal is to reduce the overall polluting emissions by half. This emission reduction has to be allocated between the two firms. The choice of the instrument will determine the individual abatement for each firm, as well as the overall cost to the economy.

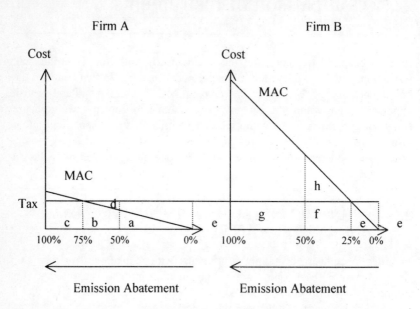

Figure 2.1 Marginal abatement costs (MAC) and the instrument choice

Uniform Regulation

Let us first examine the case in which the government has no information on the cost functions of the firms. It introduces a uniform regulation, which compels each firm to reduce its emissions by 50%. The total emissions will be equal to the objective, which is half the initial emissions. In Figure 2.1, the abatement cost will be equal to area (a) for firm A, and area ($e+f+h$) for firm B. The total cost for the economy is ($a+e+f+h$).

However, this is not the cheapest solution for achieving the objective of half the initial emissions. Indeed, as shown in the figure, with this solution marginal abatement costs (MAC) are not equal for the two firms. Thus, it would be less costly, from a global point of view, if A reduced its emissions a little more, and B a little less. If A decreases its emissions by 75%, and B by only 25%, the total emissions would be the same, but the overall abatement cost would be smaller. It would be equal to only ($a+b+e$), which is smaller than the previous cost of ($a+e+f+h$). More generally, it can be shown that, in order for the total abatement cost to be minimal, firms have to reduce their emissions up to the point where their marginal abatement costs are equal.

Perfectly Differentiated Regulation

Suppose now that the government knows the MAC functions of both firms exactly; it will be able to impose a perfectly differentiated regulation, according to which A has to reduce its pollution by 75%, and B by 25%. In this situation, marginal abatement costs are equal for both firms. Therefore, the total abatement cost will be minimized.

The comparison between a uniform and a perfectly differentiated regulation shows that, with the regulation, abatement costs will only be minimized if the government knows the cost functions of each firm, and is able to impose perfectly differentiated standards. Information needs are important; it may be in the interest of firms not to give this information to the government, or to give misleading information; moreover, it may be difficult for a government to justify a different treatment for each firm. For all these reasons, in practice, regulations do not minimize environmental protection costs. They may come close to this minimization, when the information is shared by firms and the government, and when there are few firms; but regulations that try to minimize costs are very complex.

Economic Instruments

With economic instruments, marginal abatement costs are equalized; therefore, total abatement costs are minimized. For example, with a tax, each firm reduces its emissions exactly to the point where a supplementary reduction is more expensive than the tax payment. In the figure, A reduces its emissions by 75%. If it reduces them by a smaller amount, paying the tax will be more expensive than reducing the pollution a little more; and if it reduces them too much (for example, by totally suppressing all emissions), that will be more expensive than paying the additional tax between 75% and 100%. For firm B, the mechanism is the same, and it will be in B's interest to reduce its emissions by exactly 25%. As we see in the figure, marginal costs are equalized, and thereby total abatement costs are minimized.

Cost minimization is one great advantage of economic instruments in comparison to regulations. Taxes, subsidies, and emission permits share this characteristic. Beyond the cost of environmental protection, there are other differences between economic instruments and regulations:

- Distributive aspects are different. With a standard, the cost for the polluter is limited to the cost of reducing its emissions. With economic instruments, there is an additional monetary transfer, which can be positive, or negative.

- When there is an emergency, only regulations are able to deal with the situation, while economic instruments are more propitious to long-term actions.
- Economic instruments make relatively modest informational demands on the regulatory authority (Oates, 1985). If, on the contrary, standards are to take abatement costs into account, the informational demands are very high.
- Economic instruments give polluters an incentive to reduce their emissions more and more, through research-development and technological innovation; with regulations, polluters have a tendency to be content with the level attained, and regulations have to become increasingly restrictive in order to avoid that.

In practice, differences between regulations and economic instruments are not so clear-cut. Regulations are often defined in such a way that they take cost differences into account, which makes them closer to economic instruments. Moreover, when the government does not have sufficient information, it may discuss or even negotiate regulations; this will increase the flexibility of regulations, and improve their acceptability (OECD, 1989). On the other hand, economic instruments, in order to be implemented, also have to make compromises; this decreases their efficiency and makes them closer to regulations.

2.2   TAXES VERSUS SUBSIDIES

Taxes and subsidies are two economic instruments which are capable of inducing firms to reduce their emissions to the same level. As seen in the preceding section, if the government imposes a tax on the polluting emission, each producer reduces its emissions up to the point where the marginal abatement cost is equal to the tax (Figure 2.1). Now, suppose that the government gives producers a subsidy for each unit of pollution reduced, compared to the initial pollution. This subsidy will increase the marginal cost of the emission in exactly the same way as the tax: if the producer wants to increase its emissions, he will have to give up part of the subsidy. If the level of the subsidy is the same as the level of the tax, both cases will result in the same level of pollution.

In this first analysis, taxes and subsidies lead to the same result. However, this comparison is rather restrictive, being made only from an allocative point of view, in the short term, and in a partial equilibrium framework. If we go beyond this restrictive framework, significant differences do exist. All these differences make taxes more favourable:

- When an abatement technology is available, the two instruments are not equivalent. By subsidizing abatement activities, the government reduces the marginal production cost of firms, which will give them an incentive to increase their production beyond the optimal level. Taxes, on the contrary, reduce the production of polluting goods.
- Subsidies increase the revenue of producers, which in the long term will bring new producers into this market. Overall, subsidies may in fact increase the pollution! On the other hand, by increasing their production costs, taxes may eliminate some producers, hence less pollution.
- Whereas taxes raise revenues for the government, subsidies have to be financed. In order to finance the subsidies, one solution is to increase other taxes, for example, income taxes, or sales taxes; however, most taxes cause economic distortions, and increasing them will increase the distortions in the economy.

Distributive aspects are also fundamentally different for the tax and the subsidy. In the case of the tax, the polluter has to bear the emission abatement costs, as well as pay the tax on the remaining emissions. In the case of the subsidy, he also has to bear the abatement costs, but he gets a subsidy from the government. Overall, he may even make a profit. Thus, firms will be better off with the subsidy than with the tax. However, it may be difficult, from a moral point of view, to subsidize a polluter. Also, subsidies depart from the polluter-pays principle (see Chapter 5).

Overall, subsidies suffer many drawbacks in comparison to taxes. If subsidies are used, it is because they are appealing to the industry, which does not have to bear the same cost increase as with other instruments. Therefore, the political acceptability from industry is high. However, we will see that other economic instruments can also be acceptable to industry.

2.3   TAXES VERSUS EMISSION PERMITS

Taxes and emission permits (hereafter permits) are the main economic instruments for environmental protection. Here we will examine their main difference, which is the control of prices versus the control of quantities. We will then show that the main advantage of permits, the reduced burden on the polluting industry, disappears when an appropriate refund of the tax revenue is considered.

Prices versus Quantities Control

Taxes limit pollution through an increase in prices, and permits through a limitation of quantities. From an allocative point of view, we know that, without uncertainty and administrative cost, both instruments result in the same emission reduction, and at the same cost. However, as soon as there is an uncertainty with respect to cost and benefit functions, one instrument becomes preferable.

With uncertainty, increasing prices and limiting quantities are not equivalent any more. For a given externality, the best instrument will depend on the relative slopes of the benefit and cost functions (Weitzman, 1974). The tax will be a better choice if the marginal damage curve is relatively flat, and the marginal abatement cost (MAC) curve is relatively steep. Conversely, permits will be the better instrument if the marginal damage function is steep and the MAC is relatively flat.

A steep marginal damage function characterizes some toxic effluents and wastes, which can be very harmful if a certain threshold is passed. In this case, setting a tax too low can result in the threshold being exceeded; emission permits are a better instrument, because they directly control the quantity emitted. The advantage of a permit system is that the pollution reduction is known in advance (although the cost is unknown). Permits are also attractive for the regulatory agency, because of this direct control on the quantity of emissions. On the other hand, when the damage curve is not so steep, more attention should be paid to the MAC curve. A system of emission permits may impose very high costs on the economy if the number of available permits is too small. Taxes do not pose this problem, because the maximum cost to the polluters is known in advance, and is equal to the tax.

In practice, low-cost clean-up measures have already been taken in industrialized countries. Most studies show that we are now operating along rapidly rising segments of MAC curves (Oates, 1990). This suggests that in the future, errors are likely to be more costly with a permit system, than with a tax one.

However, the theoretical distinction between prices and quantities is not so clear-cut in practice. Many existing taxes also incorporate a 'quantity' feature:

- Many environmental taxes are based on the 'charges and standards approach'. With this approach, the government sets an environmental quality objective (i.e. a quantity objective); then, the tax level necessary to attain this objective is estimated (see Chapter 4). Whereas taxes are a price instrument, a charges and standards approach is closer to a quantity instrument.

- Some taxes are combined with regulations, such as the American CFC tax: the tax gives the necessary incentive, but a regulation ensures that a certain (quantitative) production level will not be exceeded. The regulation may be viewed as insurance against the limitations of the tax in the presence of uncertainty.
- Some taxes are also set with the possibility of increasing their level, if they are not effective enough in reducing the quantity of emissions. In this case, we have a price instrument, with a quantity in mind. This is the case with the Swiss tax on volatile organic compounds (VOC).

These 'quantity' features ensure that, in the presence of uncertainty and lack of information, the cost due to the choice of the wrong instrument will not be too high. For the same reason, emission permits may also incorporate some 'price' features, such as a reserve of permits which can be used, should the price of the permits reach an unacceptably high level.

Distributive Consequences

A traditional argument against taxes is that polluters not only bear the costs of abatement, but they also have to pay the tax on their remaining emissions. This seems to be a compelling argument, since the tax payments can be as high as 10–15 times the abatement costs! However, as we will see, this is a flimsy argument, since the tax payments can be refunded to the polluters.

With emission permits, distributive consequences will vary according to whether pollution rights are initially sold to the polluters, or distributed without charge according to past emissions, a system called 'grandfathering'. If emission permits are sold to the polluters by means of an auction, it can be shown that distributive consequences are exactly the same as with an emission tax (see for example Barde, 1992, p. 301); in a static approach, and in the absence of uncertainty and transaction costs, a tax is equivalent to auctioned emission rights. On the other hand, with grandfathered permits, polluters will not pay anything to the government in compensation for the pollution emitted. Therefore, the distribution of free permits lowers the environmental protection cost for businesses; it also increases its political acceptability (Baumol and Oates, 1988, p. 179).

However, if emission permits seem to be politically more attractive than emission taxes, it is because the tax revenues have not been considered. We will consider them now, and compare, in a partial equilibrium framework, the distributive consequences of (1) an emission tax, (2) free emission permits, and (3) a tax with lump sum refund of the tax revenue. In order to do that, we will use the same figure that we used to compare regulations and economic instruments (Figure 2.1).

1. The tax

Suppose that the government imposes a tax on polluting emissions. Firm A will reduce its emissions up to the level at which a supplementary reduction will be more expensive than the tax, which is a 75% reduction. Firm B will act similarly and reduce its pollution by 25%. The government will receive the tax revenue, amounting to $(c+g+f)$. If the tax is set to the level of the marginal external cost, resources will be allocated optimally. In this example, the total pollution is decreased by half.

With the tax, firms are the big losers. Not only do they have to bear the abatement costs, they also have to pay the tax on the remaining emissions. The government is the big winner, since it gets the tax revenue. Distributive consequences for the two firms and for the government are presented in Table 2.1.[1]

Table 2.1 Emission tax

	Emission abatement cost	Tax	Total
Firm A	-a-b	-c	-a-b-c
Firm B	-e	-f-g	-e-f-g
Government	--	+c+f+g	+c+f+g
Total	-a-b-e	0	-a-b-e

2. Distribution of free permits

Permits can be granted according to different criteria, but distributing an equal quantity of permits to each polluting firm makes no sense. In the United States there are several examples of permit systems, such as the control of national SO_2 emissions or the control of effluents in the Fox River in Wisconsin; those permits have been distributed in proportion to past emissions (grandfathering). As past emissions are not modifiable, such a distribution takes on a lump sum character. Any other distribution that would influence the marginal costs of firms would have an impact on their choices, and would therefore lead to a non-optimal situation. In our example, with the hypothesis of a proportional distribution according to past emissions, each firm would receive permits granting the right to emit 50% of the initial pollution.

If each firm reduces its emissions by half, total emissions will also be reduced by half (this corresponds to the reduction level achieved with the tax). However, individual emissions corresponding to the initial distribution of permits, i.e. 50% for A and 50% for B, are not optimal, since marginal abatement costs are different. It will be in the interest of the firms to exchange permits until their marginal costs are equal. This will happen if A reduces its emissions by 75% and B by 25%. The price of the permit will be equal to the level of the tax.

For the firms, private costs are much smaller than in the case of the tax. For firm B, the cost is equal to $(e+f)$, which is smaller than the cost $(e+f+g)$ incurred with the tax. For firm A, the cost is also smaller $(a-d,$ vs. $a+b+c)$; firm A may even make money from the environmental protection if $a<d$.[2] A tax will never lead to this result. On the other hand, as permits are distributed free, the government will not get any revenue. Distributive implications of this emission permit scheme are presented in Table 2.2.

Table 2.2 Distribution of free permits

	Emission abatement cost	Sale / Purchase of permits	Total
Firm A	-a-b	+b+d	-a+d
Firm B	-e	-f	-e-f
Government	--	--	0
Total	-a-b-e	0	-a-b-e

Note: In the figure, area f is equal to area $(b+d)$.

3. Tax with refund of revenues to polluters

If the government wants to refund the tax revenue to polluters, different possibilities exist. It may refund the same amount to both firms. It may also refund according to any other criterion, such as the number of employees, the capital, the sales, etc. To make comparison with the permits scheme, we will look at a particular refund: for each firm, the refund is proportional to its initial emissions (it corresponds therefore to the amount implicitly granted by means of a distribution of free permits, which is also proportional to the initial pollution).

This refund is considered a lump sum by firms. It should not influence their choice (similarly, freely granted emission permits should not give an incentive for firms to pollute more, solely in order to obtain more permits). In our example, as the initial level of emissions was the same for both firms, each one will receive the same amount, i.e. $(c+b+d)$, which is also equal to g_3. It can be verified that the total amount refunded is equal to the tax revenue. The welfare analysis is modified as in Table 2.3.

Table 2.3 Tax with refund of the tax revenue

	Emission abatement cost	Tax	Revenue refund	Total
Firm A	-a-b	-c	+c+b+d	-a+d
Firm B	-e	-f-g	+g	-e-f
Government	--	+c+f+g	-c-b-d-g	0
Total	-a-b-e	0	0	-a-b-e

Note: Area f is equal to area $(b+d)$.

As shown in Tables 2.1–2.3, the allocative consequences are identical in the three cases studied here (the total surplus variation, which is the total abatement cost of the pollution, is identical in all cases and equal to a-b-e). As for distributive implications, they are identical in the case of the tax with refund of revenues to polluters, and in the case of grandfathered permits.

This conclusion is not counter-intuitive: to the extent that the allocation of resources is identical in both cases, it is always possible to find a refund of the tax revenue that has the same distributive impact as emission permits. Because this refund is considered by each firm as a lump sum, it will have no impact on the allocation of resources; it will only have a distributive impact. *When tax revenues are refunded to polluters, distributive differences are no longer an argument in favour of one or the other instrument. The instruments 'tax + refund' and 'grandfathered emission permits' become equivalent from an allocative and from a distributive standpoint.* Therefore, both instruments should achieve the same political acceptance.[4]

Other Factors

Other factors distinguish taxes from tradable permits, especially in the long term:

- The level of the tax has to be regularly adjusted in order to keep up with economic growth and inflation; in contrast, with permits, the equilibrium price of the permit will automatically take growth and inflation into account (advantage of permits). However, if economic growth is strong, a shortage of permits can occur, which will considerably increase their prices and even give rise to speculation (advantage of the tax).

- In practice, markets for emission permits do not function smoothly; permits are not traded as much as they should be in order to maximize the cost savings. Some firms take advantage of their dominant position and monopolize permits. A well-designed system of taxes does not present this problem (advantage of the tax).
- One additional argument against emission permits is that they create an artificial shortage that is more characteristic of a war economy than of a market economy. For example, if CO_2 emissions of vehicles are limited by means of a tradable permits system, each motorist would receive gasoline coupons in a limited number at the beginning of the month (or year). Such a process may call to mind the food stamps that were used in some countries during World War II; it would certainly not be popular. Tradable permits are more feasible for firms, since in most countries firms have anyway to obtain an emission authorization from the government.

Finally, as we will see in Chapter 6, there are other reasons, of an ethical and cultural nature, that differentiate the instruments and influence the choice.

2.4 COVENANTS VERSUS OTHER INSTRUMENTS

Voluntary agreements between polluting firms and authorities can be found in the area of waste recycling, the reduction of the use of some substances (phosphates, CFC), or the progressive withdrawal of some types of packaging. One particular type of voluntary agreement is called a 'covenant'. A covenant is an agreement between polluting firms and the government, which defines a certain reduction in polluting emissions. We will see that, from an economic point of view, covenants are similar to the assignment of free emission permits.

In order to be effective, a covenant requires a well-defined group of polluting firms. If they are organized in an association or consortium, the government can negotiate with this association and agree on a maximum level of polluting emissions. Such a covenant is a straightforward solution for the government, which does not have to worry about distributive implications, or tax revenues. However, for businesses, this is not so easy: How will firms distribute emission reductions? Should they compensate those with higher abatement costs? How can they agree on a fair reduction?

Three solutions are possible: (1) all firms reduce their emissions by the same proportion; (2) firms reduce emissions until the marginal abatement costs (MAC) of the pollution are equal; and (3) firms reduce emissions until their MAC are equal, and compensate each other.

Reduction of Emissions by the Same Proportion

Each firm reduces emissions by the same proportion, for example, 50% as in
the previous examples. If firms abide by the agreement, this leads to exactly
the same result as with a uniform regulation, with which the government does
not have the necessary information to differentiate firms according to their
costs. As we have seen in the regulation case, this solution is not efficient.

In fact, if firms negotiate with the government, it is precisely in order to
avoid the uniform and rigid emission reductions associated with a regulation.
The solution presented here will therefore not be chosen by the firms. On the
contrary, it will be in their interest to negotiate with each other until their
marginal abatement costs are equal.

Equalization of Marginal Costs (Without Compensation)

Firms which are part of a covenant generally attempt to take their MAC into
account. Firms with the lowest marginal abatement costs reduce their
emissions by a greater proportion than others, but without any financial
compensation from the other firms for this supplementary reduction. Going
back to Figure 2.1, firm A would ideally reduce its pollution by 75%, and
firm B by 25%, in such a way that marginal abatement costs are equal for
both firms.

This situation is identical to the one in which the government has access
to complete information, and is therefore able to implement a perfectly
differentiated regulation, with which the individual level of abatement
depends on marginal costs. However, a substantial problem exists with this
solution. With a covenant that equalizes marginal abatement costs, for firm A,
the cost increases by an amount equal to area $(a+b)$, while with a uniform
reduction of the pollution, it increased only by (a). It is therefore in the
interests of firm A to oppose this system, and to encourage the adoption of a
uniform regulation which is more favourable to A. Firm A will not want to
participate in the covenant.

For this reason, we examine a third system, in which it will be in the
interests of both firms to participate.

Equalization of Marginal Costs with Compensation

Here, firms equalize their marginal abatement costs; but as firm A reduces its
emissions proportionally more than B, it receives a financial compensation
for this supplementary effort.[5] In order for A to agree to reduce its emissions
more than B, the compensation has to be at least equal to the cost increase,
that is, at least equal to area b in Figure 2.1 (this amount is equal to the
difference between the total abatement cost with a uniform regulation and

with an equalization of marginal costs). This compensation has to be financed by firm B.

Now consider firm B. If the compensation it has to pay is greater than $(f+h)$, B will prefer to decrease its emissions by a supplementary 25% (i.e. from 25% to 50%), rather than to pay this compensation. This means that it will prefer a uniform regulation to this covenant. In order for the two firms to reach an agreement, the compensation will have to be an amount between (b) and $(f+h)$. Now suppose that the compensation paid by firm B to firm A is equal to area $b+d$ (which is also equal to area f). This compensation scheme will be accepted by both firms. It is based on an implicit unit price of emissions, which is the same for both firms. The compensation corresponds exactly to the amount involved in the purchase or sale of emission permits.

With this particular type of covenant, for the firms, the situation corresponds to the grandfathered permits scheme from the preceding section (Table 2.2). In both cases, the individual emission levels are the same; and the compensation required by the covenant corresponds exactly to the purchase and sale of the permits. Table 2.4 compares the two instruments.

Table 2.4 Comparison between grandfathered permits and covenant with compensation

Grandfathered permits		Covenant with compensation	
The government		The business association	
	issues X permits		agrees with the government on a maximum overall emission of X
the firms		the firms	
	receive the permits, determine if they have too many or too few of them;		receive individual emission reduction targets;
	and buy or sell permits.		and compensate each other.

Although their economic impact is similar, there are significant differences between the two instruments. From a judicial standpoint, emission permits require a law, whereas covenants are only a contract between the environmental agency and the business association. As a result, the consequences of non-compliance are different. In the case of emission permits, the government issues the permits and is responsible for ensuring that no firm pollutes without the corresponding number of permits. In the covenant case, the business consortium may be given the responsibility of ensuring that all members respect their obligations. Indeed, the temptation for firms to behave as 'free riders', and not reduce their emissions, is strong. In order to be successful, covenants require that there are relatively few firms, and that a trusting relationship exists between firms, the consortium, and the government. For this reason, covenants are mainly found in small countries.

Giving firms a greater responsibility may also lead to some abuses if a firm misuses its dominant position inside the association, or adopts a strategic policy to take maximum advantage of the system. In this case, other instruments may be preferable. Another difference stems from a possible failure to respect the agreed objective. With permits, the firm which pollutes more than its permits allow is subject to an individual fine. On the other hand, with the covenant, there is a collective responsibility. All the participating firms will have to suffer the consequences of the non-compliance of one firm, for example, through the introduction of an emission tax or a stricter regulation.

2.5   ECONOMIC INSTRUMENTS: A SUBSTITUTE OR A COMPLEMENT TO REGULATIONS?

When trying to implement taxes or other economic instruments, the following question always arises: is it better for taxes to replace or to complement regulations? Generally, economic instruments cannot work without being accompanied by a regulatory framework. Regulations may make the taxes more focused, or may suppress some of their undesirable effects. The tax can also be a means to give polluters an incentive to reduce their emissions beyond the level fixed by the regulation. In this case, the regulation is maintained, and the tax provides a supplementary incentive.

In comparison with a unique instrument, a combination of instruments will often allow a better environmental quality at a given cost, or, alternatively, the same environmental quality at a smaller cost:

- When the localization of the pollution is a consideration, a uniform tax cannot differentiate between places, such as the pollution in the city centre and in the countryside. In order to do that, it will often be necessary to use several instruments, for example, a tax accompanied by a regulation ensuring a minimal level of environmental quality everywhere. Preserving an existing regulation, or even an older one, avoids the appearance of 'hot spots' (significant pollution in some locations).

- Because of the uncertainty of its impact, a tax can be profitably complemented by a regulation. For example, in the United States, the tax on ozone-depleting chemicals has been accompanied by a quantitative cap that has reassured those who did not trust the price mechanism (Fullerton, 1996).
- A combination of tax and regulation provides more flexibility, as each instrument can be adjusted over time to attain the targeted objective (Brown and Johnson, 1984).
- A combination of tax and regulation is advantageous in a decentralized system, where each level of government has limited decision-making power. Brown and Johnson (1984) thus assert: 'more policy instruments are better than less'.
- Following the Tinbergen rule (Tinbergen, 1952), each instrument should be assigned only one objective. If there is more than one environmental objective, more than one instrument will be needed. For example, in the case of road traffic, a gasoline tax cannot simultaneously address the problems of CO_2, NO_x, VOC, O_3, particulates, lead, noise, and congestion. More than one instrument is needed.
- Giving up existing regulation when introducing a tax may induce undesired substitutions. For example, with automobiles, a policy aiming at the reduction of one pollutant may lead to the increase of another one; therefore, if the existing regulation is abandoned when introducing a tax, an increase in the emissions of some pollutants may be the result (Wallart, 1997).

Instruments other than regulations may also be used in addition to the tax. For example, a policy of household waste reduction may simultaneously combine a tax on garbage bags with education, persuasion, and the providing of recycling facilities. However, if a tax is efficient, it will bring about an evolution towards cleaner technology, which in the end makes existing regulations unnecessary.

2.6   SUMMARY AND CONCLUSION

In economics, the environmental problem may be viewed from the standpoint of the public goods theory, the externalities theory, or the property rights approach. The common approach of treating the environment as an externality to production and consumption leads directly to the 'Pigouvian tax' instrument. However, a different perspective on the instrument can be taken by considering the environment as a public good, of which a certain quantity, or quality, is produced as the result of a political process.

The comparison between environmental policy instruments leads to the following conclusions. In the absence of uncertainty and transaction costs, there is equivalence between:

- auctioned emission permits;
- an emission tax.

The following instruments are also equivalent:

- a tax, the revenues of which are refunded to the polluters, in proportion to their past emissions;
- a system of marketable emission permits distributed without charge, in proportion to past emissions;
- a covenant between the government and polluting businesses, under which businesses compensate each other for their cost differences.

All these instruments minimize the overall emission abatement cost. Even though their basic ideas are very different, they have similar economic effects. From a political economy perspective, the main difference between them, which is the distributive impact on firms, does not remain when appropriate redistributions are considered. Once this is acknowledged, attention can be focused on the other differences which are relevant from an implementation perspective, such as the instrument choice in the presence of uncertainty, or the detailed definition of the instrument. In the third part of the book, we will see that, beyond those economic aspects, cultural and judicial traditions also influence the instrument choice. This last element will be all the more important when the economic impact of the instruments is similar.

In the long term, especially from a sustainable development perspective, technological progress is crucial to the solution of environmental problems. In this respect, the long-term adaptation of businesses to environmental protection instruments is probably much more important than the short-term impact of the instruments. More than regulations, economic instruments provide long-term incentives for the development of more effective environmental technologies. Milliman and Prince (1989) show that taxes and auctioned emission permits are the two most effective instruments for promoting technological change, because they give innovative firms the greatest financial advantage if they engage in R&D activities. Since, in practice, emission permits are not auctioned off but rather distributed without charge, it seems that, in practice, taxes are more likely to provide the necessary long-term incentives for technological progress.

NOTES

1. Note that the total indicated in the table is negative. This does not mean that the emission tax is not efficient, but only that, for the distributional analysis, we did not take into account the benefits of a reduction in the pollution, which are greater than the abatement cost.
2. This may happen if marginal abatement costs differ significantly between the two firms.
3. The same result is obtained in the more realistic case in which the initial pollution is different for each firm. The essential point here is that, in order to obtain the same distributive impact as with freely granted permits, the tax revenue has to be refunded according to the same rule as the initial distribution of permits.
4. With the refund of the tax revenue to polluters based on past emissions, not only does the distributive impact become similar to that of grandfathered permits, but some of the problems of grandfathered permits also arise. For example, the distribution of free permits causes equity problems. Indeed, a firm that would have made an important effort to reduce its emissions in the past would not receive more permits than another that made no such efforts; the first firm would therefore be penalized. Moreover, a new firm which enters the market will have to buy permits, while the old ones got them free. These equity problems also exist with a tax whose revenues are refunded to polluters. Indeed, in order to have the same distributive consequences as permits, the tax revenue has to be distributed in the same manner as the grandfathered permits. Polluting firms would get a refund proportional to past emissions; new firms would not get any refund, and firms which have undertaken an important reduction effort in the past would not receive a refund that takes their efforts into account. Some firms would therefore be penalized in the same way as with grandfathered permits. On the other hand, firms exiting the industry would continue to get the refund forever. However, in practice, it should be possible to design creative mechanisms that limit those problems, as has been done in the implementation of emission permits.
5. Although not very widespread, such a system exists in the Netherlands, where firms compensate each other for differences in their abatement costs.

PART TWO

Models of Environmental Taxes

3. Pigouvian Taxes and the Internalization of External Costs

3.1 INTRODUCTION

Environmental taxes, or green taxes, are generally classified according to their tax base. We have (OECD, 1989):

- Emission charges, or emission taxes, are levied on polluting emissions. The tax base is the pollution emitted.
- Product charges, or taxes, are used for products or equipment when their consumption, utilization, production, or destruction, result in pollution. Here, the tax base is not an emission but a product. There are particular cases of product charges. Tax differentiation increases the price of products which are harmful to the environment, when other less polluting products exist; this instrument can be applied to products, which are close substitutes, when their environmental impact is different. Deposit-refund systems increase the price of some products when they are not disposed of in an environmentally appropriate manner.
- The objective of user fees, or user charges, is to finance some public services related to the environment. The tax base is the public service in question.
- Finally, administrative fees are paid for the governmental authorization of some products or processes. They are a type of user fee.

These taxes can be specific (that is, levied in relation to the weight or number of the taxed product), or *ad valorem* (as a percentage of the value of the product).

In practice, a wide range of existing and prospective taxes can be observed throughout the world. Barde and Owens (1996) list 32 different areas where environmental taxes exist in OECD countries. It is not always easy to relate an existing tax to a specific theoretical reference. As a result, the ambiguity in the definition or objective of a prospective tax often leads to its rejection.

In what follows we use a microeconomic perspective and try to clarify the environmental tax jungle. We begin with the Pigouvian tax, which is a direct application of the economic theory of the environment. We explain how to estimate the level of the tax in practice. Then we present some of the rare examples of existing Pigouvian taxes. However, in practice, Pigouvian taxes are difficult to implement, and also have theoretical flaws. Therefore, we show how the limits of these taxes give rise to the 'charges and standards' approach (Chapter 4). Finally, Chapter 5 explores the diversity of taxes used in practice, and shows how they are related to the economic theory.

3.2 HOW DO PIGOUVIAN TAXES WORK?

In Chapter 1, we saw that pollution can be seen as an external cost which accompanies economic activity, i.e. an externality. The presence of externalities drives producers and consumers to make decisions that do not lead to an optimal allocation of resources: the pollution level is greater than the optimal level. (Although this may seem strange for non-economists, the optimal level of pollution is always greater than zero, since zero pollution means no factories, no cars, no planes, no trains, etc.)

As a rule, economic efficiency in the market of a good is attained if, for this good:

Supply (marginal private cost) = Demand (marginal willingness to pay)

With environmental externalities, this is no longer true, because the external costs to the environment are not taken into account. In order for economic efficiency to be attained in the presence of pollution, the total cost of the good has to be considered, not only the private cost. That is, the following condition must be met:

Marginal private cost + Marginal external cost = Demand

where the sum of the private cost and the external cost is defined as the social cost.

However, when making their decisions, producers and consumers consider only the private cost. They do not take external costs, such as environmental costs, into consideration. For example, when choosing to buy a big sport utility vehicle, the buyer considers only his private costs and benefits, but does not take into account the additional environmental burden or the increased fatality risk to other drivers. In the same way, when deciding its level of production, a polluting factory does not take into account the environmental burden resulting from its production. As a result, the production, hence the pollution, will be higher than the optimal level.

In order to re-establish efficiency, the government can impose a tax to 'internalize' these externalities, that is, to integrate them into the production cost of producers and into the purchase price of consumers. If this tax is set at a level equal to the external cost at the optimal level of production, it is called a 'Pigouvian tax', named after Arthur Cecil Pigou (1918). Where external costs exist, the Pigouvian tax re-establishes economic efficiency in the following manner:

Marginal private cost + Pigouvian tax = Demand

Therefore, the objective of the Pigouvian tax is to re-establish economic efficiency through the internalization of external costs. The tax forces consumers and producers to take into account not only the private cost, but the total cost related to their activities, that is, the social cost.

How does a Pigouvian tax affect the production, consumption, and pollution level? The tax works essentially through three mechanisms: (1) reduction of the quantity exchanged, (2) incentive to implement abatement technologies, and (3) incentive to engage in research and development activities.[1]

Reduction of the Quantity Exchanged

Figure 3.1 shows the market of a good, the production or consumption of which is polluting. There is no abatement technology; therefore, the polluting emission is proportional to the quantity produced. For simplicity, we assume that the marginal private cost, as well as the marginal external cost, is constant with respect to quantity. Without pollution, the optimal quantity is Q_0, which corresponds to the intersection of the demand curve and the marginal private cost curve. However, as soon as pollution is taken into account, Q_0 is no longer optimal. With the external cost of pollution, the optimal quantity will be determined by the intersection of the demand curve and the marginal social cost curve, i.e. Q_1. As we see, Q_1 is smaller than Q_0. This means that economic efficiency requires smaller production and consumption of the polluting good.

Suppose that the government knows the level of the marginal external cost (MEC) in Figure 3.1. It imposes a tax equal to the MEC. As a result, for each unit produced, firms will have to pay a tax equal to the MEC. Therefore, when choosing the quantity to be produced, firms will not consider the marginal private cost, but will instead consider the marginal private cost plus the tax, that is, the marginal social cost. They will produce the optimal quantity Q_1 instead of the initial quantity Q_0. In addition, they will have to pay the tax to the government, which is an amount equal to Q_1 multiplied by the tax.

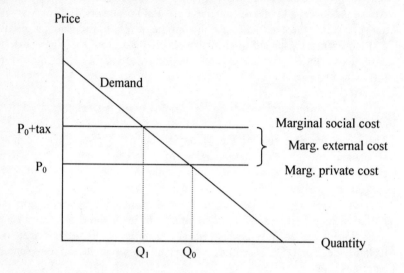

Figure 3.1 The optimal production of a polluting good

We see that the tax reduces the production of the polluting good. This reduction depends on the market structure: it is greater when the price elasticity of demand or supply is high. The quantity exchanged will be smaller when there are close substitutes (elastic demand) that are not polluting and will not be taxed. It will also be smaller in a very competitive market which is open to trade (elastic supply).

Two supplementary facts, which are rarely emphasized, should be added about Pigouvian taxes:

- We know that Pigouvian taxes increase social welfare by causing a reduction in the pollution level. However, even if they increase total welfare, the quantity of produced goods decreases, that is, material welfare is reduced.[2] This remark already raises the question of the acceptability of environmental taxes: if material welfare decreases, those who have an interest in this material welfare will oppose environmental taxes.
- Instead of seeing the tax as a payment, the opposite view may be considered: in the absence of an internalization measure such as the tax, firms do not bear the entire (social) production cost, and the rest

of society has to bear part of it. Therefore, introducing the tax can be seen as the *elimination of a subsidy*. Without the tax, firms do not pay for the cost of their pollution, which means that their pollution is subsidized. And we know that eliminating subsidies brings efficiency gains for the economy.

Incentive to Implement Abatement Technologies

Suppose now that there exists an abatement technology, which allows firms to reduce their polluting emissions and thus to avoid the payment of part of the tax. There will be an abatement cost function corresponding to this technology. This case is shown in Figure 3.2, where polluting emissions are measured from left to right, and emission reduction from right to left. The initial level of emissions is e_0, which reflects the situation without any abatement activity. In the absence of government intervention, firms will choose this level. However, from this level e_0, emissions can be reduced significantly at a small cost.

Now suppose, as in the preceding case, that the government imposes a tax equal to the marginal external cost. For the initial level e_0, the marginal reduction cost is smaller than the level of the tax, and it will be cheaper for firms to purify their smoke than to pay the tax. Such is the case until the level of emission e_1 is reached, where the marginal reduction cost is equal to the level of the tax. At this point, firms minimize their costs, paying an abatement cost of e_0Be_1 and a tax of Oe_1BD. We see that the tax gives an incentive for firms to use an abatement technology, to the extent that the clean-up cost is smaller than the tax they would otherwise have to pay between e_0 and e_1. As a general rule, taxes induce firms to modify the structure of their productive capital so that their production generates fewer emissions.

Incentive to Engage in Research and Development Activities

Firms, at the emission level e_1, still pay a substantial tax amount to the government. However, they think that they are able, with technological innovation, to reduce the pollution abatement cost. Therefore, they engage in research and development activities, and find a means to move the marginal abatement cost curve downwards, from MAC to MAC'. This allows them to further reduce their emissions, and therefore to pay a smaller tax amount. The new equilibrium will be e_2. At this point, firms pay Oe_2CD to the government, and bear an abatement cost of e_0e_2C.

As a result of this technological innovation, firms save an amount equal to e_0BC, less the cost of the R&D. We see that the tax favours technological progress: it gives an incentive for firms to develop less polluting products and processes. If the tax did not exist, firms would not get any benefit from environmental R&D. Therefore, they would have no interest in undertaking this kind of research. It can also be shown that the firms' gain from technological innovation is greater with the tax than with other instruments such as regulations or grandfathered emission permits.[3] As a result, the tax gives more incentives for technological innovation than other instruments (for a formal proof see Milliman and Prince, 1989).

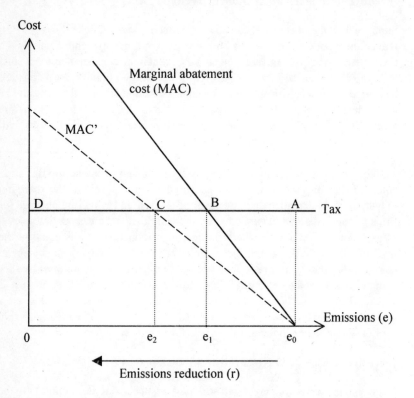

Figure 3.2 The optimal level of pollution with an abatement technology

In the cases presented here, the marginal external cost (MEC) has been assumed to be constant. With a constant MEC, the tax is equal to the MEC for every pollution level. However, if the MEC is increasing with the production (or pollution) level, this is no longer true. A tax calculated for the current production (or pollution) level will no longer be optimal; instead, it will be necessary to evaluate the tax for the socially optimal level of production (or pollution). From then on, the optimal Pigouvian tax will be smaller than the currently measurable MEC. Later, we will discuss the practical problems this implies. However, the mechanisms exposed here (reduction in demand, utilization of clean-up technologies and incentive for technological progress) work in the same manner, whatever the shape of the MEC curve.

3.3   HOW TO ESTIMATE THE EXTERNAL COST IN PRACTICE

In order to impose a Pigouvian tax, it is necessary to evaluate the external cost of the polluting emission. That is, the damage caused to the environment has to be translated into a monetary value. We need answers to questions such as: what is the value of clean air in city X? What is the value of endangered species Y? Or what is the present value of avoiding a 3°C increase in the average temperature of the earth in 100 years?

As the environment is not part of the market, its value cannot be directly observed. Yet estimations of external environmental costs have to be sufficiently reliable, because they will be used to calculate the level of the tax which people and businesses will effectively have to pay. Valuation methods for environmental goods can be classified into two broad categories, according to whether the behaviour of individuals is observed or hypothetical. In the first case, the methods are based on the observation of markets which are linked to the environment, and in the second the methods use questionnaires which pose hypothetical questions (see Freeman, 1993, or Markandya, 1991).

Market-based valuation methods

Market-based valuation methods look at existing markets for goods, the prices of which are related to the environment. The following methods can be used:

- The hedonic pricing method isolates environmental factors from observable prices. This method is mainly used for the valuation of the environmental quality by looking at differences in housing prices (because houses in polluted areas cost less), and the valuation of an increased mortality risk by looking at differences in wages in the labour market (because dangerous jobs pay more). For example, with the housing market it is possible to isolate environmental factors, such as noise or air pollution, from rents or house prices. This is done by eliminating all other factors which influence the price of a unit, such as the size of the housing unit, the age of the building, the quality of the neighbourhood, the distance from downtown, etc.

- With the travel cost method, the demand for environmental goods is estimated on the basis of what people spend to visit some sites with a specific environmental quality, especially national parks, lakes, forests, etc.
- With dose-response methods, first the impact of the pollution on 'real' (biological or physical) aspects such as health, mortality, or agricultural output, has to be estimated; natural science researchers are in charge of these estimations. In a second step, economists evaluate the economic losses from these modifications.
- Another method is based on the prevention expenses incurred in avoiding specific environmental damage. For example, the expenses of households which install insulating material or filters to protect themselves from noise or air pollution will be estimated.

Despite the multiplicity of these methods, they only allow the valuation of environmental goods when they are somehow or other related to a market. Yet, many environmental goods are not related to a market. For example, the value of most living species is difficult to estimate with these methods.[4] Also, the mere 'existence value' of a resource, besides its actual or future use value, is difficult or impossible to determine if it is not related to a market.

Contingent valuation methods

On the other hand, with contingent valuation methods, all aspects of the environment can be estimated, including existence values which are problematic with the other methods. Contingent valuation methods are also useful to confirm, or invalidate, the results obtained with other methods. There are two broad types of contingent valuation methods:

- One method is based on the individuals' willingness-to-pay or willingness-to-accept. It uses questionnaires to ask individuals in a population what price they are willing to pay for a certain improvement in the quality of the environment. Alternatively, individuals can be asked what amount of money they would require as compensation for specific deterioration of the environment.
- Individuals may also be asked to classify different alternatives according to their order of preference, when at least one of them is associated with a price.

There are formidable technical difficulties associated with contingent valuation methods. However, these difficulties can be significantly reduced by careful use of such methods (Zerbe and Dively, 1994). Nowadays, an increasing number of estimations of external costs, obtained with various methods, is available. Together, these estimations give an approximate picture of the value individuals attach to certain aspects of the natural environment.

3.4   PROBLEMS AND DIFFICULTIES

In this chapter, in order to simplify, we have made the assumption of a constant marginal external cost (MEC). However, in reality, the MEC is a positive function of the level of pollution. As a result, the MEC for the optimal level of pollution will be lower than for the actual level, and the Pigouvian tax should be set equal to the MEC at the optimal level of production and pollution, not at the current level. In order to determine this optimal level, it is necessary to know both the marginal damage and the marginal abatement cost functions, for the whole economy. This means that, in order to calculate the amount of a Pigouvian tax, we should have extensive information about both the damage and abatement functions.

In practice, if one tries to evaluate the damage at the optimal emission level, the procedure is the following (Coase, 1988, p. 182). First, it is necessary to estimate, for different levels of emissions, the damage suffered by the polluted, the measures they would take to protect themselves at each damage level, as well as the exact cost of these measures. It is also necessary to evaluate whether, following a change in the pollution level, new households would settle in (or leave) the polluted zone. It would then be necessary to show polluters the function obtained with those calculations, and each polluter would have to decide his emission level by comparing the clean-up cost with the external damage, for different emission levels. With the help of this information, the government could finally calculate the level of the tax.

As we see, this is not an easy process. Most of this information is not known, especially the damage suffered. Even if the victims and the polluters have access to this information, it may not be in their best interest to disclose it. Therefore, even if it is theoretically possible to start this procedure in order to estimate the level of the Pigouvian tax, the task is extremely difficult and expensive. Also, as the optimum is not static but dynamic, it would be necessary to continually repeat this procedure, because the optimal production level is never the same.

However, with the help of monetary valuation techniques, it is possible to evaluate the marginal environmental damage at the current production level. A tax can be set equal to this level of damage. Following the response of polluters, the marginal damage can be re-estimated, and the tax level adapted.

By repeating this procedure many times, we have an iterative process. It may be hoped that this process converges towards the optimum.

Such an approach may be attempted in practice, but it would be hampered by formidable difficulties. First, a tax equal to the marginal damage at the current production level is necessarily higher than the Pigouvian tax. Consequently, it imposes costs that are too high for the economy. Then, at each stage of the iterative process it would be necessary to have information which is difficult to acquire, and not always accurate. Consequently, at each stage of this process, it would be impossible to know if, following a modification of the tax level, one would be closer to, or further from, the optimum (Baumol and Oates, 1988, p. 161).

There are other problems. Buchanan showed in 1969 that, in the case of a monopoly, the internalization of external costs by means of a Pigouvian tax could in some cases decrease welfare. The reason is that a monopoly can in some cases choose a production level that is smaller than the social optimum (taking externalities into account); in this case, a Pigouvian tax will make the monopoly reduce its production even more. One finds in Baumol and Oates (1988) a complete discussion of the different cases in which results are influenced by market imperfections.

Furthermore, Baumol and Bradford showed in 1972 that the very presence of externalities of a sufficient magnitude could give rise to multiple local optimums, between which it is very difficult to choose. In the presence of significant externalities, the production possibilities frontier can change from the usual convex form to a concave one, with several implied optimums. Therefore, it is no longer known in which direction to go in order to have an increase in welfare, and imposing corrective taxes does not change anything about this problem. Baumol and Bradford conclude that the choice of an equilibrium point for the economy has to be the result of a collective decision, and not the result of an automatic economic adjustment process.

For all these different reasons, it is generally impossible, in practice, to reach the social optimum with the help of a Pigouvian tax. The estimation of external costs can only give some indication of the direction of the change. In the next chapter, we will see how a charges and standards approach may in practice replace Pigouvian taxes.

3.5   EXAMPLES OF PIGOUVIAN TAXES

Despite the evident problems of putting the Pigouvian theory precisely into practice, the following taxes are attempts to do it:

- *The British landfill tax*. In Great Britain, the external costs of dumping garbage in landfills have been estimated with the help of a research program. A tax has been introduced, at a level equal to the corresponding external costs (European Foundation, 1996). To our knowledge, this is the best current example of a Pigouvian tax.[5] Should we be surprised that it was introduced in Pigou's country?

- *Airport noise taxes*. In some airports (for example in Switzerland), noise taxes are added to landing taxes. Noise taxes are calculated according to the type of the plane, and are directly linked to the noise emitted during landing and takeoff.

- *Gasoline taxes*. The most often quoted example of a Pigouvian tax is the internalization of external costs caused by motor vehicles. Available estimations of external costs justify an increase in the gasoline tax in many cases. However, this tax is not the best example of an internalization of external costs, because gasoline consumption is not accurately related to polluting emissions (Wallart, 1997). The internalization of external costs by means of an increase in the gasoline tax reduces gasoline consumption, but does not provide an incentive for motorists to install abatement devices, nor does it give an incentive for manufacturers to engage in research and development activities to reduce pollution. Furthermore, an internalization should ideally differentiate between the automobile utilization in cities and in rural areas, because external costs are much higher within cities than outside them; with a gasoline tax this is not possible. As an exact Pigouvian tax is not possible in the case of road transportation, the gasoline tax can be viewed as a second best solution, as part of a combination of instruments. This tax has other positive economic effects, such as a reduction in greenhouse gas emissions, a reduced dependency on oil producing countries, a reduction in the social cost of noise and accidents, as well as an increased conservation of a non-renewable resource. The global warming issue strengthens the justification for an increase in the gasoline tax, even if its rationale corresponds more to the rationale of the charges and standards approach (see next chapter) than to that of the Pigouvian tax.

NOTES

1. One finds in Von Weizsäcker et al. (1992) five channels, through which an energy tax influences the energy consumption. To the three channels mentioned in the text, these authors add the following: (4) they distinguish between development activities (on the basis of known technologies) and research and development activities (the development of as yet unknown technologies); (5) they introduce a cultural change in the very long term, which

will influence consumption (several decades).

2. The same result can be shown with a general equilibrium model (Weder, 1995).

3. In theory, emission permits can be auctioned off, in which case they provide the same incentive for technological innovation as taxes do. However, in practice, emission permits are generally distributed without charge, instead of being auctioned off.

4. However, some people suggest valuing biodiversity as a genetic reservoir for the pharmaceutical industry. By doing this, biodiversity is linked with the market.

5. However, a truly Pigouvian tax should be equal to the external cost at the *optimal* level of production and pollution. In Great Britain, the external cost could only be measured for the *actual* level. Therefore, the British tax is probably too high to be a true Pigouvian tax.

4. The Twofold Rationale of the Charges and Standards Approach

The charges and standards approach is a practical and cost-effective method for achieving an environmental goal. This goal can be an approximation of the Pigouvian optimum, which is unknown. Alternatively, the charges and standards approach can be used to achieve any goal decided by society, such as a given sustainability objective.

4.1 CHARGES AND STANDARDS INSTEAD OF PIGOUVIAN TAXES

Rationale of the Charges and Standards Approach

As we have seen in the preceding chapter, it is almost impossible to calculate the marginal damage at the optimal production level, which is necessary to set a Pigouvian tax. The only practicable approach would be to base a tax on the current evaluation of the marginal damage; in response to this intervention, polluters would reduce their emissions; the government would then adjust the tax to the new level of marginal damage, observe the reaction of polluters, adjust the tax, and so on, via an iterative process. However, this approach is complex; the information needed to determine the direction of the adjustment at each stage of the process is difficult to obtain. In addition, tax rates cannot in practice be adjusted easily by the political process. One would never know if, following a modification of the tax rate, the economy would be closer to, or further from, the optimum. In short, this approach is impracticable.

In 1972, Baumol and Oates (hereafter: B&O) proposed another approach, which had the great advantage of feasibility. They suggested setting an 'acceptability standard' for the polluting emissions, then imposing a charge to reduce emissions down to the chosen level. Following the imposition of the tax, the regulatory authority observes the outcome; if the tax does not achieve the target reduction in pollution, the tax rate is adjusted, by means of successive iterations, until the objective is achieved. For each adjustment in the tax rate, the only information required is the current level of pollution;

and contrary to the information needed to calculate the Pigouvian tax, the current level of pollution can easily be measured.

The charges and standards approach is not only feasible, it is also efficient. As it equalizes the marginal cost of reducing emissions across all activities, it can be shown that this method is the least-cost method to achieve the desired result (B&O). However, despite its cost-effectiveness, this approach does not generally lead to the optimal level of pollution; this approach is efficient, but not optimal. The optimal situation remains the one in which the external costs are internalized at the optimal production level. As clearly stated in B&O (1988, p. 159-161), the charges and standards approach is only proposed because of the lack of a better alternative. For those authors, *the theoretical reference remains the Pigouvian tax.*

With the charges and standards approach, the level of emissions has to be set so as to achieve 'a reasonable quality of life' (B&O, 1972). But what is a reasonable quality of life, in relation to the environment? Unfortunately, there is no answer from a strictly economic point of view. Yet, B&O emphasize that the same problem exists for the provision of nearly all public goods. Citizens do not easily reveal their willingness-to-pay for public goods. This prevents the government from learning the (economic) demand for public goods, which is required to determine their optimal level of production. As the government does not know the demand, it has to use other methods in order to learn the preferences of the public. As a general rule, the quantity of public goods is chosen by way of a political process, such as direct majority voting, or voting through elected representatives.

In the same way, as the economic demand for the environment is not known, it is necessary to use a political process in order to determine the desirable quality of the environment. Even if it does not lead to the optimal environmental quality, because of its legitimacy, a procedure such as majority voting may be preferred to the Pigouvian procedure. For this reason, a charges and standards approach, where the environmental objective is decided by majority voting, may be more readily accepted than a Pigouvian tax.

From this discussion, we see that the charges and standards approach has three compelling advantages over the Pigouvian tax:

- With a charges and standards approach, there is no need to estimate damage functions. The government has only to observe the effective level of emissions. Administratively, this approach is easier, and it is often the only feasible approach to tax pollution.

- The charges and standards approach minimizes the cost of achieving a certain objective of pollution reduction, whatever the conditions of competition in the market. This approach is efficient whether there is a monopoly or perfect competition (remember from the preceding chapter that in the presence of a monopoly, a Pigouvian tax could actually decrease welfare).

- With the charges and standards approach, the environmental objective is decided by a political process. In this sense, it may be viewed as more democratic, more comprehensible, and more legitimate, than a Pigouvian tax, whose level is determined by technicians (on this subject, see also Chapter 6).

On the other hand, the advantage of the Pigouvian tax is that, under ideal conditions, it leads to the economic optimum. However, with a charges and standards approach, the standard can also be modified if it is viewed as too far from the optimum. After the following examples, we will see that the concept of sustainable development provides another rationale for the charges and standards approach.

Examples

Different emission taxes and charges follow the rationale of the charges and standards approach:

- A good example is the Swedish tax on NO_x emissions of large combustion plants for energy production. The level of the tax has been set by considering, for each level of potential emission reductions, the corresponding abatement costs. Abatement costs varied between 3 and 80 SKr per kilo of NO_x, and the tax level has been set at 40 SKr per kilo. The tax has been very effective, decreasing the emissions of the installations concerned from 24,000 to 15,300 tons between 1990 and 1992. This reduction was greater than anticipated. However, the scope of the tax is rather limited, as only 6.5% of Swedish NO_x emissions are taxed (Olivecrona, 1995).
- The tax on ozone-depleting chemicals in the United States covers 20 different chemicals. For each one, the tax rate is proportional to the potential of destruction of the ozone layer (the ozone-depleting factor). The objective of this tax is to reduce the production of those chemicals, in order to comply with the Montreal Protocol of 1987.[1]
- CO_2 taxes already exist in northern European countries (Denmark, Norway, Sweden, Finland, and the Netherlands). The Kyoto Protocol signed in December 1997 requires the industrialized countries to reduce their emissions of CO_2 in order to limit global warming. The emission target for the period 2008–2012 is 7% below 1990 levels for the United States, 8% below for the European Union, and 6%

below for Japan. As the target is a quantitative reduction, one appropriate instrument is the charges and standards approach (for CO_2 taxes, see also below).

4.2   THE SUSTAINABLE DEVELOPMENT CRITICISM

A charges and standards approach is justified when the Pigouvian approach is not feasible; it can also be justified by some weaknesses of the neoclassical model, which does not treat ecological sustainability in an appropriate manner.

References to the limits to economic growth are ancient: they were mentioned by Malthus and Ricardo at the beginning of the nineteenth century. Malthus argues that the finiteness of agricultural land imposes a limit on the total population; for Ricardo, the limit comes from the fact that with population growth, farmers have to cultivate land of steadily worsening quality, hence decreasing returns. The introduction of technological progress appears with John Stuart Mill, who argues that technological progress can offset decreasing returns. With the introduction of technological progress, economics is not the 'dismal science' any more.

From 1870, with a few exceptions, the sensitivity to the limits to growth disappears completely from the thinking of mainstream economists, most of whom agree on the fact that growth can continue indefinitely. Actual growth models, such as the popular Solow-Swan model, totally ignore the issue of natural resources and the environment, and concentrate solely on population growth, capital accumulation, and technological progress.

The modern realization of the problem dates from 1966, with the theory of Boulding on the Earth as a closed system. Public consciousness increased especially after 1972, the year in which the report to the Club of Rome was published (Meadows et al.). On the basis of extrapolations, this report brought to the fore the limits of an economic growth that was at risk of running into the finiteness of natural resources. Also, concerns emerged about the growing accumulation of waste, which was a byproduct of the mass consumption society. Only recently, however, has this accumulation begun to cast some doubt on economic growth, under the threat of a possible change in the global climate. Since 1972, a majority of economists have continued to think that economic growth remains possible and even desirable. However, the vision of a different kind of growth, one compatible with the imperatives of environmental protection, has forced its way into economic thinking.[2]

The notion of sustainable development has spread since the report 'Our Common Future', also called the 'Brundtland Report' (World Commission for Environment and Development (WCED), 1987). Sustainable development is defined as follows:

> Sustainable development is development that meets the needs of the present without compromising the ability of future generations to meet their own needs.

This generally accepted definition contains two concepts: the concept of needs, and that of intergenerational equity. The concept of 'needs' can be interpreted in many different ways; therefore, it does not provide precise, practical guidance. Also, today it is impossible to anticipate the needs of future generations. 'Intergenerational equity' can be understood as a formal principle that is intended to restore the old links between generations, which have been broken by a growing mobility, as well as the loss of traditional values (Passet, 1994). Like the concept of needs, this concept also offers little precise guidance. More precise, but also more controversial, definitions of sustainable development exist. In their book, Pearce et al. (1989) quote about thirty of them, corresponding to different philosophies. All these definitions contain a normative objective of wealth distribution over time.

The issue of sustainable development is derived from weaknesses in the neoclassical theory, which, even when integrating the concept of internalization of external costs, is not able to satisfactorily respond to many criticisms relating to the natural environment.

Some Problems with the Neoclassical Approach

In the neoclassical production function, the degradation of the environment takes the form of a diminishing natural capital about which the neoclassical approach remains fundamentally optimistic. Indeed, according to this approach, there are two possibilities according to which production can grow despite a diminishing natural capital: (1) technological progress compensates for this decline; (2) even in the absence of technological progress, a declining natural capital can be replaced by an increasing manufactured or human capital, because they are substitutes.

Solving the sustainable development problem with technological progress supposes that progress will always advance at a sufficient pace to compensate for the diminishing natural capital, so as to guarantee a non-decreasing production. However, it is necessary to be optimistic to think this way; indeed, the Ehrlich equation shows that the constraints imposed by an increasing population and an increasing consumption per capita, are very important.[3] Also, even though technological progress solves some environmental problems, it creates other problems, which did not exist previously. These different considerations already show that, if technological progress is necessary to significantly reduce environmental pressures, it may not compensate fully for the diminishing natural capital.

According to the second possibility, sustainable development is possible by substituting different forms of capital.[4] With a usual, Cobb-Douglas type production function, a declining natural capital requires more and more manufactured and human capital to maintain a certain level of production. However, substitution possibilities do always exist, even if only a very small amount of natural capital remains. Sometimes, models suppose the existence of a 'backstop technology', which prevents this substitution from being more and more costly as natural capital declines (solar energy or nuclear fusion are examples of backstop technologies).

Facing these optimistic considerations, the following criticisms can be stated:

1. First of all, neoclassical theory assumes substitutability between the different forms of capital. However, in order to be useful, the physical capital often has to be accompanied by natural resources. Natural and physical capital are complements and not only substitutes: what is the usefulness of an oil refinery, if oil is no longer available?

2. The model that advocates the internalization of externalities is mainly based on a certain world. Yet uncertainty aspects are inherent in environmental problems. Uncertainty affects the reserves of natural resources, the future technological progress, the consequences of global pollution, and also the preferences of future generations (Faucheux and Noël, 1995, 12). Often, the causes of an environmental problem are insufficiently understood, and their consequences are difficult to quantify. For example, after the detection of a hole in the ozone layer, and before internalization measures can be implemented, many steps have to be taken. First, it is necessary for scientists to understand and quantify the phenomenon precisely; then, they have to forecast and quantify its exact consequences; then, economists have to translate these consequences into accurate estimations of external costs; and finally, a corresponding tax must be legislated, passed, and implemented. Each stage of the process is uncertain, and diminishes the probability that the tax will ever accurately reflect the external costs.

3. In many cases, the environment is characterized by irreversibilities. Irreversibilities can be observed in physical, chemical, biological or climatic processes. The extinction of a species is an irreversible process. Similarly, the accumulation of many pollutants is irreversible for human beings. If a pollutant is emitted in quantities that exceed the assimilative capacity of the environment, there will be an irreversible reduction in this capacity. However, the economic calculus does not take into account

these kinds of irreversibilities, and when uncertainty comes into play with irreversibility, it compounds the difficulty of the problem.

4. Environmental problems are characterized by complexity and multidimensionality. Natural phenomena involve multiple and complex interactions, not all of which are known. Yet the neoclassical approach reduces the environment to the sole dimension of the internalization of quantifiable, and known, external effects. This approach ignores combined effects, which are caused by complex chemical processes, leading to new pollutants.[5] It also ignores the link (implied by the first law of thermodynamics) between the extraction of natural resources and the production of waste. Complexity and multidimensionality challenge choices based on a unique criterion.

5. The neoclassical approach is confronted with the problem of intergenerational equity. It is impossible to know the preferences of future generations. And even if they were known, this would not solve the question of how to distribute natural resources and welfare among generations. We will tackle these problems later in the book (Chapter 10), and for the moment only illustrate this situation with an example from Von Weizsäcker et al. (1992, p. 16). These authors graphically represent the evolution of the world population and the world consumption of resources, over a period of several thousand years. They question our right to use up, in just a few decades, resources which our planet took millions of years to create.

6. Through discounting, the future is assigned a lower value than the present; the further in the future a cost or a benefit occurs, the more it is reduced by this process. In the case of the environment, this can be criticized for several reasons. First, environmental protection spending is discouraged since its benefits occur in the long term, whereas its costs have to be borne today. Second, the interest rate influences the speed at which natural resources are depleted; if economic policies favour high interest rates, natural resources are depleted more rapidly. Finally, potentially catastrophic consequences have little influence on a decision if they occur in the distant future (Faucheux and Noël, 1995, p. 217).

Each of these criticisms substantially reduces the scope and the application potential of the externality theory. This is especially true when environmental problems simultaneously involve several elements, such as uncertainty, complexity, irreversibility, and intergenerational equity. In this case, the internalization of external costs is not sufficient to adequately respond to the problem. Two approaches attempt to answer these criticisms: the London school approach, and the approach of the ecological economics school.

The London School Approach

The neoclassical approach supposes that physical capital is a substitute for natural resources. This has been frequently contested. Critics of a perfect substitutability between the different types of capital have got together with David Pearce to create the London school. Because of the non-substitutability between forms of capital, the authors of the London school propose ensuring sustainability by maintaining a constant stock of natural capital.[6] Each generation has to bequeath to the following a stock of natural capital, which is at least as important as the one it inherited. With such an approach, it is possible to take into account what is uncertain, irreversible, intergenerational, as well as values other than utility (Faucheux et al., 1995).

In addition to the constant natural capital, authors of the London school use concepts such as critical natural capital, safe minimum standards, and precautionary principle. Because of the imperfect substitutability between physical and natural capital, it is necessary to define which components of the natural capital are too critical to be replaced by physical capital. In order to protect this critical natural capital, 'safe minimum standards' have to be defined. Those standards are physical indicators, which impose minimal constraints on the economic activity. They provide the reference needed to maintain a minimal level of key resources, in order to ensure the stability of ecosystems. The 'principle of precaution' is used when at the same time there is uncertainty about benefits and costs, irreversibility of damages, and high values of the natural capital; in this case, it is necessary to take precautionary measures, instead of doing nothing and waiting until more scientific evidence is available – or some catastrophic event occurs.

Once the principle of a constant stock of natural capital has been accepted, it is necessary to know how to interpret this rule. That is, we should have answers to the following questions: Should the natural capital be constant in physical or in economic terms? Is it possible to aggregate different kinds of resources, such as oil and copper? Can an increase in a renewable resource (say, forests) compensate for a diminishing non-renewable natural resource (oil)? In order to define more precisely what a constant stock of natural capital is, the London school authors have proposed various interpretations. All of them use monetary evaluations of the natural capital.

However, the main criticism of the neoclassical approach was precisely related to the use of monetary valuations of the natural capital. Thus, even if the London school has clearly shown the importance of preserving a constant natural capital, by trying to evaluate this natural capital, it falls back on the monetary valuations it had previously criticized (Faucheux et al., 1995). The problem of measuring the natural capital is more than a technical one; it is a conceptual problem, which questions the very concept of a constant stock of natural capital. For Victor (1991), this problem is impossible to solve; another approach is necessary, one which integrates economics and the laws of nature.

The Ecological Economics Approach

The main criticism of the neoclassical approach and the London school approach is that, somehow or other, one always falls back on monetary valuations of nature. Yet, with monetary valuations, the physical environment is not adequately taken into account, especially when there are irreversibilities or uncertainties. Economic approaches based on monetary valuations always try to integrate the environment into the economic sphere; yet economic systems are part of ecological systems, not the other way round (Turner, 1993). If economic systems are part of ecological systems, then sustainable development depends on the preservation of these ecological systems, i.e. on ecological sustainability. Yet, ecological sustainability depends on certain physical (or biophysical) limits and constraints. These constraints are needed to ensure a minimal stability of ecosystems, to maintain a minimal reserve of resources, and to preserve the Earth's capacity to assimilate waste. It follows that, in order to ensure a sustainable development, these physical limits and constraints must be binding criteria.

The idea of physical constraints is not new. We have seen that classical authors such as Malthus, Adam Smith, Ricardo or Mill already mentioned the constraints imposed by the diminishing quality of arable land. More recently, Galbraith claimed that, for environmental problems, the only possible solution is 'to continue economic growth, but to specify by legislation the parameters within which it can occur' (Galbraith, 1975, p. 306). Similarly, Passet (1979, p. 228) describes in detail quantitative and qualitative constraints, within which the economic calculus has to take place. A similar idea can be found in the works of the thermodynamic school (Victor, 1991), as well as in those of the London school (Turner, 1993).

What do these physical constraints look like? Environmental mechanisms involve threshold effects, above which irreversibilities occur. When a pollutant is discharged into the environment, the effect is often reversible up to a certain threshold (the 'critical load'). Once this threshold is exceeded, the pollution accumulates and can no longer be assimilated into the environment. For example, nitrates and phosphates dumped into a lake cause an overproduction of seaweed. When the seaweed decomposes, it exhausts the oxygen of the water. As long as there is a sufficient quantity of oxygen, some life will subsist in the lake. But if the effluents exceed the critical load, seaweed will multiply to such a point that it will exhaust all the oxygen, and life will disappear from the lake. This process is almost irreversible. Similar thresholds exist in the case of climatic change or the extinction of species.

The notion of critical load is supported by scientific consensus, and therefore has also to be used by economists. Sometimes, the threshold is not related to known ecological consequences, but to an unknown risk zone, in which costs are potentially catastrophic. For example, in the case of global warming, the 'known' zone corresponds to the temperature variations the Earth has experienced over the course of its recent history. Beyond this threshold is the zone of risk, in which nobody can predict what may happen.

Nowadays, ecological economics is based on a collection of theories, which all have the study of physical foundations in common. This school of thought involves a plurality of visions of the world and of nature. It is largely based on interdisciplinarity, but also on different forms of rationality; it is not limited to economic rationality (Faucheux et al., 1995). Ecological economics is not yet precisely defined, but it has already allowed important advances in knowledge. As Gowdy and Olsen (1994) state:

> Perhaps the most important contribution of ecological economics is the notion of environmental sustainability as a binding criterion.

4.3   THE CHARGES AND STANDARDS APPROACH FOR SUSTAINABLE DEVELOPMENT

As we see from this discussion, sustainable development involves various dimensions. The issue goes far beyond the mechanical internalization of known and quantifiable external costs in specific markets, as the neoclassical analysis suggests. The analysis of both the London school and the ecological economics school emphasizes the need to determine the specific conditions under which ecosystems can survive. Meeting these conditions will, in turn, guarantee that the economy can prosper, and that future generations can benefit from a minimal surviving level of the natural environment. Later we will address the fundamental question of how to define these conditions; for the moment we will examine the appropriateness of charges and standards to achieve the sustainable development objective.

Charges and Standards, and Sustainable Development

One important element in the analysis of the London school and the ecological economics school is the set of physical sustainability constraints, or ecological constraints, which society places on its own activities. But ecological constraints are themselves a sort of standard; therefore, they can be achieved with the help of a charges and standards approach. Remember that the charges and standards approach advocated by Baumol and Oates (B&O) depends on the definition of acceptability standards, which society places on its activities in order to achieve a 'reasonable quality of life'. With charges and standards aimed at achieving sustainable development, the 'reasonable quality of life' objective is simply replaced with a 'sustainable development' objective. With an appropriate definition of the constraints, any particular sustainable development objective can be achieved.

The philosophy underlying the B&O approach is quite different from the one underlying the sustainable development approach. B&O propose to use standards because of the difficulty of obtaining the information necessary to calculate optimal Pigouvian taxes. Yet, with sustainable development in mind, the choice of standards comes from considerations about ecological sustainability. Therefore, the theoretical difference between the usual charges and standards approach, and the sustainable development approach, is fundamental. On the one hand, the concern is approximating the economic optimum, on the other, it is placing ecological constraints on the economic activity.

Even though the philosophy of these two approaches is different, in both cases the instrument and its application work in the same way. In both cases, the point is to set certain environmental standards, and then to achieve them with the help of taxes or charges. The environmental goals will be determined in one case by a political choice (B&O, see section 4.1 above), in the other case by ecological constraints (sustainable development).

In addition to the ecological constraints, other elements are important for the sustainable development issue. Thus, we saw that technological progress is crucial in solving environmental problems; also, sustainable development requires the substitution between natural capital and other forms of capital. Table 4.1 shows that the charges and standards approach effectively deals with those elements. It addresses the concerns of the neoclassical approach, the London school approach, as well as the ecological economics approach.

Take the example of a tax on fossil energy. By increasing the price of fossil fuels, fuel consumption is reduced through a modification in individual behaviours, and through a substitution between fossil fuels and other sources of energy (point 2 in the table). Therefore, natural resources are saved. By reducing fuel usage, the tax also reduces CO_2 emissions. As CO_2 emissions are responsible for global warming when a certain climatic threshold is exceeded, this tax results in compliance with an ecological constraint (point 3). The tax also encourages technological progress in the field of energy saving (point 1).

Even if the charges and standards approach effectively addresses most of the sustainable development issues, this instrument is not the solution to all problems. As mentioned earlier, a combination of instruments is often preferable. For example, the charges and standards approach is not adapted to the management of other sustainable development components, such as biodiversity, high industrial risks, or demographic growth (Barde, 1992, p. 38).

Table 4.1 Sustainable development and the charges and standards approach

Sustainable development implies	Adequacy of the charges and standards approach
1. Encouragement of technological progress (neoclassical approach; London school).	Charges not only encourage technological progress, but, with the sale of emission permits, they are the most effective instrument in this respect. Without economic incentives, firms have little interest in undertaking research and development activities and implementing clean technologies.
2. The substitution between different forms of capital (neoclassical approach; London school).	Charges and standards, by increasing the price of natural capital, encourage producers and consumers to substitute natural capital with other types of capital. The extent of this substitution will depend on the price increase due to the charges.
3. Compliance with certain ecological constraints (London school; ecological economics).	Charges and standards, by reducing the production and consumption of polluting goods, brings their use down to a level compatible with ecological constraints.

Defining the Ecological Constraints

If the objective of the charges and standards approach is to comply with ecological constraints, two fundamental questions arise: how can these ecological constraints be defined? Who has to define them? Two authors, Pearce and Hueting, made seminal contributions on the question of defining ecological constraints.

Pearce and the assimilative capacity of the environment

The article of Pearce (1988) was written in response to the Daly criticism that an optimal allocation of resources does not imply ecological sustainability. Pearce distinguishes externalities which are relevant from an ecological point of view from those which are not. He is interested solely in the ecologically relevant externalities which may bring an irreversible reduction in the assimilative capacity of the environment. He calls these 'ecological externalities'. Ecological externalities represent a cost imposed on future consumers of environmental goods.[7] This cost is zero if the environment can return to its original state; it becomes positive only when the assimilative capacity is irreversibly diminished.

The Pearce model is original in its integration of the assimilative capacity of the environment in physical terms. In this model, the assimilative capacity is a threshold (A). When polluting emissions (e) are smaller than the assimilative capacity of the environment, that is when $e<A$, the marginal external cost is zero. Ecological externalities occur as soon as $e>A$. If $e>A$, there will be a decrease in the assimilative capacity, and this reduction is irreversible.

If this irreversible degradation of the ecosystem has to be avoided, the only solution is to prevent polluting emissions greater than the level A. This can be done with a charges and standards approach; in this case, the charge has to be set high enough so that A is not exceeded. It is important to note that the tax level which is needed to keep emissions below the assimilative capacity of the environment is higher than the Pigouvian tax. The charges and standards approach is chosen because the Pigouvian tax is not sufficient to comply with the assimilative capacity.

Hueting and the social preference for sustainability

Another method has been developed by Hueting (1991) with a more practical objective, the correction of national accounts for environmental degradation. It is based on a normative vision, according to which the assimilative capacity of the environment must not be exceeded (Faucheux and Noël, 1995, p. 307). Hueting starts with a criticism of the neoclassical theory with arguments such as irreversibility, uncertainty, and complexity. According to him, it is not possible to estimate a demand for environmental functions with the help of monetary valuations based only on individual preferences. A pragmatic approach has to be adopted, and physical standards of sustainability have to be defined. Within these physical limits, economic activity can take place freely.

As the demand for the environment is not known, Hueting proceeds as follows: in a first step, physical standards are defined for environmental functions, based on their sustainable use; and in a second step, the measures necessary to reach these physical standards are chosen. With this approach, a level of availability of environmental functions (*B*) is defined, which reflects a social consensus on the degree of sustainability. *B* is defined as a sustainability standard; Hueting interprets it as a demand function stemming from society; this demand function replaces the (unknown) traditional demand.

Comparison

The Pearce approach bears some resemblance to the Hueting approach, to the extent that both define sustainable development as the compliance with physical standards, and not as the result of an economic optimization. For both authors, the main point is the compliance with certain sustainability standards; the difference between those two approaches is related to how these sustainability standards are defined.

For Pearce, the assimilative capacity of the environment is determined by natural scientists. The threshold *A* is the level above which the assimilative capacity decreases. On the other hand, the Hueting approach is derived from the pragmatic need for environmental indicators, which are necessary to make political decisions. The threshold *B* results from a social preference for sustainability. In this sense, this approach is akin to the one proposed by B&O, who define the desirable pollution level as the result of a political process. If we take the example of CO_2 emissions, with Pearce, the critical level of emissions would be determined by climatologists, and with Hueting, it would emanate from society.

With both approaches, the difficulty is choosing the critical level of emission; however, this difficulty is common to any concrete definition of sustainable development. With the Pearce approach, the assimilative capacity of the environment is determined by natural scientists. Such an approach is possible in the presence of a scientific consensus; however, without such a consensus, the choice may be difficult. The lack of public debate and information could even give rise to a sort of 'dictatorship' of scientists, which would bring to mind George Orwell's '1984'.[8] Moreover, a solely scientific approach may cause disproportionate costs to the economy, costs which could be avoided if a public debate were to take place. With Hueting, the physical sustainability standards are not determined by scientists. Instead, they 'come from society', which presupposes the idea of a social consensus as the rationale for the choice. But this kind of consensus may be difficult to reach.

Examples

Some environmental problems are lessened with economic growth, others grow worse. Concerns about sustainable development arise because of the second type of problems. These problems are mainly: CO_2 emissions, waste production, the nitrate content of water, the consumption of energy, aluminium, paper, and plastic, and the use of land (World Bank, 1992; Binswanger, 1993). The following examples are charges and standards aimed at sustainable development:

- The landfill tax in Denmark. Unlike the British landfill tax (see Chapter 3), the Danish tax level has not been set with reference to the external costs of dumping waste, but with the intention of achieving the government objective concerning a sustainable development of landfills.
- In the case of CO_2 emissions, the emission reductions agreed upon at the Kyoto summit in 1997 correspond to a consensus on a certain level of emissions. However, these reductions will not be sufficient to stabilize the concentration of greenhouse gases in the atmosphere. The approach of Von Weizsäcker et al. (1992) corresponds to the objective of a stabilization of the global climate, i.e. to the compliance with an ecological constraint. These authors propose the introduction of a dynamic energy tax in Germany, with the objective of increasing energy efficiency. The tax level would be raised by 5% to 7% per year in real terms.
- There are some proposals for a tax on the consumption of natural resources, or 'Virgin Materials Tax', which could be levied on the consumption of water, iron, aluminium, silver, nickel, cadmium, sand, gravel, or timber. Some people also propose to tax land covered with asphalt/concrete.[9]
- Finally, the most ambitious approach is certainly that of the Carnoules Declaration (Factor 10 Club, 1994), which proposes increasing the productivity of resources by a factor of 10, on average, in the next 30 to 50 years. The objective is to 'dematerialize' the economy, through an increase in the longevity of products and the intensity of their utilization. To achieve that goal, one of the proposed instruments is an ecological tax reform.

NOTES

1. Initially, the United States Congress introduced quantitative restrictions, and the tax was intended to avoid excessive profits for the producing firms. But gradually the tax became the predominant instrument, achieving reductions beyond the initial objective (Fullerton, 1996). For this reason, this tax has now become an application of the charges and standards approach.
2. The same evolution happened with businesses. See for example *Changing Course* by Schmidheiny (1992).
3. The Ehrlich equation tells us that the total environmental impact is $I=P \cdot C \cdot T$, where P is the

population, C is the consumption per capita, and T is the environmental impact per unit of consumption. If P doubles, and C is multiplied by 4, then T has to decrease by a factor of 16 in order for global pollution to be reduced by half (see for example Bürgenmeier, 1994, p. 96).

4. This approach is called *weak sustainability*.
5. One example is ozone pollution, which appears mostly during hot summers. The chemical reaction producing ozone requires nitrogen oxides (NO_x), hydrocarbons (or Volatile Organic Compounds), and sunlight to be present. If one element is missing, no such reaction occurs. But not all hydrocarbons react with nitrogen oxides in the same way: some are more reactive than others. Moreover, the ozone concentration is *positively* related to the NO_2 level in the air, but *negatively* related to the NO level, which makes the problem even more complex! The ozone concentration is not uniform; and some of these processes are not exactly known by scientists. With all these interacting factors, it is impossible for the economist to exactly internalize externalities from NO_x or hydrocarbon emissions in order to reach the economic optimum.
6. This approach is called *strong sustainability*. See for example Pearce et al. (1989, p. 37).
7. The 'sustainability user cost'.
8. Passet, 1979, p. 231.
9. The objective of a tax on asphalt or concrete-covered land is to regulate water flows in populated areas. These examples are from Umwelt- und Prognose-Institut Heidelberg (1988), and Meier and Walter (1991).

5. Other Environmental Taxes

Beyond Pigouvian taxes and the charges and standards approach, a variety of environmental taxes exists in practice. In most cases, these taxes are efficient, given the existence of certain constraints. There are taxes on goods and services related to pollution, user charges, combinations of taxes and subsidies, and revenue-raising environmental taxes.

5.1 TAXES ON GOODS AND SERVICES RELATED TO THE POLLUTION

Faced with problems such as the high cost or the impossibility of measuring emissions, or a lack of political or social acceptability, different solutions exist. One is to tax the concentration of the pollutant; as the environmental damage is closely linked to the concentration, this solution is efficient, but requires the pollution to be easily traced to an individual polluter. Other solutions include taxes on the production, the revenue, or the capital of polluting firms; yet, as these measures are not closely linked to the polluting emissions, they are not very effective. Where pollution cannot be taxed directly, the usual approach is to tax products which are linked to the polluting emissions. There are product charges, equipment taxes, and taxes on complements or substitutes of polluting goods.

Product Charges

When it is impossible, or too costly, to directly tax the polluting emission with the help of an emission charge, which is the best solution, a tax may be imposed on a related product. Information needs will be much smaller than with an emission tax. From the environmental standpoint, this solution will be all the more effective when:

- the link between the emission and the product is strong (if the link is not strong enough, the tax will not be efficient in the short term; and producers will not have enough incentives to introduce new environmental technologies in the long term);

- there are close, non-polluting (and therefore non-taxed) substitutes, to which consumers will be able to turn.

Examples

Product charges may be imposed on inputs, or on finished goods. Examples include taxes on heating oil with high sulphur content (Norway, Sweden, and Switzerland); taxes on plastic bags (Italy); taxes on solvents and paints containing Volatile Organic Compounds (Switzerland); taxes on drink containers, single-use cameras and disposable razors (Belgium); taxes on fuels according to their carbon content; taxes on fertilizers, batteries, tyres, used oil, paper, chlorine, etc.

In these examples, the link between the tax and the environment is not always clear. For example, the link between the consumption of fertilizers and ground water pollution is problematic, because the pollution does not only depend on the quantity of fertilizers used, but also on the type of soil, the quantity of rain, the geological characteristics of the land, etc. Consequently, a tax on fertilizers alone may not be the most efficient instrument. Similarly, with taxes on plastic bags as in Italy, the link with the pollution is indirect and the main effect of the tax is to reduce the consumption. A good example is the perfect link existing between the quantity of gasoline burnt and CO_2 emissions. As the link is perfect, a tax on the CO_2 emissions of gasoline, and a tax on gasoline consumption, are equivalent.

Equipment Taxes

Pollution is often generated by equipment goods, or durable goods, during their utilization. When emissions cannot be taxed, sometimes the equipment responsible for this pollution can more easily be taxed. This solution will be especially appealing when there are several models of the same equipment good (such as cars or refrigerators), which provide the same service but cause different emission levels. The tax will bring about a substitution between the polluting products and the less polluting ones. It will be all the more efficient as there are close substitutes on the market, which are non-polluting.

Equipment taxes are based on the 'presumption principle', according to which the possession of a piece of equipment is tantamount to its utilization (IEA, 1993). When purchased, the equipment is taxed at a level equal to the expected environmental costs, and the tax is refunded only if the owner proves that he has polluted less than this level. For example, if a car is taxed on the basis of future environmental costs, and the car is destroyed soon after its purchase, part of the tax will be refunded.

Examples

- A tax on fuel-inefficient cars exists in the United States and in Ontario (Canada). In the United States, this 'gas guzzler tax' covers cars with a fuel consumption higher than 10.4 litres/100km. It has been very effective in reducing the consumption of passenger cars; however, it does not apply to the increasingly popular sport utility vehicles (SUVs), and is therefore much less effective than intended. Similarly, in Canada, the Government of Ontario has tried to apply a progressive 'tax on fuel-inefficient vehicles' to all cars with a consumption of more than 8.5 litres/100km. Following vigorous opposition from the industry, and also from automotive unions, the following measures made the tax more acceptable, but also less effective: (1) the tax rate for SUVs was strongly reduced; (2) a small subsidy was introduced for the most efficient vehicles, which consume less than 6.0 litres/100km; and (3), the name of the tax was changed to the less ominous 'tax for fuel conservation' (Bregha and Moffet, 1995).
- Supplementary taxes on the most polluting new cars exist in Norway and in Finland. We have also proposed a tax on new cars, which consume more fuel and emit more NO_x and noise than a certain level (Wallart, 1997).
- Taxes can be imposed on all polluting objects, for which there are good substitution possibilities, such as mopeds, motorbikes, refrigerators, light bulbs, lawn mowers, etc.

Taxes on Complements, Subsidies on Substitutes

Another possible solution is to tax a complement of the polluting good, or to subsidize a substitute. Since a direct emission tax is not possible, a tax on a complementary good will be optimal if the taxed good is a perfect complement to the polluting good. Similarly, if a perfect substitute exists, it can be subsidized in order to reach the optimum.[1]

Examples

The classic example is road traffic in cities. Congestion and pollution in cities are responsible for high levels of external costs, which would ideally require an internalization by means of a Pigouvian tax. However, for different reasons, this is not easy to do; tolls at city entries are exceptional (they exist in cities like Singapore, Cambridge, or Bergen, but mostly as experiments). From an administrative standpoint, as well as from a political one, it is easier to tackle the problem through complements and substitutes:

- Public transport is a close substitute for individual transport; as a result, most cities subsidize public transport.
- Parking places in city centres are a good complement to the use of cars in the city. Parking places in city centres can be taxed, in order to internalize external costs (pollution, noise, and congestion); alternatively, their quantity can be limited.[2]

However, because of the simultaneous presence of a substitute (public transport) and a complement (parking), economic theory is not conclusive; the optimality of subsidizing public transport vs taxing parking places is an empirical question (Wijkander, 1985). In practice, subsidies to public transport are common, but parking taxes are not; quantitative and regulatory limitations are preferred.

There are other examples of taxes on complements and subsidies on substitutes:

- Following the Kyoto Summit in 1997, the U.S. government proposed a temporary subsidy (between $3,000 and $4,000) on the most energy-efficient cars, which are substitutes for 'gas guzzlers'. This timid measure is far easier to implement politically than an increase in the gasoline tax.
- Repairing a product is a good substitute for purchasing a new one. For example, by repairing a car or a fridge, there is no need to buy a new one. Yet, the environmental impact of the repair is often much more favourable than that of the purchase (because purchasing a new product implies scrapping the old one, hence waste; also, the production and delivery of the new product can be polluting, or energy-intensive). Therefore, maintenance and repair activities involve external benefits. For this reason, one could subsidize, or remove taxes from, maintenance and repair activities. By decreasing the cost of repair and maintenance, the lives of the products are prolonged, and waste production decreases.

5.2   USER CHARGES AND THE POLLUTER-PAYS PRINCIPLE

There are many existing environmental taxes, the primary goal of which is not to reduce the pollution, but rather to raise revenue from polluters. This revenue will then allow the public sector to finance environmental activities, such as waste water treatment, or waste incineration. These user charges (also called user fees, or cost-covering charges) are a direct application of the polluter-pays principle.

The Polluter-Pays Principle

Basically, when pollution is emitted, three categories of economic players may take measures to reduce it, and bear the costs of doing so:

1. The polluters can reduce their polluting emissions, according to the polluter-pays principle.
2. The government (i.e. the taxpayers) can finance pollution reduction measures.
3. The victims of the pollution can pay the polluters so that they reduce their emissions; they can also take measures to protect themselves from the surrounding pollution.

Solution 3, where the victims subsidize the polluters, is unfair: the victims not only have to suffer the pollution, but also have to pay those who are responsible for it. This solution is also potentially ineffective, to the extent that it is generally easier for polluters to reduce their emissions, than it is for the victims to protect themselves. Thus, in the case of air pollution, the victims cannot easily protect themselves (unless by wearing gas masks), while polluters can easily install filters on their chimneys.

Solution 2 also has drawbacks. If the government pays, polluters have no incentive to reduce their pollution. Also, they will probably choose a production method with a pollution level greater than the optimal. Furthermore, it is unfair that the people who do not consume polluting goods have to bear part of their cost, by paying taxes to finance clean-up facilities.

For these different reasons, which are related to equity, economic efficiency, and also ethics, in 1972 the OECD formulated the polluter-pays principle, which is widely accepted nowadays (solution 1). The polluter-pays principle states that 'the polluter should bear the cost of measures to reduce pollution decided upon by public authorities to ensure that the environment is in an acceptable state'. Polluters have to bear the clean-up cost, whether they clean up the environment themselves, or whether the government cleans it up for them. Note that, according to this definition, environmental protection measures have to lead to an 'acceptable' quality of the environment: there is no mention of an optimal level, which would correspond to the optimum of the economic theory. The acceptable state is defined by public authorities (Pearce et al., 1989).

User Charges in General

With the internalization of external costs by means of a Pigouvian tax, each polluter individually compares the payment of the tax with the abatement cost. He will choose to reduce his pollution if the abatement cost is smaller than the tax; otherwise, he will continue to pollute, and will pay the tax. This solution will be optimal with the usual economic hypothesis of decreasing returns (i.e. the marginal cost and the average cost increase with the quantity produced).

However, in the environmental area, there are many common cases of increasing returns to scale (or economies of scale, i.e. decreasing costs). With increasing returns, a standard Pigouvian tax, or even a charges and standards approach, will not be optimal. A typical example is waste water treatment plants (Baranzini, 1996). A unique waste water treatment plant for a whole town is generally cheaper than one treatment plant in each district. With decreasing costs, the treatment is cheaper if centralized; for this reason, waste water treatment is often provided by the public sector, with only one plant for the entire town. But waste water treatment plants have to be financed somehow or other.

Faced with decreasing costs, the economic rule for an optimal resource allocation is that the user pays a price equal to the marginal cost of production of the service. However, as the marginal cost is decreasing, it will always be smaller than the average cost; for this reason, with a price equal to the marginal cost, the public utility service will always lose money.

Even without increasing returns to scale, there are many cases in which it is the government that provides environmental benefits. Indeed, as a general rule, the environment is a public good: on the one hand its consumption by an individual entails no diminution of the consumption of another individual (non-rivalry of consumption), on the other hand, it is impossible to exclude from its consumption someone who does not pay (impossibility of exclusion). If the environment is a public good, its production or its restoration by the market will be insufficient. For example, waste will not, or too rarely, be disposed of in an ecologically acceptable way. Therefore, the government has to take care of the disposal of waste, which again poses the question of financing.

Two possibilities exist to finance these services, both being largely applied in practice. The first is financing from the general budget of the government, that is, with revenues from general taxes such as the income tax or the value added tax. These taxes are based on the ability to pay principle, according to which taxpayers are asked to pay, relative to their economic capacity. The second possibility is to finance this public service with a tax linked to the service in question, according to the polluter-pays principle. For example, the disposal of old batteries, cars, or refrigerators can be financed by a tax paid by those who buy the good, instead of being paid by all the taxpayers.

With the environment, the old debate about whether to sell public services for a price, or to offer them free of charge, reappears (see for example Weber,

1988). Selling public environmental services for a price has the following advantages over providing them free of charge:

- It puts the polluter-pays principle into practice.
- The production costs of the public service are covered; at the same time, the price mechanism gives information about the demand for this service.
- Offering some public services at no charge results in an increase in apparent needs. The illusion of free services results in excessive demand, which in the end increases production capacities through over-investment, encouraged by the political process (Bird, 1976). On the contrary, when public services are priced, individuals have to make a choice, and there is no illusion that they are free.
- If a price is charged, it is possible to add external environmental costs to this price (Herber, 1983). This increases economic efficiency. For example, waste water treatment plants or incineration facilities may ask the waste producers, not only to cover the cost of treatment, but also to pay for the external costs of the residual pollution, which subsists even after treatment. This is impossible when the service is offered for free.

Selling public services also has disadvantages. First, there is the administrative cost of the tax collection. If the administrative cost is high, another source of financing may be preferable. Fullerton (1996) criticizes the high administrative cost of the collection of environmental taxes in the United States. Because of economies of scale in the tax collection, the administrative cost is (proportionally) high with taxes that raise small revenues. For this reason, most existing U.S. environmental taxes entail a high administrative cost.

Distributive aspects are another drawback of the pricing of public services. The traditional argument is that, if low-income people pay as much as high-income people, it is inequitable, because their ability to pay is different. However, it can be argued that a free supply of public goods is not always fair; and when the free supply is fair, this is often associated with a waste of resources (Weber, 1988). Also, it can be argued that there are means to correct income distribution other than the free supply of public goods. For example, equity considerations may favour a zero (or low) price for water consumption. However, with a low price, water is wasted. The solution is a progressive price structure: a low price is charged for basic water needs, and a higher price is charged for any additional consumption, so that all the costs are covered.

Examples of user charges

- User charges often cover the costs of waste water treatment. The charges may be proportional to the size of the household, to the area of the house, or to the consumption of water. As the charge covers the cost of waste water treatment, but is not closely related to the pollution emitted, it is a user charge and not an emission tax.

- Another example is given by taxes on oil and chemical products in the United States. The tax revenues finance the clean-up of old toxic waste landfills and oil spills. These taxes are user charges in a very broad sense, since whole industries are targeted and not specific companies. The rationale of taxing whole industries is that, often, the firms responsible for existing toxic landfills do not exist any more.

User charges are also used for household waste. Two fundamental tendencies coexist nowadays.

- On the one hand, there is a tendency towards taxing waste at the time of its collection, dumping or incineration. This corresponds to the end of a product's life: products are taxed when they are not used any more. One example is unit pricing for garbage collection and disposal, which exists in many municipalities (in the United States, Canada, Ireland, Germany, Switzerland, etc.). Another example is the landfill tax existing in France which applies to household waste entering landfills (industrial waste was exempted because of industry opposition).

- On the other hand, there are examples of disposal and recycling taxes paid *at the moment of the purchase*. This happens with refrigerators, batteries, computers, automobiles, oil, and beverage containers. These taxes cover the cost of treatment or recycling at the end of a product's life. The treatment or recycling can be done either by public firms, or by private, competing firms.

Is it better to tax goods when they are produced and sold (*ex ante*), or when they have become waste (*ex post*)? Taxing waste *ex post* is probably easier, and can be done at a decentralized level. However, waste is not only a local problem. Moreover, if the tax is due when entering the recycling or treatment process, there is a strong incentive for illegal dumping, which can be extremely harmful to the environment. A careful study of household responses to pricing garbage by the bag in a U.S. city shows that in response to unit pricing, households reduce the volume of garbage much more than the weight. Additional illegal dumping accounts for 28 to 43 per cent of the reduction in garbage weight (Fullerton and Kinnaman, 1996). As the treatment cost increases because of concerns for a better environment, the incentive for illegal dumping will increase as well.

Moreover, by taxing waste *ex post,* consumers, not producers, will pay the tax. While consumers can choose between different goods, they have no means to reduce the 'waste content' of a product; only producers can do that. In addition, consumers will often get rid of the goods many years after their purchase, sometimes as much as 50 years later; for this reason, their purchasing decisions are not, or hardly, influenced by the cost of the later disposal or treatment (consider older people, who have accumulated objects during their lives: did they ever think about the future costs of disposal?) *Ex post* waste charges do not provide a direct relationship between production and consumption decisions, and the production of waste.

For those reasons, it is worth thinking about taxing goods *ex ante,* since every good will sooner or later end its life as waste. This is already done in some countries for cars or refrigerators, but it could be extended to many other products, such as tyres, motorbikes, furniture, stoves, TVs, CDs, paper, packaging, toys, light bulbs, clothes, mattresses, etc.

User Charges when Polluting Emissions can be Directly Taxed

In practice, many taxes are a combination of the three following characteristics: (*a*) their main objective is to raise revenues; (*b*) the tax level is low; and (*c*) the revenues are earmarked for environmental spending in the area of the tax (Hahn, 1989). All these three characteristics do not correspond to the logic of Pigouvian taxes, which (*a*) should provide incentives instead of raising revenue, (*b*) should be at a sufficiently high level to provide these incentives, and (*c*) should not be earmarked for environmental spending.

Although these taxes do not correspond to the logic of Pigouvian taxes, their existence and frequency cannot be ignored. (We give examples at the end of this section). Here, we will present a simple model, which combines the three above-mentioned characteristics. The model shows that these taxes will result in the optimal level of pollution.

Figure 5.1 represents the marginal abatement cost (MAC) and the marginal external cost (MEC) for a pollutant. Initially, without any clean-up measures, the emission level is E_0. With the traditional Pigouvian solution, the government imposes a tax equal to the marginal external cost existing at the optimal pollution level. As the optimal emission level is E_2, the Pigouvian tax will be at a level t_2. With this Pigouvian tax, firms reduce their emissions to the level E_2.

Suppose now that the government sets the tax at level t_1. (This may happen for example if the high rate of a Pigouvian tax causes acceptability problems.) This tax will bring emissions down to the level E_1, which is higher than the optimal level E_2. But at this level E_1, the government gets tax revenues, which are equal to area $C+D$.

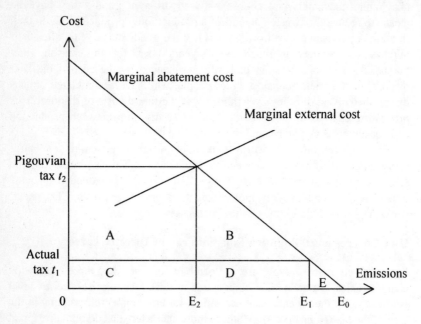

Figure 5.1 Optimality of a particular type of user charge

Suppose that the government uses these revenues to build supplementary emission treatment facilities, which will abate emissions from E_1 to E_2. The cost of these facilities will be equal to area $B+D$. If the tax level t_1 is such that this supplementary expense $(B+D)$ is equal to the tax revenues $(C+D)$, then the result will be exactly the optimal pollution E_2. We have then the following result:

A suboptimal tax (t_1) results in the optimal pollution level (E_2), provided that its revenues are used for abatement spending, and that the tax level is set adequately. (Adequately means $B+D=C+D$, that is, $B=C$.)

The solution outlined here, and the Pigouvian solution, both result in the same optimal pollution level. However, the distributive impacts are different:

- In the Pigouvian case (t_2), polluters pay $(B+D+E)$ to reduce their emissions, and $(A+C)$ as a tax on the remaining emissions. They pay a total of $(A+B+C+D+E)$.
- With the tax t_1, whose revenues are used to finance additional abatement, polluters pay (E) to reduce the emissions, and $(C+D)$ as tax. They pay a total of $(C+D+E)$.

By choosing the Pigouvian solution (t_2) instead of t_1, polluters bear an additional cost equal to area $(A+B)$. Therefore, polluters have a strong preference for solution t_1 instead of the Pigouvian solution. On the other hand, the government prefers the Pigouvian solution, with which it can keep the tax revenues.

The condition $B=C$ suggests another remark. With the tax t_1, whose revenues are used to abate emissions, firms save an amount $A+B$. This amount is equal to $A+C$, which corresponds to the tax payment on the remaining emissions from the Pigouvian case. This means that, with solution t_1, firms save the tax on the remaining emissions. On the other hand, with solution t_1, firms bear a total cost of $(C+D+E)$. But this amount is also equal to $(B+D+E)$, which is the cost of reducing emissions in order to attain the optimal level of pollution. This means that, with solution t_1, firms have to bear only the abatement cost *(B+D+E)*, but not the tax on the remaining emissions *(A+C)*.

For the polluters, this solution corresponds to other instruments, which do not require a tax payment on the remaining emissions either: grandfathered emission permits, or a tax whose revenues are redistributed to polluters (see Chapter 2). As polluters save an amount *(A+C)*, they will favour such a system, instead of a Pigouvian tax, whose revenues fill the coffers of the state. Other advantages include a smaller cost increase for firms, hence fewer firms going bankrupt, and a smaller loss of consumer surplus. Also, the price hike due to the tax is smaller.

Contrary to the user charge of the preceding section, here the tax is levied on the polluting emission. Therefore, the tax itself causes a reduction in emissions. Traditional user charges also raise revenues from polluters, but they are not directly levied on polluting emissions (for example, they are levied on water consumption). The tax revenue is the main objective of traditional user charges, and there is little or no incentive effect. In practice, it is not always easy to make a distinction between those two types of user charges; often, the incentive and the revenue characteristics will be present simultaneously.

Examples
- Waste water taxes levied on industries in France and Germany. In these two countries, the tax level depends on both the quantity and the harmfulness of effluents. Some incentive is provided by the tax, and a supplementary improvement in water quality is made possible through subsidies for waste water treatment, which are financed by the tax. In France, the charges are set so as to balance the pollution control budget of the river basin agency (as is the case in our model). The toxicity of industrial effluents is taken into account. (Households pay a traditional user charge: a uniform charge is simply added to the price of water, hence little incentive effect.)
- When highway traffic noise is a problem, an increase in the gasoline tax may finance noise barriers along highways: the higher gas tax reduces the number of miles travelled, hence less noise, and the noise barriers bring about a further noise reduction.
- A carbon tax can finance energy efficiency measures, reforestation or preparation for global warming. As highlighted in the study 'Preparing for an uncertain climate' of the U.S. Office of Technology Assessment (1994), it is politically very difficult to stabilize the emissions of CO_2, and unthinkable to stabilize the concentration of CO_2. It is therefore necessary for people and ecosystems to adapt to higher global temperatures. This adaptation could be financed with the revenue of a carbon tax.
- After the fall of the communist regime, Russia wanted to introduce taxes on different air pollutants, which it did in 1991. The country could choose between a tax based on the estimated cost of the pollution (a Pigouvian tax) and a tax to finance regional pollution control programs (a user charge). Since the level of the user charge was 10 to 15 times lower than the level of the Pigouvian tax, the choice was made quickly: firms were simply unable to pay the Pigouvian tax (Golub and Strukova, 1994).

5.3   TAXES COMBINED WITH SUBSIDIES

Besides the mere combination of a tax and a subsidy, we will also present deposit-refund systems, as well as differential taxes. With all these systems, the political acceptability is greater than with usual emission taxes; the reason is that the government does not receive any supplementary revenue.

Deposit-refund Systems

With a deposit-refund scheme, for example on beverage containers, the individual pays a tax (the deposit) when he buys a beverage in a container. Later, when he returns the container for recycling or proper disposal, the deposit is refunded. In other words, returning the container for recycling or proper disposal is subsidized. A deposit-refund scheme combines a tax and a subsidy, but the incentive element is the subsidy; the tax only raises the revenue which pays for the subsidy. The deposit has to be high enough so that the consumer returns the container.

Why choose a deposit-refund scheme and not a Pigouvian tax? With beverage containers, the Pigouvian solution would be to impose a tax on littering and improper disposal. However, this is impossible to control. Therefore, the recovery of empty containers is subsidized (with the revenue of a tax paid at the time of purchase). As littering and improper disposal cannot be avoided with a tax, they are avoided with a subsidy (the refund). And contrary to a traditional subsidy, the consumer himself, not the taxpayer, pays for the refund.

Examples
- Deposit-refund systems are widely used for beverage containers.
- In addition, they are appropriate for all the products for which the costs of improper disposal are high, such as: lubricating oil, chlorinated chemicals, solvents, batteries, or refrigerators.

Combination of a Tax and a Subsidy

The next instrument is the combination of a tax and a subsidy, in relation to a critical level of emission (C). If the polluter emits more than C, he pays the emission tax on the level exceeding C; and if he emits less than C, he receives a subsidy according to his clean-up effort (Sorensen, 1993; Faucheux and Noël, 1995, p. 206). Here, the incentive comes from both the tax and the subsidy: the tax gives an incentive to reduce the pollution level to C, and the subsidy offers a supplementary incentive to go beyond C (remember from Chapter 1 that a tax and a subsidy can bring about the same result).

The advantage of this system is the possibility of obtaining budgetary neutrality, hence a better political acceptability than usual emission taxes. However, budgetary neutrality is not attained easily; more likely, the government will have to constantly adapt the level of emission C if it wants to obtain a neutral impact on the budget. If it does not, the tax revenues may decrease regularly while the subsidies increase; from then on, this system faces the same type of criticisms as the pure subsidy (see Chapter 2).

Tax Differential

The tax differential, also called feebate,[3] introduces a price differentiation for similar products, according to their environmental impact. The classic example is the tax differential existing between unleaded and leaded gasoline. The tax differential combines two mechanisms:

- a tax is levied on a product for which there is a close substitute, which is less polluting;
- the tax revenues pay for a reduction in the price of this substitute.

The tax increases the price of the more polluting good, and the subsidy decreases the price of the less polluting substitute. There is a modification in the relative price between the polluting and the less polluting good, which shifts the consumption towards the cleaner good. This is generally done with a neutral impact on the budget.

From a theoretical point of view, the tax differential can be related to one of the two following rationales:

1. The tax differential can be linked to the Pigouvian theory, by decomposing it into a classic Pigouvian tax, and a lump sum subsidy. Take the following example: in the market for new cars, there are two models, one polluting more than the other. During the expected life of these cars, the external costs of the polluting emissions are estimated at $2,000 for the first car, and $5,000 for the second. A Pigouvian tax, equal to these external costs, is therefore imposed on each car. Also, a lump sum subsidy (the same for both vehicles) is introduced. If equal quantities of these two models are sold, the subsidy will be equal to ($2,000 + $5,000)/2 = $3,500 for each car. For the cleaner vehicle, the buyer will therefore pay:

   price + tax - subsidy = price + 2,000 - 3,500 = price - 1,500

   and he will get a bonus of $1,500. For the more polluting car, the buyer will pay:

   price + tax - subsidy = price + 5,000 - 3,500 = price + 1,500

   which is a price increase of $1,500. In effect, we have a tax differential, with a neutral effect on the budget of the government. The Pigouvian component internalizes the external costs of the pollution. As for the subsidy, it does not introduce distortions between each car, since it is a lump sum. However, because of the subsidy, this scheme is not equivalent to a usual Pigouvian tax. It does not correct distortions between cars and other non-polluting goods. For this reason, when possible, pure Pigouvian taxes are a better choice; only when they are not feasible, for example because of political constraints, can a tax differential be considered.

2. Besides the (static) internalization of external costs as in the above example, the tax differential can also be justified from a dynamic perspective, as an incentive towards technological progress. The tax differential encourages the substitution with cleaner products. Its objective is therefore not a static optimum, but rather a dynamic incentive for technological change.

Examples
- A tax differential between leaded and unleaded gasoline exists in many countries.
- A tax differential according to emissions for new cars exists in Sweden and Germany. This measure can be seen as a complement to gasoline taxes, which apply indiscriminately to all cars, whatever their emission level.
- Other areas may be considered: light bulbs (some consuming much energy and others not), detergents (with or without phosphates), paints (with or without volatile organic compounds), electric household appliances (according to their energy consumption), etc.

5.4   REVENUE-RAISING ENVIRONMENTAL TAXES

Finally, there are taxes, such as the energy tax, for which the primary objective is not environmental but fiscal. The objective is to raise revenue, independent of environmental considerations, or beyond the level required from an environmental point of view. In order to define and plan the details of the tax, as well as to avoid any conflict, it is important that the fiscal objective is clearly established and publicized.

Of course, even if it is not their main objective, these taxes will also affect the environment. They will improve the quality of the environment, because they decrease the production and consumption of polluting goods. For example, energy taxes reduce the production and consumption of energy; this, in turn, reduces the polluting emissions associated with this production and consumption.

As the objective of these taxes is fiscal, they have to be compared with other taxes (new taxes, or an increase in existing taxes). As we will see in section 9.4, the question of whether environmental taxes are better adapted to raising tax revenues than existing taxes, is rather controversial. Most studies conclude that, if it can be advantageous in some cases to replace a bad tax (which creates important distortions) with an environmental tax, often a traditional tax will be better adapted to raising revenue.

Indeed, environmental taxes, which are levied on a relatively narrow tax base (for example, gasoline), may cause greater distortions than traditional taxes, which are imposed on a very large tax base (income, consumption, or wealth). For this reason, environmental taxes are not always adapted to raising revenue. However, this may change once the environmental benefits are included in the analysis. Therefore, when comparing a revenue-raising environmental tax with traditional taxes, the environmental benefits should never be neglected in the analysis.

Examples

In order to be favourable from a fiscal point of view, the environmental tax must have several characteristics: it must have a large tax base, which is relatively unaffected by the levying of the tax; it has to be fair with regard to income distribution; it has to raise stable revenues; and it has to be levied with small administrative cost.

- Energy taxes have existed for a long time in many European countries. Governments have taxed energy because of fiscal considerations[4] (fiscal objective), but sometimes also to reduce the energy dependence of the country (incentive objective). Most of the time, the tax revenues flow into the general fund of the government.
- Gasoline taxes may be used to raise revenue. However, they are often earmarked for road traffic expenses (in which case they are user fees or user charges) or they have an incentive goal (in which case, they correspond to the Pigouvian approach, or to the charges and standards approach).

5.5   CONCLUSION

We have seen that Pigouvian taxes, aiming at optimizing the pollution by internalizing external costs, are difficult to apply in practice. Implementation problems and difficulties, as well as theoretical flaws, prevent easy achievement of the optimal level of pollution. On the other hand, we have seen that with the charges and standards approach, it is possible to achieve a given environmental objective in a cost-effective manner. The charges and standards approach can be used either to replace Pigouvian taxes, or to achieve a sustainable development objective. In both cases, they rely on the same procedure: the political process defines the environmental objective, and with the tax, it is possible to achieve it at the least cost.

Can we forget the concepts of a Pigouvian tax and the internalization of external costs? In our opinion, these concepts remain useful as references, to which actual instruments can be compared. For example, the level of a gasoline tax can be compared to the estimated external costs of road transport; this will provide a reference for the government, which may, or may not, change the tax rate towards this presumed optimum. However, when facing issues related to sustainable development, the estimation of external costs is seriously insufficient, because it does not take into account irreversibility, uncertainty, multidimensionality, or intergenerational equity. In this case, the precautionary principle and the adoption of safe minimum standards are better guides for action.

As we have seen in this chapter, existing environmental taxes do not follow one unique pattern, but are remarkably diverse; and there are even more possibilities of introducing new ones. Existing taxes often combine a revenue-raising objective, incentive characteristics, a differentiated treatment of different groups in the economy, and regulatory features. Many reasons have induced practitioners to depart from the theoretical models. We have already examined the technical and economic reasons. Also, we have often mentioned acceptability problems, but without going into detail. We will now address the issue of the acceptability of environmental taxes.

NOTES

1. If a complement and a substitute are simultaneously present, the situation is not straightforward; in order to reach the optimum, it is necessary to take into account the interactions between the complement and the substitute (Wijkander, 1985).
2. Limiting price and limiting quantity result in the same allocative impact, but the distributive impact is different: if the quantity is artificially limited, owners of parking places will get a scarcity premium, and if parking places are taxed, the government will get revenue.
3. Feebate is a contraction of fee and rebate.
4. Energy taxes levy substantial revenues at a very small administrative cost. Also, the price-elasticity of energy demand is low, hence small distortions.

PART THREE

The Acceptability of Environmental Taxes

6.   Two Categories of Opposition

6.1   INTRODUCTION

Economic instruments for environmental protection, such as environmental taxes, increase society's welfare; as we have seen in Chapter 3, under some conditions, they lead to an optimal situation. Also, they have allocative advantages in comparison to regulations: they give firms the choice of paying the tax or taking clean-up measures, which a uniform regulation does not. In achieving a certain pollution reduction objective, the implied cost for the whole society is smaller with taxes than with regulations; in other words, for a given cost, the pollution can be reduced more with taxes than with regulations. Furthermore, taxes are also more effective than regulations from the point of view of long-term prevention of environmental damage.

Given these multiple advantages, environmental taxes should therefore gain the approval of a large majority. However, in practice, important acceptability problems are observed. As noted by Cropper and Oates (1992), while the 'intellectual structure' of environmental economics has been both broadened and strengthened in the past 20 years, its contribution to the design and implementation of environmental policy has been mixed and confusing:

> It reveals a policy environment characterized by a real ambivalence (and, in some instances, an active hostility) to a central role for economics in environmental decision making.

This mixed record applies to tradable permits as well as environmental taxes. There are several reasons for this.

One reason for the rejection is certainly the relative novelty of the instrument. As illustrated by the French adage *'un bon impôt est un vieil impôt'* [a good tax is an old tax], the acceptability of taxes improves over time, as they are adapted to deal with various situations, as taxpayers become accustomed to paying them, or to modifying their behaviour in order to avoid paying them. In this respect, environmental taxes are probably no different from other taxes. However, the problem of the novelty tends to solve itself as the utilization of economic instruments spreads. And it is always possible initially to introduce a tax at a low rate, to gain experience with the instrument, and later modify the tax or increase its rate.

Another often mentioned reason has to do with taxes and their acceptability in general.[1] Taxes are one means for the government to raise revenue. Yet, the government is often perceived as an inefficient and bureaucratic organization, which wastes resources. This explains why some individuals reject any increase in its resources. If this is the case, environmental taxes will cause acceptability problems if they add new resources to the government budget. However, it is easy to avoid these problems by redistributing tax revenues in the economy; the different redistribution options will be analysed in detail in the fourth part of this book.

Some opposition is for technical reasons, such as the difficulty of calculating the optimal level of the tax, the regressivity of some environmental taxes, the uncertainty of their impact, or the fear that they will not prevent further deterioration of the environment. Tax projects are often complex or ill-advised; they often mix environmental and fiscal objectives, or they entail heavy administrative costs (Pearson, 1995). In order to avoid a rejection based on technical considerations, the tax project has to be prepared carefully, and the affected players have to be consulted.

Other factors influence the acceptance or the rejection of an environmental tax project. For example, the education level of the population influences the tendency towards a vote favouring the environment. The same is true with the economic health of the region or the country: when people are unemployed, they will rather vote for jobs than for the environment (Frey and Schneider, 1996). Psychological considerations are also important. Surveys show that the more visible taxes are less willingly accepted by the population. Also, the acceptability of taxes does not seem to be related to an objective measure of fairness: indirect taxes are probably more popular and are considered as more equitable, although they are less progressive than direct taxes (Lewis, 1982).

Moreover, taxes are increasingly accepted only in return for public benefits, whatever they may be. Indeed, many citizens are not fully aware of the relationship between public revenues and expenditures. Taxes will be more readily accepted if citizens realize this relationship. Thus, individuals are more inclined to accept new taxes in return for supplementary benefits, than without a counterpart. A question such as 'Are you willing to pay new environmental taxes?' will probably result in a negative answer, while the following forms are more favourable: 'Are you willing to pay new environmental taxes if the revenues are used to reduce another tax?' or 'Are you willing to pay new environmental taxes in order to finance this environmental protection activity?'. Already, these considerations show us that we have to pay attention to the utilization of tax revenues.

In the field of automobile taxation, a critical factor is the restricting nature of the instrument. A survey of Swiss households showed that the measures which are the least restricting for motorists are the most easily accepted (Bütschi and Kriesi, 1994). Thus, technological improvements, car-pooling and electrical vehicles are judged favourably by the population, while taxes of any kind, as well as supplementary speed limitations, are less readily accepted.

In the same context, Witherspoon (1995) shows that those who use cars are much less inclined to accept traffic reduction policies than those who do not use them. Furthermore, this author shows that the acceptability of environmental policy measures is not so much influenced by the knowledge of environmental problems, but rather by attitudes in general towards the intervention of public authorities. On the other hand, for Diekmann and Preisendörfer (1991), information as well as environmental ethics increase the acceptability of environmental measures, even if they are less efficient than economic incentives. Thus, pricing garbage by the bag is more readily accepted by people who are informed and educated about environmental problems, than by others. Information and education cannot be neglected as environmental policy instruments.

In practice, four distinct groups are basically opposed to environmental taxes (Hahn, 1989; Kelman, 1981; Stähelin-Witt, 1991). The strongest opposition to any type of environmental tax comes first of all from the *industries* adversely affected by environmental protection measures. More surprisingly, a certain opposition comes from *ecologists*, although they are divided on this matter. Also, *members of left political parties* seem to have a limited trust in the market mechanisms and prefer an intervention by the government. When the automobile is involved, there is also opposition from *motorists and automobile associations*; they oppose any measure that increases the costs of road transportation.

The existence of these four groups enables us to distinguish between two fundamentally different kinds of opposition:

- The opposition from those who consider the economic approach as inadequate to solve environmental problems. These people are opposed to environmental taxes for philosophical, moral or ethical reasons. Their criticism is supported mainly by the 'licence to pollute' argument (see below). Ecologists and leftists belong to this first category.
- The opposition from those who are interested in preserving the status quo, because they are the losers, if an environmental protection policy is implemented. Industrialists and motorists belong to this second category.

6.2   OPPOSITION FOR PHILOSOPHICAL, MORAL OR ETHICAL REASONS

The opposition to environmental taxes for philosophical, moral or ethical reasons is related to the use of market mechanisms in order to protect the environment. According to this argument, by paying the tax or buying the permit, individuals or firms buy a 'licence to pollute'. By contrast, traditional instruments, such as emission standards, directly control the maximum allowed amount of emissions, and do not rely on market mechanisms.

Indeed, there are several ways to make decisions in a democracy. The market is one such way, but the political process, social mechanisms and non-profit organizations can also produce and allocate goods and services. The protection of the environment, as well as any other issue in our society, can be governed through the use of markets, or other mechanisms. The question of economic instruments vs regulations is, therefore, part of the fundamental issue of the importance our society wishes to assign to the market as a means of organizing itself.

Economic instruments for environmental protection are based on market mechanisms. However, for some people, the use of market mechanisms to protect the environment causes uneasiness and concern, which are related to the very idea of extending the use of the market. In the end, this results in the rejection of economic instruments. In what follows, we will try to understand the causes of this uneasiness; we will see how they are inherent in the economic approach, and if it is possible to take them into account when designing the instrument. In order to do that, it is necessary to begin with the foundations, principles, and values of the market system, and see what they imply when they are applied to the environment.

First of all, the philosophical tradition behind the economic approach is anthropocentric (human-centred), as opposed to an ecocentric perspective which sees the human species as part of an ecosystem. In the anthropocentrist tradition, human beings have more rights than other species, and nature is widely available to satisfy human needs. However, today many people do not adhere to this view. Those known as 'deep ecologists' adhere to ecocentrism. From the ecocentric perspective, the human species is only one species among others, and has no more rights than others.

The economic theory of the environment clearly refers to the anthropocentric framework: in economics, the environment is a concern only if it causes external costs to human beings. As noted by Bürgenmeier (1994b), the mere use of the term 'environment' instead of 'nature' is a reference to a society which has integrated the transition from a natural world to an artificial one. Indeed, the term 'nature' applies to what exists without human intervention, while the term 'environment' refers to the human environment. Implicitly, talking about the environment presupposes the adoption of an anthropocentrist framework. Such an approach is clearly normative, hence debatable.

Next, the usual approach in economics is to consider environmental problems as a market failure, preventing an optimal functioning of the market. The government has to intervene only when there is a market failure, and not when the market can function normally. This approach refers to an underlying philosophy that views the market as the guiding reference for the organization of society. As the market is after all only the reflection of consumer sovereignty, the action of the government has to be defined according to this sovereignty (Weber, 1991).

This sovereignty of the market reflects an individualistic idea of society. For example, when considering the environment as external to the market, the environment enters the economic sphere only if individuals realize the existence of a cost related to the environment (Bürgenmeier, 1994, p. 85). The environment has a value only if individual costs or benefits are associated with it. It has to be protected through the translation of these costs into monetary terms, and their aggregation. However, there is no direct relationship between individual and social behaviour. When individuals maximize their utility, this does not entail a social rationality (Kirman, 1992). Moreover, the market system also influences society through the way in which it rules relationships between individuals. Economic incentives not only leave more room for individual freedom than standards and regulations, but also tend to promote self-interest.

The main economic characteristics of the market system are the private ownership of capital, and the price mechanism as the main incentive mechanism. The advantages of an allocation of resources through the market are widely known. However, even in a market economy, not everything is governed through the markets. Not only are many things not for sale, but many incentive mechanisms are not based on prices. The reasons which explain why some things are not part of the market system also apply to the environmental debate. Not surprisingly, many opponents of the economic instruments are found among those who are hostile to 'the market' in general.

More precisely, the uneasiness caused by economic instruments for environmental protection has to do with the relationship between the environment and the fundamental principles that are the basis of the market system. This uneasiness comes from the following factors: (Kelman, 1981; Goodin, 1994; Frey and Schneider, 1996; Bürgenmeier et al., 1997)

1. The first objection is related to the ownership of the environment. Many people feel that the environment does not belong to anybody, that nature has its own rights. And what is not owned cannot be sold. As the

government does not own the environment, it has no right to give it away, and still less of a right to benefit from its sale.

2. Using economic instruments for environmental protection often means bringing the environment into a system of markets and prices of which it previously has not been a part. However, for many people, putting a price on some things causes, at least intuitively, an uneasiness that is related to a high 'value' of these things. For example, most people do not sell their help to their friends, because it would dramatically reduce the 'value' of friendship. Most things can be bought or sold, but for some special things, we say: 'this is not for sale'. The natural environment possesses such a high value.

3. By integrating the environment into the market, society refuses to pass a value judgment on the polluting behaviour. To the extent that the price has been paid, it becomes as acceptable to pollute the environment as to consume any other good, and thus there is nothing wrong with polluting the environment. However, such an attitude is considered as cynical, or even unacceptable, by many people who believe that society should stigmatize polluting behaviour.

4. Often with economic incentives, rich people will pay the tax and continue polluting as before, while poor people will have to modify their behaviour in order to avoid paying the tax. For the economist, the environment is primarily viewed as an allocative problem: there is a pollution problem because the external costs of production or consumption are not taken into account by the market. Dealing with environmental problems from an allocative point of view tends to neglect distributive considerations. Quoting Bürgenmeier (1994, p. 18), it is often 'first efficiency, then equity'. If the market is the realm of freedom, it is also the realm of inequality. However, as nature is part of a common heritage, many people believe that its consumption does not have to depend on a very unequal ability to pay. Law, on the other hand, has to be egalitarian with all individuals, whatever their income or wealth.

5. Finally, by pushing people into protecting the environment in order to save money, society tends to make a statement of indifference towards the motives of people, and to be interested only in the results. Yet, society cares about the motives of people. This can be noted clearly in criminal law: killing someone accidentally is not the same as killing someone intentionally. Using economic instruments can result in the endorsement of self-interested behaviour, instead of other motives, for obtaining the result desired by society. This may even lead to the opposite result: if people were motivated to protect the environment without incentives, rewarding them for this action might destroy this intrinsic motivation.

These objections are not only characteristic of the environment, but explain why many aspects of society are not relegated to the market. They explain why human beings cannot sell themselves into slavery; they explain why votes, freedom of speech, and natural reserves, cannot be legally bought and sold.

Implications for the Design of Instruments for Environmental Protection

Each of the above mentioned objections could lead to a simple and straightforward recommendation: the rejection of economic instruments for environmental protection. However, given the undeniable advantages and considerable potential of those instruments, it is worth adopting a more positive attitude and trying to integrate, as much as possible, these ethical considerations into the design of economic instruments. Each of the five objections enables us to present some implications for the design of economic instruments.

Proposition 1. *The design and the name of the instrument reply, at least partially, to the criticism of selling the ownership of the environment.*

Giving a right to pollute, and especially selling a right to pollute, can be considered as wrong, to the extent that only what is owned can be sold, and nobody owns the environment. First, note that, if it is claimed that economic instruments give the right and the freedom to pollute insofar as the corresponding price has been paid, this has to be compared with the alternative, which is regulation. Yet, regulations also grant the right to pollute the environment, as long as it is not beyond the standard. Hence the following question: Are granting the right to pollute free of charge, and selling the right to pollute, fundamentally different?

Second, we already discussed the question of whether the tax had to replace or to complement existing regulations (Chapter 2). When introducing a tax, if previous regulations are ruled out, polluters are given a potentially unlimited freedom to pollute. On the other hand, if the tax complements a regulation, the freedom given to polluters is limited; and it is the idea of selling a potentially unlimited right to pollute that is especially frightening. If the existing standard (or even an older, less strict standard) is preserved when the tax is introduced, the change is less radical, and the criticism of selling the ownership of the environment loses some of its relevance. By preserving the regulation, the innovation is more moderate and more readily accepted (this is what happened with water taxes in Germany, see Brown and Johnson, 1984).

Finally, concerns about granting the right to pollute imply that the tax is a more acceptable instrument than emission permits. For Goodin (1994), transferable emission permits are the most 'dramatic' form of the economic approach. Transferable permits are closest to the very idea of selling that which cannot be sold. In this respect, the terms and the formulation chosen are important. For example, in order to improve the political acceptability of emission permits, the American Clean Air Act uses the expressions 'emission reduction credit' and 'allowances', rather than the expressions 'pollution rights' or 'permits' which have more emotional connotations (Crandall, 1983; Stritt, 1997).

Proposition 2. *It is more acceptable to modify the price of something that is already traded in markets or priced, than to put a price on a pollutant that has never previously been traded in markets or priced.*

One objection came from putting a price on something that was not priced before, such as pollution. However, many polluting goods are already exchanged in the marketplace, and have prices. For example, there is a market for oil, coal, gasoline, automobiles, solvents, CFC, batteries, fertilizers, herbicides, pesticides, etc. Moreover, most of these products are taxed in one way or another, be it through general consumption taxes, or through specific ones (gasoline tax, energy tax). As the pollution is already associated with the price of the good, it cannot be claimed that the pollution is 'not for sale', or priceless. If the prices of these products are modified through a product charge, the criticism of putting a price on something that has not been previously traded or priced does not apply with the same strength.

The same observation can be made with waste, and waste water. In the case of waste water treatment, before effluent charges were introduced households and industries already paid for the treatment cost. The cost of operating treatment plants was financed for example with the income tax, the property tax, or a higher water price. This means that, even without an effluent charge, a price was already associated with the pollution. Today, when effluent charges are introduced, they do not introduce the pollution into the price system (this has already been done before), but they only require that the waste water treatment cost is paid with an effluent charge, rather than with a more traditional tax.

And it can be observed in practice that the vast majority of existing taxes and charges can be found in areas that were already associated with a price, such as gasoline, automobiles, CFC, energy, waste water, or batteries. There are far fewer examples of economic instruments in areas that were never priced before, such as noise[2] or air pollution.

Proposition 3. *Taxes combined with regulations, as well as a charges and standards approach, are more acceptable than Pigouvian taxes.*

One objection came from the fact that, by introducing pollutants into the market system, society refused to pass a value judgment, refused to assert that it is 'wrong' to pollute. This problem is not so strong with regulations: regulations distinguish what is allowed from what is forbidden, in other words, what is right from what is wrong. With a regulation, the degradation of the environment, beyond some level, is comparable to a 'sin'. On the other hand, with economic instruments any pollution is allowed if the polluter has paid the corresponding tax. There is nothing wrong *per se* with polluting the environment.[3]

Let us first note that our societies have an ambiguous attitude towards taxation: indeed, taxes are usually levied on activities useful to society, such as working or investing. But there are also 'sin taxes', which are levied on more harmful activities such as gambling, smoking, or drinking. This ambiguous attitude also exists with environmental taxes: does taxing pollution imply a value judgment on the polluting behaviour, or not? And if tobacco and alcohol are taxed, why not pollution?

On the other hand, if the tax complements an existing regulation instead of replacing it, society does not cease to make a value judgment on the polluting behaviour. Indeed, if a regulation subsists parallel to the tax, up to a certain level the pollution will be tolerated (and taxed), and beyond this level any supplementary pollution will be forbidden (as in the pure regulation case). It is especially when the tax replaces the regulation that the value judgment is weakened.

For Goodin (1994), the 'philosophy' of the tax determines the existence of a value judgment. With the Pigouvian approach, the tax is set at a level which ensures that polluters bear the social cost of their activities. As soon as polluters bear the full social cost, polluting the environment becomes socially optimal. Yet this idea of a socially optimal level of pollution is problematic. By using the concepts of optimal level of pollution, and optimal Pigouvian taxes, what was wrong is rendered right. A charges and standards approach, on the other hand, does not pose this kind of problem: to the extent that the tax solely aims to achieve a pollution reduction objective, the tax becomes a simple means to reduce pollution, and does not aim at the more ambitious objective of optimizing pollution. By using environmental taxes as 'policy enforcement', instead of 'policy choice', the instrument is insulated against the criticism of turning wrongs into rights.[4]

Finally, the difference between a Pigouvian tax and a charges and standards approach has another significance. As we have seen in Chapter 4, with a charges and standards approach, the quality of the environment is decided by means of a political process, through a democratic mechanism. On the other hand, with the Pigouvian tax, the quality of the environment depends on the individuals' monetary valuation of external costs; the willingness to pay on the part of individuals determines the quality of the environment. The difference between the Pigouvian tax and the charges and standards approach is more than a technical choice:

- With the Pigouvian tax, the choice of the quality of the environment is decided through the market (the principle: one dollar = one vote).
- With the charges and standards approach, the quality of the environment is decided democratically (the principle: one person = one vote).

Before going into the technical details of Pigouvian taxes vs the charges and standards approach, society has to decide whether the quality of the environment should be decided through the monetary valuations of individuals, or democratically.

Proposition 4. *It is essential to take equity considerations into account when designing the instrument.*

In a shortage situation, the economic approach limits demand through prices, which many people consider as unfair. This explains why many services do not increase their prices even when demand largely exceeds capacity (Frey, 1986). This happens with theatres, operas, festivals, ski resorts, museums, exhibitions, historical monuments, restaurants, etc. Rationing quantities is often more easily accepted, even if less efficient. In the area of the environment, economists recommend the introduction of urban tolls or parking taxes in order to decrease the costs of urban congestion. Such an approach is economically efficient, but the result is that only those who can afford it will use their car in the city. The congestion causes costs, but is more egalitarian: everybody can take his car and enter the jam.

If equity considerations are not taken into account in the design of a tax, this can be fatal to the project. Yet, with some imagination, it is often possible to combine economic incentives and social justice, by using economic incentives while allowing everybody, rich and poor, some basic consumption of the good. For example:

- For water pricing, some people advocate a progressive pricing structure: a basic consumption is invoiced at a low price (under the cost of providing water and treating waste water); and beyond this level the price increases rapidly, so that in the end the total cost is covered.

- The American 'gas guzzler tax' is only levied on the most fuel inefficient cars; those cars are generally more expensive than average.

The impact of the tax on income distribution can also be corrected by redistributing tax revenues to the poorer people (see the fourth part of this book).

Proposition 5. *Ill-conceived environmental protection instruments may discourage people from acting in favour of the environment by themselves. In contrast, a well-designed tax may actually increase the awareness and responsibility of polluters.*

Often, individuals act in favour of the environment by themselves, without any reward other than their personal satisfaction. They are 'intrinsically motivated' to protect the environment. Note that people act by themselves in an ecological way especially when the associated effort is not too great: thus, most people agree to sort their waste (small effort), but do not so easily forgo the use of their car to use public transport instead (the effort is too great).

When individuals act in favour of the environment by themselves, the introduction of economic incentives can in some cases deter them from doing so (Frey, 1992; Frey and Schneider, 1996). Indeed, for people who are already prone to act by themselves, the introduction of an external reward may undermine their intrinsic motivation; this is a well-known mechanism in psychology: the introduction of a reward undermines rather than enhances intrinsic motivation.

Psychologists have shown that it is possible to avoid the loss of intrinsic motivation, and even to enhance motivation, if the reward is satisfying to the one who receives it, or if it recognizes success, competence, or superior performance. The reward has to give certain information to the one who receives it, but not control the individual. For example, a scholarship or a wage increase is a positive reward, which can enhance the motivation of the beneficiary by acknowledging his competence (see for example Baron, 1989).

Is it possible to apply these findings to environmental taxes? The question is not of so much concern for industries, for which rational calculation is of greater importance than intrinsic motivation; however, it is important for consumers. For them, it is likely that some tax designs are more favourable than others. Also, the way in which the tax is presented may affect intrinsic motivation. Therefore, psychologists may be needed in designing a tax project that will affect consumers. A complement to environmental taxes could be some kind of environmental information, or education, aimed at strengthening intrinsic motivation.

A successful example that did actually increase the awareness and responsibility of polluters is that of water charges in France, implemented as early as 1964. Two charges are levied by the River Basin Agencies according to the polluter-pays principle: a pollution charge, based on the estimated quantity of pollution of households and industries, and a use charge, based on the consumption of water. Tax revenues subsidize waste water treatment. These charges

> played and indeed still play a crucial part in guiding the behavior and attitudes of users and polluters. . . . It has increased the sense of responsibility of all those who damage the natural environment. . . . The system has also led to a restraining influence on abusive use by others in the same vicinity. (Tuddenham, 1995)

A Cultural Choice

Last but not least, the choice of an instrument for environmental protection is also influenced by cultural considerations. Indeed, depending on each country, the importance of the market as a mechanism of social regulation varies. For example, in the United States, the market rules most issues of resource allocation, even to some extent in areas such as education, prisons, police, churches, and political life. On the other hand, in Europe and Asia, political, cultural, and social mechanisms are also deemed essential in addition to the market. Attitudes regarding the market will influence the choice between environmental protection instruments, and whether they will give more or less importance to the market. The choice between regulations, covenants, taxes, and emission permits is also a cultural choice.

Concerning the choice of a tax versus emission permits, the cultural influence originates from the fact that Coase is American, while Pigou was British. For Coase, externality problems are due to the non-existence of markets, while for Pigou, it is rather the ill-functioning of a market. For example, for Coase, the pollution of a river occurs because the river does not belong to anybody, while for Pigou, it is because the polluter did not pay the total cost of his activity. Therefore, Coase suggests giving a greater importance to the market than Pigou: by assigning property rights to polluters (or to the victims), the problem will disappear. The market is seen as the dominant form of social regulation, capable of regulating not only the economic activity, but also pollution problems. The pollution is not seen as a malfunction of the market (Pigou), but as the non-existence of a market (Coase).

In this respect, it is revealing to consider that Coase taught at the University of Chicago. Its economic school may be viewed as ultra-liberal, with thinkers such as Milton Friedman or Gary Becker. The ideological and institutional context of the Coase article is the American reaction that followed many years of Keynesian domination (Vivien, 1994, p. 60). As for Pigou, he was influenced by the Cambridge school (or partial equilibrium school), associated with the name of Alfred Marshall. The Cambridge tradition, while being faithful to the principles of liberalism, recommends some government intervention, for example in the area of wealth redistribution or other market failures. In this sense, it is more in agreement with the French economic tradition, which often places more trust in the government than in the market.

Such cultural and economic traditions have strong implications for the environmental policy. It is a fact that European governments (for example in France, Germany, and The Netherlands) have not shown great confidence in the most market-orientated approach (i.e. emission permits) to solving pollution problems. Indeed, they consider markets to be responsible for pollution problems, rather than to be a solution to them; for this reason they often prefer taxes to emission permits. Another reason for this preference for taxes is that the government plays a more active role with taxes than with emission permits (Chichilnisky and Heal, 1995).

On the other hand, most examples of emission permits are found in the United States, a country where society and government are ruled by the realm of the contract (Le Mouël, 1991). Emission permits have been applied to the lead in gasoline, to national SO_2 emissions and to various pollutants in California.[5] There are other examples of permits in Canada and Australia. However, in Europe, experiences are remarkably limited. In the Swiss Canton of Basle, a modest experiment has been tried to limit VOC and NO_x emissions beyond federal standards by means of emission permits, but without success: there has been practically no exchange of permits.[6]

When considering economic instruments, the European approach is based on taxes rather than on permits, whether it be to limit the air pollution, the water pollution, or the lead in gasoline. Recently, Russia also made a move towards a utilization of environmental taxes to combat air pollution (Golub and Strukova, 1994). Also, for a long time, China has been using a system of taxes to fight air and water pollution, although it does not follow the principles of a market economy (Potier, 1995).

It is tempting to draw the following parallel between instruments chosen in the United States and Sweden in similar situations: the problem of SO_2 emissions in the United States, and the problem of NO_x emissions in Sweden.

- The United States has a system of tradable permits for SO_2 emissions. Initially, the permits (called allowances) were grandfathered to existing businesses, i.e. distributed according to past emissions.
- In 1992, Sweden introduced an emission charge on the NO_x emissions of large combustion plants for energy production. The revenues from this tax are refunded to the plants in proportion to their energy production.

Remember from Chapter 2 that a system of grandfathered emission permits had the same result as a tax, the revenues of which were refunded to the polluters; and such a tax with refund is exactly what exists in Sweden.[7] Here, we have two similar economic instruments for similar air pollution problems, but one solution implements a tax, the other an emission permit system. If tradable permits are the American solution to this pollution problem, the European response is a charge, the revenues of which are refunded to the polluters.

6.3   OPPOSITION FROM THE LOSERS

Those who lose as a result of environmental protection measures form the second basic category of opposition. Even if overall society is better off as a result of a certain environmental measure, within society some groups will be worse off than before, and it will be in their interest to oppose the measure. In this sense, environmental protection is no different from other economic policies, which also generate winners and losers.

Despite the overall gain in society's welfare, some groups will lose because of the distributive effects of environmental taxes. These distributive effects can take several forms. One of them is the regressive impact of some taxes. Recent history of fiscal policy in most industrialized countries suggests that there is always a great political resistance to levying higher taxes on the poor (Poterba, 1991). In any case, the impact of environmental taxes on rich and poor people has to be assessed. If the taxes are regressive, additional measures should be taken in order to correct this regressivity (see Chapters 9-10).

Many other groups in the economy are potential losers. Losers may use the democratic system and oppose the introduction of an environmental tax. In this case, the tax will be rejected if:

1. A majority of the population is worse off with the environmental tax than without it (even if society overall is better off).

2. A majority of the population is better off with the environmental tax, but the losing minority is able to impose costs on the majority. There can be three reasons for this:[8]

   a. The majority does not yet exist (future generations, who cannot vote, form the majority).

   b. The majority exists, but does not know that it is better off with the tax than without it (for a long time, this has been the case with pollution problems).

   c. The majority exists and is well informed, but is less organized than the losing minority (for example, industries often manage to acquire or to preserve advantages to the detriment of the rest of the population, just by being better organized).

In order to understand the reasons behind the rejection of an environmental tax, it is necessary to focus on the losers, regardless of whether they are the majority or a well-organized minority.

In the two following chapters, we will discuss how environmental protection measures can be adopted in a democratic system. We will make a distinction between direct and representative democracy. Direct democracy is based on direct majority voting, a system in which people can influence the environmental policy by using their voting right; basically, if the majority is better off with the tax than without, it will vote for the tax. On the other hand, a representative democracy involves more complex relationships between elected politicians, civil servants, and lobbyists.

Special attention will be devoted to industry, which is a powerful interest group. Industry belongs to the case of the well-organized, losing minority (see *2.c* above). In contrast to the population, industry cannot vote. In order to be heard, it has to organize itself and form lobbying groups. Another difference is that the population pays the tax, but also benefits from less pollution; a tax may bring about a welfare gain for the population, and can be accepted for this reason. On the other hand, firms pay the tax, but mostly households will benefit from a better environment. Therefore, a tax cannot bring about a welfare gain for firms; in order for firms to be better off and willing to accept the tax, the tax must be compared with other instruments.

NOTES

1. In order to avoid any reference to usual taxes, some economists prefer the terms environmental charges or fees, instead of environmental taxes.

2. Even the introduction of airport noise charges is a less radical innovation than it appears to be, because these charges are nothing more than modified landing taxes.
3. The reason why the wrong remains wrong, even after payment, is that the wrong done to the environment is not an economic wrong, but rather a wrong committed against the natural context which provides meaning to the lives of people (Goodin, 1994).
4. The reader will note that these philosophical considerations lead to the same practical conclusion as economic considerations, namely replacing Pigouvian taxes with a charges and standards approach.
5. However, emission permits remain exceptional. Regulatory measures are still the rule, even more than in Europe (OECD, 1989).
6. This was due to the existence of a strict federal regulation that was not withdrawn when emission permits were introduced in the Canton. The Canton could therefore not allow a polluter to emit more than the federal emission standard, even if he purchased the permit. For this reason, almost no exchange of permits took place.
7. With the difference that revenues are not refunded in proportion to the initial pollution, but in proportion to the energy production.
8. Boyce (1994).

7.   Voting for Environmental Taxes

7.1   ENVIRONMENTAL TAXES CAUGHT BETWEEN
MARKET FAILURE AND GOVERNMENT FAILURE

In democracies, laws, which are the result of a voting procedure, are used to implement and enforce environmental taxes. There are countries, like the United States or Switzerland, where people are sometimes asked to vote directly on a project, but most often people elect representatives who will vote for them. In this chapter, we will look at direct and indirect democracies, identify those who may oppose the introduction of environmental taxes, and try to understand the reasons behind their opposition.

As we have seen in Chapter 1, pollution is an external cost associated with economic activity. When external costs exist, the market equilibrium is not optimal, and the production level is excessive. Externalities are a market failure. As a rule, in the presence of a market failure, economists advocate governmental intervention as a means to correct it. In the case of pollution, they advocate the internalization of the external costs of pollution, in order to force polluters to take the entire cost of their activities into account. For example, with road transportation, an increase in gasoline taxes is recommended, as a means to internalize the external costs of pollution.

When the government has to intervene, it is necessary to understand how this intervention works, and what the associated problems are that might prevent this intervention from happening or being successful. One of the biggest problems is adopting and implementing an environmental tax, which generates losers. Even if society, as a whole, is better off with the environmental tax than without it, some people will be worse off, and therefore will oppose the project. If the losers are numerous or powerful, they may be able to have the project thrown out. In this case, we not only have a market failure, but also a government failure.

In this chapter, we use a hypothesis which is central to the public choice theory, namely that individuals vote according to their own individual interest. They will only vote for an environmental tax if they are better off with this change, otherwise they will vote against it. If the losers vote against an environmental tax, the first question we should answer is then: Who are the losers?

Environmental taxes increase society's welfare, because they bring pollution down to its optimal level. (A monetary value can be placed on this welfare increase.) However, environmental taxes increase the price of polluting goods for consumers, and decrease the price at which producers can sell those goods. Following the introduction of the tax, the consumers' and producers' surpluses are reduced. For consumers and producers, the loss in their surpluses is an approximation of the cost of environmental taxes for them.

Because of their loss of surplus, consumers and producers of polluting goods are the losers from environmental taxes. The loss of surplus (which can be assigned a monetary value), will result in acceptability problems for environmental taxes. However, the surplus' loss is not a cost for everybody. Part of this cost is nothing but the tax revenue, which is a transfer to the state. Therefore, the use of the tax revenue is an essential issue in understanding acceptability problems. Now let us examine what happens in a direct democracy (Section 7.2) and in a representative democracy (Section 7.3).

7.2   DIRECT MAJORITY VOTING

Those who lose as a result of the introduction of environmental taxes are the consumers and producers of polluting goods. If the losers are a minority of the population, it may be a problem if they are well organized and able to impose their will on the rest of the population. Yet, the problem becomes more serious if a majority is worse off, because the losing majority will oppose environmental taxes, even without having to organize itself in any particular way.

The Majority of the Population Loses

The losing majority case is best highlighted by the example of the automobile. The internalization of the external costs of automobile transportation is advocated by a number of economists as a welfare-improving measure. However, in practice, a majority of people seem to be opposed to it. Automobile associations, automobile manufacturers, as well as motorists, oppose any attempt to increase taxation on cars. The market is unable to attain the social optimum (there is a market failure), but a government intervention, intended to correct this market failure, is not accepted by the voters, even if it improves social welfare.

This situation reflects the paradox between individual and social behaviour. Buchanan (1962) shows that a democratic solution to externalities may lead to a non-optimal situation. Indeed, in a majority voting system, any vote will result in a situation where the majority imposes its choice on the minority, and with external costs caused by the majority, a majority vote will result in external costs being imposed on the minority. Buchanan even shows that externalities are inevitable if the voting rule is not unanimity.

In the case of automobile transportation, such considerations are illuminating. In fact, in industrialized countries, the majority of citizens who have the right to vote use cars. Therefore, a tax aimed at internalizing external costs of car pollution will affect the majority of voters. On the other hand, a reduction in pollution will benefit the whole population. But as car drivers are the majority, they will be able to impose costs on the rest of the population, if a majority vote takes place.

Let us now use a simple model to determine what influences the acceptability. A democratic country is composed of x identical polluting citizens, and y identical non-polluting citizens. In the case of the automobile, x is the number of motorists (car owners or car users) and y the number of non-motorists (non-owners or non-users). We suppose $x>y$, that is, there are more motorists than non-motorists.

Next, let us consider the market for gasoline in this country. We suppose that the supply is infinitely elastic (which may be the case in a small importing country). Driving cars causes polluting emissions which are proportional to the gasoline consumed. The marginal damage (or marginal external cost, or MEC) of the pollution is assumed to be constant. The pollution emitted by cars affects the whole population, i.e. the motorists (x) as well as the non-motorists (y). Every citizen votes according to his self-interest, and is perfectly informed.

In the initial market equilibrium, the x motorists impose external costs on the $x+y$ members of the society. They act individually in a rational way, and do not take into account the pollution they emit. This initial situation is not optimal. In Figure 7.1, this non-optimal equilibrium is point (p_1, q_1), where q is the quantity of gasoline and p its price.

Suppose now that the government proposes a direct majority vote, on the introduction of a Pigouvian tax (t) equal to the marginal external cost of the polluting emission. Following the introduction of this tax, the optimum at point (p_2, q_2) is reached. Each motorist pays an amount of tax t for every unit consumed. The pollution reduction benefits the whole society, i.e. the motorists as well as the non-motorists.

The use of the tax revenues will determine who is a winner and who is a loser. Therefore, we will examine the three following cases, in order to see when the democratic solution leads to the economic optimum:

- The government does not refund the revenues from environmental taxes.
- The government refunds the tax revenues in a lump sum manner to all citizens.
- The government refunds the revenues in a lump sum manner, solely to motorists.

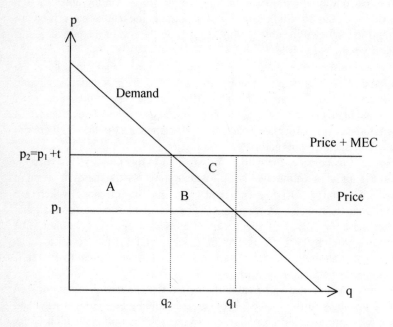

Figure 7.1 Environmental tax and direct voting

The Government does not Refund the Tax Revenues

In this first case, the government does not refund the tax revenues; it uses them to cut its deficit or pay off its debt.[1] The introduction of the tax modifies the welfare of all players: motorists pay the environmental tax, the government receives the tax revenues, and the resulting reduction in pollution benefits all citizens, including non-motorists. As gasoline consumption decreases from q_1 to q_2, the damage of the pollution is reduced by an amount equal to $(B+C)$. From the point of view of the whole society, we have an optimal situation, with a welfare increase equal to area C.

However, from a public choice perspective, we are not interested in the total welfare increase, but in the welfare change for each group of voters. Remember that x is the number of motorists (the majority), y is the number of non-motorists (the minority), and $x+y$ represents the whole group of voters.

Let α stand for $\dfrac{x}{x+y}$, i.e. the proportion of motorists in the population, and δ stand for $\dfrac{y}{x+y}$, i.e. the proportion of non-motorists in the population, with $\alpha+\delta=1$.

Following the introduction of the tax, the non-motorists will benefit by a proportion δ of the pollution reduction, i.e. an amount equal to $\delta(B+C)$. As they do not drive cars, they will not bear any cost. Therefore, they will vote for the tax. However, as they are the minority, their vote is not important. The government is the big winner of the tax, but it has no voting right. The motorists will see their consumers' surplus reduced by an amount equal to area $(A+B)$. On the other hand, they will benefit by a proportion α of the total pollution reduction, i.e. $\alpha(B+C)$ (see Table 7.1).

Table 7.1 The government does not refund revenues

	Impact of the tax	Pollution reduction	Total
Non-motorists	--	$+ \delta(B+C)$	$+ \delta(B+C)$
Motorists	$- (A+B)$	$+ \alpha (B+C)$	$- (A+B) + \alpha (B+C)$
Government	$+ A$	--	$+ A$
Total	$- B$	$+(B+C)$	$+C$

As motorists are the majority, a direct majority vote will result in an approval of the tax only if motorists are winners. Therefore, in order for the environmental tax to be approved, the monetary value of the pollution reduction to motorists $(\alpha(B+C))$ has to be higher than the reduction in their consumers' surplus $(A+B)$. With t being the amount of the unit tax, the reduction in the consumers' surplus of motorists is:

$$A + B = \Delta p q_2 + \frac{1}{2}\Delta p \Delta q$$

$$= t(q_1 - \Delta q) + \frac{1}{2}t\Delta q$$

where $\Delta p = p_2 - p_1 = t$ and $\Delta q = q_1 - q_2$. As the price elasticity of demand is defined as:

$$|e| = \frac{\dfrac{\Delta q}{q_1}}{\dfrac{\Delta p}{p_1}} = \frac{\dfrac{\Delta q}{q_1}}{\dfrac{t}{p_1}} \quad \text{hence} \quad \Delta q = |e| \frac{t}{p_1} q_1$$

the reduction in surplus is then: (in the following, e replaces its absolute value $|e|$)

$$A + B = t \left[q_1 - e \frac{t}{p_1} q_1 \right] + \frac{1}{2} t e \frac{t}{p_1} q_1$$

$$= t q_1 \left[1 - \frac{1}{2} \frac{et}{p_1} \right]$$

The reduction in the external costs of pollution amounts to:

$$B + C = t \Delta q$$

$$= t q_1 \left(\frac{et}{p_1} \right)$$

Motorists (the majority) will then vote for the environmental tax if the following condition is verified:

$$\alpha(B + C) > A + B$$

$$\alpha \, (t q_1 \frac{et}{p_1}) > t q_1 \left[1 - \frac{1}{2} \frac{et}{p_1} \right]$$

By simplifying, we obtain the following condition:

$$\boxed{\frac{p_1}{et} < \alpha + \frac{1}{2}}$$

which is relatively easy to test empirically. The formula shows that the tax will be more readily accepted if demand is elastic, because the pollution will be reduced all the more as demand is more elastic. In contrast, if demand is inelastic, the environmental gain will be small compared to the tax revenue; this explains why gasoline tax increases are not easily accepted. The formula also shows that the tax will be more easily accepted if there are many motorists among the voters, because they get a larger share of the environmental gain. If the condition is not verified, then the political process will give the same solution as the market, and nothing will be done to combat the pollution.

Lump Sum Refund to All Citizens

With this second possibility, the government refunds tax revenues in a lump sum manner to the whole population (a system sometimes called 'ecobonus'). Motorists pay the tax, and get back part of the revenues; the rest of the revenues goes to non-motorists. The reduction in the pollution benefits all citizens (see Table 7.2).

Table 7.2 Lump sum refund to all citizens

	Impact of the tax	Pollution reduction	Redistribution of revenues	Total
Non-motorists	--	$+\delta(B+C)$	$+\delta A$	$+\delta(A+B+C)$
Motorists	$-(A+B)$	$+\alpha(B+C)$	$+\alpha A$	$-(A+B)+\alpha(A+B+C)$
Government	$+A$	--	$-A$	0
Total	$-B$	$+(B+C)$	0	$+C$

Total welfare is increased in the same way as before $(+C)$. Non-motorists are better off than in the first case, because now they get part of the tax revenues in addition to the pollution reduction. However, as they are the minority, their situation does not influence the final decision. Motorists (the majority) are also better off than in the first case. If the tax is introduced, they will gain, if the reduction in their consumers' surplus $(A+B)$ is smaller than their monetary valuation of the pollution reduction plus the part of the tax revenues they receive:

$$\alpha(B+C)+\alpha A > A+B$$

Compared to the case without redistribution of tax revenues, this constraint is less strict, because of the term αA added to the left hand side of the inequality. Thus, we see that the refund of tax revenues to the citizens increases the political acceptability of environmental taxes.

As

$$A = t\,(q_1 - \Delta q)$$

$$= tq_1(1 - \frac{et}{p_1})$$

the condition for motorists to be winners, i.e. the acceptability condition, now becomes:

$$\alpha\left[tq_1\,\frac{et}{p_1} + tq_1(1 - \frac{et}{p_1})\right] > tq_1\left[1 - \frac{1}{2}\frac{et}{p_1}\right]$$

which is identical to

$$\boxed{\frac{et}{p_1} > 2 - 2\alpha}.$$

Even if this condition is less strict than in the first case, it may not always be realized. In this case, the political solution is not better than the market solution. Therefore, we have to consider a third refund, which is a lump sum refund given solely to the motorists.

Lump Sum Refund to the Motorists Only

In this third case, motorists recover all the tax revenues. (This could be done by means of a reduction in the annual tax on motor vehicles). As before, all citizens share the benefits of a pollution reduction, and the total welfare is increased by C (Table 7.3).

Table 7.3 Refund to the motorists only

	Impact of the tax	Pollution reduction	Redistribution of revenues	Total
Non-motorists	--	$+\delta(B+C)$	--	$+\delta(B+C)+\delta A$
Motorists	$-(A+B)$	$+\alpha(B+C)$	$+A$	$-B + \alpha(B+C)$
Government	$+A$	--	$-A$	0
Total	$-B$	$+(B+C)$	0	$+C$

For motorists, the acceptability condition now becomes:

$$\alpha(B+C) + A > A+B$$

As $B = \frac{1}{2}(B+C)$, the condition finally becomes:

$$\boxed{\alpha > \frac{1}{2}}$$

which is the starting hypothesis, i.e. there are more motorists than non-motorists.

The main difference from the former cases is that, here, nobody will oppose the change. Motorists as well as non-motorists are better off if a pollution tax is introduced. In this simple model, if tax revenues are given back to polluters, a vote on the internalization of external effects is approved with the unanimity rule.

Thus we have shown that, when there is simultaneously a market failure and a government failure, the refund of the tax revenues may correct this government failure in such a way that everybody is better off with internalization. If distributive aspects are the cause of acceptability problems, the utilization of tax revenues corrects the government failure, which permits the correction of the market failure. The utilization of tax revenues does not modify the total welfare, but only its distribution among different groups.

Summarizing our results, an environmental tax will be more readily accepted by the voters if:

- the demand for the polluting good is elastic;
- a high percentage of the voters consists of polluters;
- the tax revenues are refunded to the population;
- the refund specifically goes to those who paid the tax.

Putting these Results into Practice: Will a Gasoline Tax Increase be Accepted in Switzerland?

In order to use the three acceptability conditions obtained, we examine the acceptability of an increase in the gasoline tax in Switzerland. Switzerland is an ideal candidate to test these conditions, because in this country citizens vote directly on tax decisions, at the federal level as well as in the cantons (states).

We use the following numbers. The gasoline price is equal to SFr1.20 per litre (that is, approximately \$0.80 per litre). The tax increase is SFr0.1 for each litre of gasoline.[2] The long-term price elasticity of gasoline demand is -0.16 (Mattei, 1994). The annual gasoline consumption is q_1=3.705 billion litres.[3] In 1990, x, the number of adults belonging to households which own a car, is 4.043 million; $x+y$, the number of citizens aged 18 or more, is 5.351 million.

Let us examine the three cases studied above.

1. If the tax has to be accepted without redistribution of tax revenues, the following condition has to be verified: [4]

$$\frac{p_1}{et} < \alpha + \frac{1}{2}$$

As $\frac{p_1}{et}$ is equal to 75 and $\alpha + 0.5$ is equal to 1.25, the acceptability condition is not verified.[5] Rational citizen-motorists, voting according to their self-interest, should not approve such a tax, because they are losers.

2. If tax revenues are refunded in a lump sum manner to all citizens, the following condition has to be verified:

$$\frac{et}{p_1} > 2 - 2\alpha$$

Taking the same numbers as before, we have $\frac{et}{p_1} = 0.013$ and $2-2\alpha=0.49$ and the model's conclusion is again an outright rejection from motorists.

3. Finally, we know that, if tax revenues are refunded to the motorists only, everybody will gain, and the tax will be accepted. Non-motorists will get a proportion δ of the reduction in the external cost of pollution, i.e.:

$$\delta(B+C) = \delta \, et^2 \frac{q_1}{p_1}$$
$$= 1.21 \text{ million SFr}$$

And motorists will win:

$$\alpha(B+C) - B = \alpha \, et^2 \frac{q_1}{p_1} - 0.5et^2 \frac{q_1}{p_1}$$
$$= 1.26 \text{ million SFr}$$

The total gain from the introduction of the gasoline tax will be the sum of both, i.e. 2.47 million SFr.

7.3 POLITICIANS, ADMINISTRATION, INTEREST GROUPS

So far, we have seen what happens in a direct democracy. In a representative democracy, we have to look at the whole political scene, which includes politicians (the elected representatives), interest groups (lobbies and political action committees), and the administration (or bureaucracy).

Politicians

According to the public choice framework, politicians are primarily interested in their election, or re-election. Therefore, they will try to please potential voters. If politicians want to maximize their chances of being elected, they will try to give subsidies or tax credits to some groups of voters. On the other hand, taxes, regardless of the type, are not popular. If politicians are vote-seekers, they will not propose unpopular environmental taxes, which may cause them to lose votes.

Moreover, the costs of environmental policies generally have to be incurred immediately, whereas their beneficial effects accrue in the long term; this is all the more true for policies pursuing sustainable development. For example, with a national carbon tax, the cost for the voters is immediate, but the benefits accrue principally to future generations, and to citizens from other countries. If politicians are vote-seekers, they will never propose this kind of policy. This is especially true when unemployment is high, because in the short term there is some probability that this policy will lead to higher unemployment. In the presence of unemployment worries, not only do politicians risk alienating their existing supporters by announcing new environmental taxes, but voters will not want to take the risk of favouring such projects. In addition, the industry will never fail to scare politicians and voters with threats of massive lay-offs following the introduction of new taxes.

These considerations will be crucial for the choice of instrument. As the instruments for environmental protection compete with each other, politicians will have a strong incentive to advocate the most popular instrument, instead of the most efficient one. They will propose subsidies and regulations, which are more popular, instead of taxes and emission permits, which are more efficient. A recent example of this is in the United States, where, after the Kyoto conference in 1997, concerns about global warming led the President to propose a temporary tax credit (which is a subsidy) on the sale of the most fuel-efficient new cars, despite the fact that the first-best policy is to introduce a carbon tax, instead of further reducing the cost of driving automobiles.

Facing this kind of problem, one solution is to introduce more elements of direct democracy and federalism into the environmental policy. If citizens are concerned enough about the degradation of the environment, it should be possible to implement a sustainable development policy through direct majority voting (Frey and Schneider, 1996). Also, we should not forget that tax revenues are a great opportunity for politicians: even if taxes are not popular, the revenues they raise may finance projects which will please their constituents. For politicians, the opportunity offered by the tax revenues may be sufficient to counterbalance the political cost of the tax.

Lobbies and Political Action Committees

With environmental and sustainable development problems, there are mainly two kinds of interest groups: industries and ecologists. Each one will try to put pressure on politicians and voters. As a rule, ecologists will try to advocate environmental taxes, but industries will systematically oppose them and favour the status quo. Sometimes, the balance of power between these two groups will determine the outcome. If ecologists want to pass a law to implement an environmental tax, they will have to be convinced about the necessity of this tax, and not be divided on the choice of the instrument, because of the 'licence to pollute' argument (see Chapter 6).

Often in this situation, industries have an advantage over ecologists. The reason is that the most effective organizations are those with few members, shared objectives, and well-defined goals. This is the case with industries, which often belong to well-established associations which are accustomed to pursuing their objectives through political action. On the other hand, associations of ecologists have numerous members, and it is more difficult for them to define common objectives (Frey and Schneider, 1996). It is also more difficult for them to fight the 'free-rider' problem: everybody benefits from the achievements of ecologists, not only the members of their associations.

However, if the government wants to introduce a tax that is opposed by industry, there is always the possibility of designing the project in such a way that some firms will gain from the environmental tax, and other firms will lose. If industrialists are united, they are likely to be stronger than ecologists, but if they are divided, ecologists may have the advantage.

Administration and Bureaucracy

According to the defenders of the public choice theory, the administration will try to promote solutions that put forward its interests. As bureaucrats cannot maximize their profit (like private sector managers) or be re-elected (like politicians), they will try other ways to achieve personal success and satisfaction in their jobs: each department will try to maximize its size and its budget. Therefore, the administration will try to push forward environmental protection instruments that require a great amount of administrative work.

Environmental taxes are potentially very intensive with respect to administrative work. Because of concerns about international competition, some industries may be exempted from the tax payment; others may be assigned a reduced tax rate; alternatively, border adjustments may be made in order for domestic and foreign producers to be on an equal footing (see Chapter 8). Also, the tax level has to be set, possibly modified according to changing economic circumstances, and the tax revenues have to be managed. All these elements may contribute to the development of a large bureaucracy in charge of controlling and administering the tax. This should please budget-maximizing bureaucrats, who may also try to recover part of the tax revenues for their own use.

Because of all these elements, the administration should favour environmental taxes. However, we should stress the fact that many designs of environmental taxes are possible, some of them involving much administrative work, others none at all. The same is true for emission permits, which may also entail more or less intervention from the regulatory administration. It is also likely that other players, especially industry and liberal parties, will oppose the introduction of work-intensive taxes.

Overall

This overview shows the difficulty of achieving a favourable voting result on environmental taxes in a representative democracy: politicians are reluctant to work on programs that may turn away potential voters; the administration will try to implement solutions requiring a high administrative cost, and the industry and some political parties will do their utmost to avoid this kind of solution. Moreover, industry associations will try to favour other instruments which are less costly to them; if they use threats such as massive layoffs, they will also find support from many citizens. Against such a convergence of interests, the environmental tax has no chance of passage.

Should we be pessimistic about the chances of adopting environmental taxes in representative democracies? Not necessarily. The following remarks should provide some optimism:

- If industrialists are divided, they will not strongly oppose the project.

- Much depends on the timing: environmental taxes are more easily introduced when unemployment is low. On the other hand, new taxes are never popular among politicians, except when the public deficit is a widely shared concern.

- As environmental taxes bring about a welfare gain, part of this benefit can be used to gain the active support of civil servants or interest groups.

- The public choice rationale used here to analyse representative democracies is not free of value judgments, and is not universally accepted; politicians and citizens may sometimes try to pursue public interest instead of their own narrow self-interest. Also, each country is characterized by different political systems, habits, and values, which may leave more or less room for politicians trying to implement an environmental policy.

Most important, in this section we did not stress the existence of tax revenues, nor did we look at possible ways of making environmental taxes attractive to industry. As courting the industry is essential to the success of a tax project, we will now look at environmental taxes from their standpoint.

NOTES

1. We assume that taxpayers are 'myopic', and do not see the link between the deficit and future taxes; that is, Ricardian equivalence does not hold.
2. This number is far below the usual estimates of external costs of road traffic in Switzerland (estimates can be found in Neuenschwander et al., 1992; Maibach et al., 1992; Grosclaude and Soguel, 1992). However, the calculations done here would make little sense with the gasoline price increases necessary in order to fully internalize the external costs of road traffic.
3. In 1993, cf. Swiss Global Energy Statistics. This excludes diesel fuel, of which only small quantities are sold for cars in Switzerland (diesel cars amount to less than 3% of the total).
4. As the elasticities apply only to small variations around the equilibrium point, the following calculations can only be viewed as rough approximations.
5. Here $\alpha=0.75$. Results remain basically the same if, instead of the percentage of adults in households using a car, we take the percentage of people with a driving licence (66.6% in 1989).

8.   Industry Opposition

8.1   INTRODUCTION

Traditionally, industry has shown great resistance to environmental taxes. Indeed, it has much to lose and little to gain. Taxes imply supplementary costs for firms: not only do they have to bear the cost of pollution reduction measures, but they also have to pay the tax on the remaining emissions, which can be substantially higher than the pollution control cost. Also, there are few gains for the industry, because the environmental quality is a public good that mostly benefits the population. In addition, producers are often able to influence the contents of regulations, so as to obtain favourable clauses; this kind of political action is more difficult in the case of taxes.

The acceptability problem becomes even more serious when international aspects are considered. Firms facing international competition have little margin to implement costly environmental measures. As a result of competitiveness concerns, governments are reluctant to introduce environmental taxes at a high rate, or on a large scale. This is not only a problem with environmental taxes, but reflects a general trend: governments are increasingly reluctant to impose heavy regulatory or fiscal demands on firms that have to fight against competition for their survival in markets that have become global (Solsbery and Wiederkehr, 1995).

The opposition from polluting firms is often channelled through well-established professional associations. These associations know how to apply pressure on the government and the population, in order to avoid the passage of measures that are too unfavourable to them. By threatening to lay off workers or to move factories abroad, the industry can induce the government to withdraw a tax project. As we saw in the preceding chapter, organizations of ecologists are often weaker and more divided than industrialists, and unable to counterbalance their pressure.

In the presence of environmental problems, different instruments are always possible. As environmental taxes entail significant costs for the industry, it will be in its interest to oppose them. The industry will only accept environmental taxes if they are less costly than other instruments (especially standards), or if they have advantages that other instruments do not have. For this reason, we now compare the environmental protection instruments from the standpoint of the industry, and not with regard to social welfare as we did in Chapter 2.

8.2   ACCEPTABILITY OF DIFFERENT INSTRUMENTS

In the short term, environmental taxes increase the production costs of firms. If a firm tries to maximize its profit or minimize its expenditure, it will be concerned about any increase in its production costs. For this reason, an environmental protection instrument that entails a low cost will be more readily accepted than one which implies a higher cost. For firms, the acceptability of different environmental protection instruments depends principally on the costs.[1]

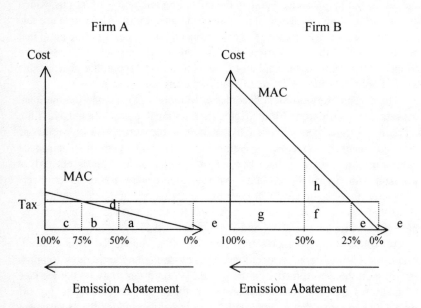

Figure 8.1 Cost of environmental protection instruments for firms

In order to compare the instruments, we take two firms, A and B, each one emitting the same quantity of a pollutant. The costs they incur in order to reduce the pollution are different, A's abatement cost being smaller than B's. Figure 8.1 shows the marginal abatement cost (MAC) of the pollution for each firm.[2] We assume that the optimal, or desired, level of pollution is a 50% reduction from the initial level of pollution; this overall reduction has to be divided between the two firms. The choice of the instrument will determine the reduction percentage for each of them. With a uniform regulation, each firm will reduce its pollution by half. With economic instruments such as a tax or an emission permit scheme, the firms will equalize their marginal clean-up costs, A reducing its emissions by 75% and B by 25%.

For each firm, the cost of the instrument for environmental protection is the sum of the abatement cost, and the financial transfer implied by the instrument:

- The cost of an emission standard is the cost of reducing emissions by half.

- The cost of a tax includes the cost of reducing the pollution down to the point where the MAC is equal to the tax, plus the tax payment on the remaining emissions.

- The cost of grandfathered emission permits is the cost of the optimal reduction (as with the tax), plus or minus the cost of the permits bought or sold.

The total cost of the different instruments for each firm is presented in Table 8.1. Remember (from Chapter 2) that under some hypotheses there is distributive and allocative equivalence between auctioned emission permits and taxes; there is also equivalence between grandfathered emission permits and taxes, whose revenues are refunded to emitters in proportion to the initial pollution.

Table 8.1 Cost of environmental protection instruments for firms

	Firm A (low AC)	Firm B (high AC)
Standard	a	e+f+h
Tax Auctioned emission permits	a+b+c	e+f+g
Grandfathered emission permits Tax with revenue refund to polluters	a-d	e+f

Notes
AC=Abatement Cost.

For each firm, the preferred instrument will be the one entailing the least cost. For firm A, which can reduce its emissions at a low cost, grandfathered emission permits, and the tax whose revenues are refunded to polluters, are the favourite instruments, with a cost equal to a-d. The next preferred instrument is the standard, which entails a cost of a. The most costly instruments are the usual tax (without refund), and auctioned emission permits, with a cost equal to $a+b+c$.

For firm B, for which reducing emissions implies a high cost, grandfathered emission permits, and the tax with refund (cost: $e+f$), are preferred to the usual tax and to auctioned emission permits (cost: $e+f+g$); they are also preferred to the standard (cost: $e+f+h$). Between the usual tax and the standard, it depends. For B, comparing the tax with the standard is the same as comparing area $f+g$ with area $f+h$. In this comparison, $f+g$ is the tax payment on the remaining emissions that occur with the tax, and $f+h$ is the abatement cost saving permitted by the flexibility of the tax over the standard. If B's MAC function is steep, or if the MAC functions of A and B are very different, then the advantage permitted by the flexibility of the tax ($f+h$) becomes more important than the additional tax payment ($f+g$).

Now, if we consider both firms, we can assert that the instruments with the highest acceptability are:

- grandfathered emission permits;

- the tax, the revenues of which are refunded to polluters.

Between the standard and the tax (without refund), the acceptability depends on the circumstances. As compared to the standard, the tax has the advantage of flexibility in the distribution of the cleanup effort; on the other hand, the disadvantage for firms comes from the tax payment on the remaining emissions. In order to compare the tax and the standard, it is therefore necessary to weigh the flexibility of the tax (which reduces the firms' compliance cost), against the payment on the remaining emissions (which increases their cost). Globally, firms will prefer the tax to the standard when MAC functions greatly differ among firms, that is to say, when the advantage of flexibility more than compensates for the disadvantage of paying the tax on the remaining emissions.

The disadvantage of the tax is the payment on the remaining emissions, and it is mainly this payment that firms oppose.[3] Therefore, the opposition to the environmental tax depends on the tax level, and the estimation of the remaining pollution that will be emitted in the future. However, if the tax revenues are refunded to polluters, the tax instrument becomes equivalent to grandfathered emission permits, and both are preferred to all other instruments.

Verification

Are these theoretical results verified in practice? Swiss businesses have expressed their preferences for environmental protection instruments.[4] They give the following order of preference:

Negotiation > Permits > Taxes > Obligations > Prohibitions

This classification confirms the theoretical result, according to which firms prefer emission permits to taxes and to standards. This is also confirmed by Barde (1993) who asserts that polluters favour marketable emission permits rather than taxes.

Concerning the comparison between taxes and standards, Swiss firms seem to indicate a preference for taxes in comparison to standards. However, Barde (1993) disagrees when he says that, in general, the aversion to taxes is greater than the aversion to standards. The ambiguity of the theoretical results also appears in practice. According to the theoretical results, a preference for taxes when compared to standards means that MAC functions differ greatly from firm to firm. However, it is generally admitted that MAC functions are relatively flat at the beginning of the clean-up efforts, and become steeper afterwards (Tobey, 1993). In industrialized countries, the cheapest clean-up measures have already been exhausted; we are currently at the beginning of a phase of rapidly increasing costs for some firms, which makes the flexibility offered by economic instruments even more necessary.

Other considerations can influence the preference for taxes or for standards. A preference for taxes can result from the fact that firms appreciate references to market mechanisms. On the other hand, firms often have the power to influence the contents of standards, while for taxes this is more difficult. Also, following Buchanan and Tullock (1975), we can mention the fact that standards serve as a barrier to the entry of new firms, while taxes do not.

Finally, Swiss firms prefer negotiation to all other instruments. This is due to the cost advantage (covenants can bring about the same results as grandfathered emission permits, see Chapter 2). But the preference for covenants also seems to reflect the importance that firms attach to their flexibility, and to the possibility of influencing political decisions, which is easier with covenants than with any other instrument.

8.3   HOW TO REDUCE INDUSTRY OPPOSITION

Several elements seem to be necessary for the acceptance of an environmental tax project. When doing the groundwork for a project, it is important to consult the sectors affected, especially those from whom strong opposition is expected. As much of the information necessary for the success of a tax project is held by the industry, the presence of an impartial commission, allowing the arbitration of the industry's views with those of the government, is a success factor. Consulting the industry is important, not only to collect the necessary information, but also to work out a consensus (Pearson, 1995).

Next, to achieve the acceptance of a tax, it is necessary to inform all sectors concerned beforehand. The details of the introduction of the tax, the expected economic advantages, and the (environmental) objective have to be widely known and communicated (OECD, 1991). Most important, the objective of the tax and its expected economic consequences have to be explained. In other words, the point is to 'sell' the tax project by stressing its advantages in comparison with other solutions.

The design of the instrument is also important: in any case, it is necessary to have a clearly defined instrument, with a precise schedule. The objective of the tax has to be to protect the environment, and not to raise revenues, which the government can spend at its own discretion. The confusion between the fiscal and the environmental objectives thus appears to be one of the key factors leading to the rejection of a tax project. In Switzerland, a carbon tax project was rejected by industry, mainly because the government wanted to benefit from the opportunity, and appropriate supplementary tax revenues.

The gradual introduction of the tax, and a gradual increase in its level, are important elements favouring the approval of taxes. In France, these elements contributed to the success of taxes on water pollutants (Hahn, 1989). Similarly, the existence of a time period before the implementation of a tax also favours its acceptability. For the industry, the 'previsibility' of environmental taxes is important in order to reduce its opposition. Currently, there are taxes in several countries which have been announced several years in advance of their implementation. As firms are sensitive to uncertainty, a foreseeable governmental action enhances the chances of acceptance.

When, despite all these measures, the industry refuses to accept the financial transfers to the government implied by taxes, three solutions are possible: a tax exemption, a reduced rate, or a financial compensation. An exemption or a reduced rate for some sectors may reduce the efficiency of the tax; for example, a carbon or energy tax, which applies to all sectors except energy intensive industries, is not efficient. The other solution is to compensate the sectors most affected so as to reduce their opposition. Unlike the exemption, a compensation to the affected sectors does not reduce the efficiency of the tax (see the following section).

This brings us to the following important point: the acceptance of a tax by the industry will depend on how the tax revenues are used. One reason for this is that businesses are generally opposed to an increase in the size of the public sector, and therefore to any instrument that leads to this result. In order to please the industry, the government has to refund the tax revenues; it may refund them specifically to the industry; it may even negotiate with the industry the criterion according to which the tax revenue will be refunded (for example, proportional to the production, to the number of employees, to past emissions, etc.).

A survey of the largest Swiss businesses shows that most of them prefer a solution where the tax revenues are used for the protection of the environment. The next preferred solutions are a reduction in direct taxes, a lump sum refund to households and businesses, a reduction in social contributions, and a reduction in indirect taxes. Finally, the least satisfactory solution is the one in which revenues are not refunded at all, and the government can use them freely (Wallart and Bürgenmeier, 1996). If revenues are used to subsidize firms for clean-up activities, firms get back as subsidies what they paid in taxes. There is a twofold impact on the environment, one with the tax and one with the environmental expenditure. This system gives the greatest political acceptability.

The last factor influencing the acceptance of a tax is the way in which the government is perceived by businesses. Indeed, in many countries businesses lack confidence in the government and the political process. This scepticism has to do with questions such as the increasing size of the public sector, the dilution of competences in the public administration, the view (warranted or not) that bureaucracy is expensive and inefficient, or just a mere distrust of the capacity of the government to control complex issues. When there is such a distrust facing the government, the earmarking of environmental tax revenues can improve the acceptance (this can be observed in the United States, where the revenues of most environmental taxes are earmarked for the clean-up of specific pollution).

For pollution problems that are specific to some industries, the mere prospect of a tax may have an effect on the polluting emissions. The threat of introducing a tax can thus be efficient, either by bringing a reduction in the pollution directly, or by prevailing on the industry itself to present proposals (for example a proposal of covenant or regulation) aimed at reducing pollution in the future, without introducing a tax. Thus, it seems that in Sweden, the mere prospect of a tax on SO_2 emissions was as effective as the tax itself (Pearson, 1995).

8.4 INTERNATIONAL COMPETITION

International aspects are important for the acceptability of an environmental tax. Generally, an emission tax will affect domestic firms, but not foreign firms doing business in the same markets; the tax changes the conditions of competition in this market. If domestic polluting emissions are taxed, but no such instrument exists abroad, domestic firms will see an increase in their production costs, and they will suffer a loss in competitiveness in comparison with foreign firms. Faced with this situation, businesses will have a tendency to move their factories to countries without environmental taxes.[5] Also, the environmental impact is not guaranteed: if firms move their factories and continue polluting in a neighbouring country, the global environment will not improve at all.

Such an evolution can be observed in practice, although the effects seem to be small. Thus, between 1965 and 1990, some firms in the most polluting industries effectively moved from industrialized to developing countries. However, this is not only the result of environmental policies, but also of changing consumer tastes (De Melo et al., 1997). Most studies show that, when accounting for the other trade determinants, pollution-control measures have exerted little or no effect on patterns of international trade (Cropper and Oates, 1992).

If a polluting emission or input (such as energy) is taxed in one country, the production price of polluting goods increases. Following that, exports will decline and imports will increase. In the short term, the country loses some of its competitiveness,[6] which produces negative effects (unemployment, currency depreciation, etc.). However, in the long term, new exporting industries will expand, and the trade structure will adapt to the new ratio of relative costs between polluting and non-polluting goods. In the long term, new patterns of specialization will emerge.

With respect to the acceptability of environmental taxes, the problem does not come from the long-term modification in international specialization and trade, but from the loss of business competitiveness subject to international competition in the short and medium terms. Because of this loss of competitiveness, businesses will have a tendency to vigorously oppose any environmental tax project that might affect them. An industry threat to move factories abroad is often enough to force governments, which are sensitive to the employment concerns of their citizens, to withdraw or postpone their prospective tax.

The more firms depend on open and competitive markets, the more likely they will oppose environmental taxes. Indeed, firms competing fiercely with their foreign counterparts have limited pricing power. The ability to shift[7] a cost increase on to consumers strongly influences the acceptability of a tax: the strongest opponents of environmental taxes can be found among businesses which are unable to increase their prices. These businesses often have energy-intensive production, and compete in international markets, such as steel and paper. Following the introduction of an environmental tax, their costs would increase significantly, but they have no pricing power to shift this cost increase to consumers. These firms have to strongly oppose additional taxes, solely in order to survive.

These problems are serious, but not insoluble. First, a tax will be more easily accepted if the main trade partners introduce the same instrument simultaneously. Also, nowadays the international context increasingly favours environmental taxes. Many countries have already adopted such taxes; all industrialized countries are studying the possibility of a CO_2 tax; Sweden has introduced an ecological tax reform with many different environmental taxes; similarly, gasoline taxes increasingly take environmental costs into account. In this context, introducing a tax can translate into a comparative advantage in the future, if other countries later introduce the same kind of taxes ('first mover advantage'). Indeed, once the national economy has adjusted to the tax, it will be in a stronger export position later when other countries also introduce the tax.

Second, relocating factories to countries which are more attractive for polluters is not as simple as it appears. It is subject to different economic and political conditions, sunk costs, as well as supplementary transportation costs. If the industry vigorously opposes the introduction of environmental taxes, it is likely that it has no intention of relocating its factories to other countries. This is supported by empirical studies, which show that pollution control costs are usually small compared to total production costs. In most pollution-intensive industries, pollution control costs run to the order of less than 2 per cent of total production costs. If pollution control costs are small relative to total costs, they do not provide a sufficient reason to move factories abroad. (However, this may no longer be true in the case of the tax: for the industry, the costs implied by a tax are significantly higher than the pure pollution control costs, because of the additional tax payments to the government.)

Third, several solutions are possible to improve the acceptability by industries concerned about their competitiveness:

1. The first solution is to introduce border adjustments: environmental taxes are levied on (polluting) imported goods, and deducted from exported goods, in order to level the playing field between domestic and foreign producers. For example, the U.S. tax on ozone-depleting chemicals applies to imported chemicals, as well as to imported manufactured products containing these chemicals; and the tax is deducted from exported products. If there is full compensation at the border for imports and for exports, domestic producers are no longer in an unfair position compared to foreign producers. Unfortunately, border adjustments are not always possible, nor easy to administer. In general, they are possible for raw materials and semi-finished products, but for finished products they may entail prohibitive administrative costs.

2. Another solution is financial compensation to polluting firms. An easy way to do this is to refund the tax revenues to the industry. Overall, this solution will neutralize the cost increase due to the tax, and may bring businesses to accept a tax project. For example, in Sweden, the revenue of a NO_x charge levied on the large combustion plants is refunded to the liable plants, in proportion to their energy production. In Chapter 9, we will see in a more detailed way how the tax revenues may compensate the polluters.
3. Finally, if the two former solutions are not feasible, exemptions or a reduced rate can be introduced for the industries most affected. However, this solution causes serious inefficiencies, in contrast to the two preceding ones. Indeed, from an economic efficiency standpoint, every polluter should confront the same price for his polluting emissions, i.e. the same tax rate. If households are subject to different rates from industries, or if different industries are subject to different rates, emission reduction costs will not be equalized, and economic efficiency is not ensured. The tax will not be cost-effective.

In order to avoid that, the exemptions can be made conditional on agreements between the government and the industries concerned, in which firms commit themselves to reducing their emissions by some percentage, in exchange for the tax exemption. In this way, economic efficiency can be re-established. The exemption can also be granted temporarily, when economic conditions are particularly difficult (for example, the German water tax makes a provision for this case).

Although they are not efficient, exemptions and reduced rates are common in practice. Northern European countries which have introduced carbon and energy taxes grant a reduction (between 25% and 90%) to the most energy-intensive industries. They even give total exemptions, for example to the metal products industry (Norway) or the electricity production sector (Sweden).

8.5   CONCLUSION

For each environmental problem, several instruments can be applied. As industry tends to favour the least costly instrument (for itself, not for society), in theory it should not favour the environmental tax. We have seen that this theoretical result is also verified in practice: taxes gain relatively little acceptance from industry, but grandfathered emission permits are more easily accepted. Industry prefers instruments which do not transfer money to the government, such as grandfathered permits. On the other hand, if the tax revenues are refunded to the polluters, the acceptability of the tax greatly improves (it should become similar to that of grandfathered emission permits, and higher than that of the other instruments).

A similar conclusion emerges from the direct majority voting case. With direct majority voting, the refund of the tax revenues improves the acceptability of the tax, especially when the refund is targeted to those who paid the tax (see Chapter 7). Moreover, we have seen that the environmental tax had to be fair in order to avoid a situation in which poor people have to modify their behaviour, whereas rich people pay the tax and continue to behave as before (see Chapter 6). But the equity of a tax cannot be evaluated without knowing what happens to the tax revenues.

An environmental tax is more easily accepted if its objective is clearly defined, and if the tax is intended to protect the environment and not to raise revenues (Chapter 8). Furthermore, industries and voters are concerned about an increase in the size of the public sector. Again, this brings us back to the issue of the use of tax revenues: if revenues are used to reduce other taxes, the size of government does not increase, and the objective of the tax is clear.

Finally, industries are sensitive to international competition. If a tax is imposed only in one country and if there is no border adjustment, the implied increase in production costs is a problem for firms which operate in competitive markets and cannot shift this cost increase to consumers. Even if there is a border adjustment, it might not completely offset the cost increase. However, the tax revenues can be used to compensate the most affected firms, and therefore improve acceptability.

As we can see, all this evidence, both theoretical and empirical, brings us to the issue of the use of tax revenues. We can therefore conclude that *an appropriate use of the tax revenues is probably the most essential factor for the acceptance or rejection of an environmental tax*. This assertion is valid in a direct democracy, as well as in a representative one. For this reason, the last part of this book deals with the issue of tax revenues.

NOTES

1. Here, we take the point of view of an individual firm which views environmental protection from a short term, book-keeping perspective. In the long term at an aggregate level, a change in the relative prices of polluting versus non-polluting goods occurs in response to the tax; new products will emerge, and old, polluting products will disappear; firms will redirect their production towards cleaner goods. In the long term, we cannot predict the impact on the profit of firms.
2. This figure is the same as Figure 2.1. It is reprinted here for convenience.
3. Transfers can be very high in comparison to the pollution reduction costs. For example, with CFCs, transfers amount to 14 times the abatement costs (Palmer et al., 1980). We should not be surprised therefore if industries protest against such payments.

4. According to a 1994 presentation from Juen, who is a representative of the 'Vorort', the leading business association.
5. This will especially happen if moving entails low sunk costs, and if there are no significant barriers to trade (Motta and Thisse, 1994).
6. Note that the environmental tax is not the only factor that affects competitiveness. We should also take into account the size of the economy, its openness to trade, the exchange rate, the importance of the taxed sector, the mobility of production factors, the market structure, innovation potential, and possible border adjustments.
7. Producers can shift part of the environmental tax on to consumers. This results in an economic incidence of the tax, which is different from its statutory incidence (see Chapter 10).

PART FOUR

Using the Tax Revenues

9.   The Possible Uses of the Tax Revenues

As we have seen in Chapter 3, under some conditions environmental taxes result in optimal environmental protection, but they also generate tax revenues. These revenues are generally a problem for governments, because they raise multiple questions: is it necessary to use the revenues to improve the protection of the environment? How can the revenues be used to compensate losers? Will the government always face the criticism of trying to use the environment in order to increase taxes? Does the macroeconomic impact depend on the way revenues are used? Should the revenues be added to the general budget of the government or earmarked for some specific additional spending? Does the size of government increase?

So far, the issue of the use of tax revenues has not received much attention in the literature. However, this issue deserves more attention than is usually paid to it. Generally, only in the analysis of large reforms, such as CO_2 taxes, is some attention devoted to the tax revenue, but this question is also important for smaller taxes.

There are many ways to use the revenue of an environmental tax. From a public finance viewpoint, we have the following possibilities:

- The government retains the new tax revenues. They are added to the other revenues of the government. This will decrease the public deficit or allow a budget surplus (see Section 9.1 below, and case *a* in Figure 9.1).

- The new revenues pay for additional public spending. This additional spending can be a financial transfer, compensating for the distributive impact of the environmental tax (Section 9.2), or an environmental policy measure, increasing the environmental impact of the tax (Section 9.3). In both instances, the revenues can simply be added to the other revenues of the government, from which the supplementary spending will be financed (case *b* in the figure); or the revenues can be paid into a special fund, separate from the rest of the budget, from which the supplementary spending will be financed (this is called 'earmarking'; see case *c* in the figure).

- The new revenues replace, totally or partially, existing taxes or social security contributions. In this case, we have an ecological tax reform (Section 9.4, and case *d* in the figure).

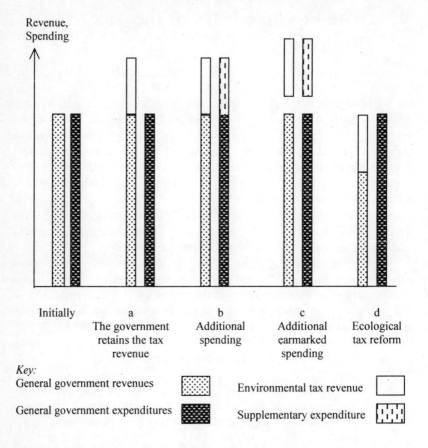

Figure 9.1 Environmental taxes and the government budget

9.1 THE GOVERNMENT RETAINS THE TAX REVENUE

If the environmental tax revenue does not pay for some other spending or reduce other taxes, introducing an environmental tax is nothing but a tax increase. With a tax increase, without a public spending increase as a counterpart, the deficit will be reduced, or a budget surplus will appear. By recognizing that this solution is a tax increase, we can already see its limitations. A tax increase is only possible if the environmental tax raises a limited amount of revenue. Indeed, a large tax increase is restricted by macroeconomic considerations (see Chapter 11) as well as by political acceptability problems (Chapters 6–8).

Should the government try to improve its budget with the revenue from an environmental tax? By reducing its deficit or its debt, the government avoids the risks of too much debt. But what are these risks?

The most likely result of excessive debt is that of the future impoverishment of society. Indeed, a deficit can shift tax burdens from current to future generations. With a deficit policy, current generations can enjoy higher public spending and lower taxes, and when in the future the government raises taxes and reduces spending because of high interest payments, some of the current taxpayers will no longer be alive; they will have shifted some of their tax burden to future generations. Moreover, a deficit policy may increase interest rates as a result of government borrowing on the financial markets; this leads to a crowding-out of private investments, and eventually to lower growth.

Furthermore, growing debt entails increasing interest costs, which add to the deficit. The deficit increases the debt, and if no deficit reduction measures are taken, this leads to the exponential growth of the debt. If there is too much debt in comparison to the size of the economy, investors will no longer want to buy government bonds, which have become too risky; this will further increase interest rates, leading to higher interest payments and higher deficit. The government will then have to resort to printing money to finance the deficit. This creates an inflationary process that also leads to the impoverishment of society.

The higher the amount of debt, the more attractive the solution of using the revenue from environmental taxes to pay off the debt. However, this solution also presents drawbacks:

- If the economy is in a period of slower growth or recession, saving the revenue from the environmental tax may worsen the economic situation, provoking a decline in the GNP. From the point of view of stabilization policy, it is therefore detrimental to retain the tax revenue. Repaying part of the debt can be a good solution, especially in a period of strong economic growth.
- The debt does not always have to be repaid. Indeed, with economic growth, the debt decreases automatically compared to the size of the economy; therefore, it becomes less and less of a problem, and never has to be repaid. If the economy grows steadily, there are probably more urgent uses for the revenue from the environmental tax than reducing the debt.

- With new tax revenues available, the government may be tempted to increase public spending instead of reducing the deficit. The availability of increased revenues is a strong incentive to pay for new programs. Indeed, as shown by Manzini and Zarin-Nejadan (1991) for Switzerland, there is a causality between public spending and public revenues. This causality means that in the presence of supplementary revenues, there is a great temptation to use these for additional spending. Spending the new revenues appeals especially to politicians in a democracy: if politicians want to be re-elected, they will try to please some voter groups with the help of additional spending. For this reason, there is some probability that the revenues from environmental taxes, even if they are initially supposed to reduce the public deficit, ultimately pay for additional programs. Even if theoretically possible, it is difficult politically not to spend the tax revenue.

Example

In Canada, Ontario has a tax for fuel conservation, which is levied on the least fuel-efficient new vehicles. The revenues from this tax reduce the public deficit of Ontario.

9.2   COMPENSATION MEASURES

When thinking about compensation, the first idea is to compensate those who suffer from the negative externalities, i.e. the victims of pollution. From the point of view of social justice, this is the best solution; it is fair to compensate those who suffer from a damage by giving them money. However, this solution is not at all efficient from an allocative standpoint; it causes many problems, and most economists reject it.[1]

The other compensation measures are: a lump sum amount to the population, an increase in social security benefits, and a compensation to businesses.

Lump Sum Transfer to Households (The 'Ecobonus')

Several authors recommend a lump sum transfer, or 'ecobonus'.[2] With this system, the revenue from the environmental tax is refunded in a lump sum manner to households (perhaps with children getting half what adults get). This lump sum transfer is an additional public expenditure.

If the whole tax revenue is refunded in a lump sum manner to households, the government does not have to be concerned about the impact of the tax on its budget. Therefore, uncertain or diminishing tax revenue does not endanger the budget. For the government, the lump sum transfer is one of the easiest ways to refund the tax revenue.

A lump sum transfer to households is similar to two other measures advocated by some economists: the 'negative income tax' and the 'basic income'. The negative income tax works as follows. Each citizen receives a lump sum (the negative income tax) from the government; and any earned income will be taxed. With this system, there is an income level I where the tax paid is equal to the negative tax received from the government. For this income level I, the taxpayer neither pays nor receives anything. Beyond I, the tax paid is higher than the transfer received, and the individual makes a net payment to the government.

Some thoughts from the negative income tax literature can be applied to our problem. The negative income tax originates from equity concerns: it may be considered fair to give an equal amount of money to everybody. However, an equal transfer to everybody does not take into account the needs of some people who need assistance they cannot afford. However, the main criticism is that, if the negative tax has to cover the basic needs of everybody, the implied tax rates have to be very high; and generally, high tax rates should be avoided, because they entail high costs to the economy.

Nowadays, negative income tax seems to be out of fashion, because of the associated efficiency problems. However, the same debate is appearing again under the name 'basic income'. A basic income is a minimal income given each period to every adult citizen, allowing him/her to survive. For its advocates, the basic income is the response to a system that discourages the unemployed people's desire to work, because they lose most of the social benefits, if they do start to work. However, the basic income faces the same criticisms as the negative income tax, that is, it cannot work without very high tax rates.

Applying these arguments to our problem, we can therefore assert that a lump sum transfer is fair, but this solution does not allow a reduction in the rate of other taxes as would an ecological tax reform. The appeal of this system comes from the income redistribution it makes possible; because of this income redistribution, a lump sum transfer can also be seen as a social policy instrument.

Example
Switzerland decided to introduce a tax on Volatile Organic Compounds (VOC), as well as one on heating oil with high sulphur content. The tax revenues will be refunded to the population on a lump sum basis, by means of a reduction in health insurance contributions (which do not depend on income in Switzerland).

Increasing Social Security Benefits

An increase in social security benefits may compensate for the negative effects of an environmental tax on some population groups. Thus, if retired people spend more on heating their homes than the rest of the population, the benefits for retired workers can be increased, so that they do not suffer more than other groups from an energy or a CO_2 tax. Similarly, if a rise in the gasoline tax disproportionately affects the populations in isolated regions, they can be compensated by means of an increase in some of the benefits they receive.

With an increase in social security benefits, the overall public spending increases. To the extent that supplementary benefits do not influence individual production and consumption decisions, they do not create economic distortions. However, when possible, reducing the taxes paid by these target groups is preferable to increasing the benefits they receive, because lower taxes imply lower costs to the economy.

Compensating Businesses

In general, serious opposition to environmental taxes comes from businesses (see Chapter 8), yet some financial compensation for the most affected businesses may bring about their acceptance. The largest polluters or energy users, who would pay the lion's share of the tax, can be compensated so as to lower their resistance. This compensation can be made on a lump sum basis, or according to other methods, but, in any case, it should not encourage firms to pollute more.

A lump sum compensation such as the one which is given to households (the ecobonus) is not possible for firms, because their size and activities are quite different. For them, a lump sum compensation should be based on the pollution initially emitted; as this compensation is proportional to the initial pollution, firms cannot influence it *ex post*. Such a compensation does not modify the firms' production decisions; therefore, there are no distortions from an allocative standpoint.[3] As we have seen in Chapter 2, with a refund based on initial emissions, the tax instrument becomes similar to a grandfathered emission permits scheme. Such a scheme is favourable from a political acceptability standpoint.

If businesses are not compensated on a lump sum basis, different criteria can be chosen to allocate the payment: revenue, payroll, number of employees, capital, cultivated land (for farmers), etc. With these possibilities, as the compensation is not a lump sum, it will always have an influence on production decisions and the allocation of resources.

A compensation proportional to the revenue of polluting firms is similar to an increase in their price: if a firm receives an amount R each time it sells a unit at a price P, in effect, the firm gets $P+R$ for each unit sold. Because the refund increases the price for which it can sell its goods, it compensates for (most of) the cost increase due to the tax. With this system, firms have an incentive to implement abatement technologies, but they are no longer penalized by the tax payment: foreign competitors do not pay the tax, but do not receive any compensation either. (Note that, if no abatement technology exists, this type of refund is ruled out, because the compensation will cancel the incentive effect of the tax.)

A transfer proportional to the payroll is similar to a reduction in social security contributions. If a firm pays $x\%$ of its payroll as social security contributions, and it receives a transfer of $y\%$ on the same payroll, it could have immediately paid $(x-y)\%$, that is, a reduced rate of social security contributions. Besides the improved acceptability of taxes, a transfer proportional to the payroll can decrease the cost of labour in comparison to capital, bringing a possible reduction in unemployment in some sectors (see Section 9.4 on the ecological tax reform).

However, a greater unemployment reduction can be obtained with a transfer proportional to the number of employees. Indeed, with a refund proportional to the number of employees the cost of labour goes down by a greater percentage for the low-income workers than for the high-income ones; and typically, the highest unemployment rates are found among the least educated people (who also get the lower salaries). Moreover, it seems that the demand for labour is more elastic in the sectors making use of a less-educated workforce. For these two reasons, employment possibilities for the less-educated workforce are particularly sensitive to the cost of labour.[4] A reduction in the cost of labour may therefore have a greater impact on unemployment if it applies especially to the low-income workers. In order to reduce unemployment, a transfer proportional to the number of employees is more effective than a transfer proportional to the payroll.

Other possibilities exist, such as a transfer proportional to the cultivated land or the energy production (see examples below). As a rule, all compensation measures other than the lump sum will result in a modification of the allocation of resources. It is necessary then to see if these modifications are regarded as desirable by society or not. They can be desirable either to compensate for some negative effects of the tax (on some groups in the economy, on the distribution of income, etc.), or to bring about changes approved by society (such as less unemployment). In any case, however, compensating the affected groups improves the political acceptability of the tax.

Examples

- Germany has introduced a tax on nitrogen fertilizers, the revenues of which are refunded to the farmers in proportion to their cultivated land. The measure is intended to give farmers who use a lot of fertilizers an incentive to reduce their fertilizer consumption, while being neutral, from a distributional point of view, for the agricultural sector as a whole. However, there is an impact on the allocation of resources, through a modification of the relative price of land in comparison to other production factors (labour, machinery).
- Sweden levies a tax on the NO_x emissions from large combustion plants for energy production. The revenues from this tax are refunded to producers in proportion to the energy produced. Although this system is widely recognized as effective, such a refund subsidizes the energy production; one may therefore wonder if a different refund, for example, proportional to the number of employees, would not have been preferable. By reducing the cost of employment in this sector, it would increase employment, instead of subsidizing energy production.

9.3   ENVIRONMENTAL POLICY MEASURES

Those in charge of environmental protection often try to take advantage of the revenues from environmental taxes, either by increasing the spending on general environmental protection, or by paying for a use directly related to the taxed pollutant. Here, we do not consider user charges, whose objective is to raise revenue, but emission taxes, whose objective is to reduce emissions (for user charges, see Chapter 5).

Spending for General Environmental Protection

The revenues from environmental taxes may allow the government to pay for additional spending for environmental protection. However, in this case, the protection of the environment is in competition with other possible uses for the additional revenues, such as social policy, transport, deficit reduction, etc. There should be a clear answer to the question: why should these supplementary funds be given to the Department of the Environment?

In fact, the environmental policy requires funding, as do the other government activities. There is no particular reason to finance it differently from other policies. The availability of tax revenues should not be a reason to increase environmental spending. Moreover, if the environmental policy is financed with the revenues from environmental taxes, it is accorded a special status; the level of spending will depend on the availability of revenues, and will not be subject to democratic choice (Hansjürgens, 1992).

Spending in the Area of the Taxed Pollutant

If a tax internalizes the external costs of the pollution, the pollution level will be socially optimal; there will be no need to use the revenues from this tax to initiate a supplementary pollution reduction, since its level is already optimal. However, in practice, there are often low taxes (at a suboptimal level), the revenues of which pay for environmental spending. Examples include water charges in France and Germany, and taxes on air pollutants in Russia. Often, political motivations can explain why the level of the tax is lower than optimal. Indeed, the lower the tax level, the lower its economic impact, and the less serious the problems of acceptability.

There are also economic reasons that may justify environmental spending in the area of the taxed pollutant. First, if the tax level is smaller than the external cost of the pollution, the pollution will be too high. If, however, the tax revenues pay for a supplementary pollution reduction, the optimal level of pollution can be reached. In order to do this, the government may either subsidize firms to encourage them to build treatment facilities, or it may build treatment facilities itself. As we showed in Chapter 5, in this way the optimal level of pollution can be attained.

Using the tax revenue for an additional emission reduction can also be justified when the tax level is high enough to internalize the cost of the pollution. Indeed, the general recommendation that the tax revenue should not be used to protect the environment, comes from static models. In a dynamic framework, technological change has to be integrated into the analysis. From a dynamic perspective, the following factors provide a rationale for using the tax revenue to promote technological change:

- We know that the tax (together with auctioned emission permits) is the instrument that gives firms the highest incentive to promote technological change. However, we do not know if the incentive for technological change is sufficient. Therefore, even with an optimal Pigouvian tax, there are reasons for using the tax revenue in the area of the environment (Carraro and Siniscalco, 1994).
- Firms react to environmental protection measures first with technological and organizational innovations, next with relocation of factories, and only finally with input substitutions and output reductions (Carraro and Siniscalco, 1994). However, static models mostly concentrate on this last stage; they are not adapted to take technological change into account.

- Simulations of the effects of a carbon tax show that even 'high' tax
  levels are not capable of stabilizing CO_2 emissions; and stabilizing
  emissions is not sufficient to solve the climatic change problem.
  However, none of the models which evaluate the effects of a CO_2 tax
  on the economic activity[5] incorporate the effect of prices on
  technological progress (Cline, 1992). By incorporating technological
  progress into the analyses, the tax levels can be greatly reduced.

In a static model, without technological progress and innovation, producers
and consumers react to the tax by reducing the quantity produced. This often
implies high tax rates, hence high welfare losses. However, in practice,
technological change and innovation seem to be more important than the
simple modification of the prices. Innovation is essential in order to solve
environmental problems. For example, the present technology is not sufficient
for solving the greenhouse gas problem at a small cost (Ossewaarde et al.
1992).

Thus, policy measures focused on increasing research and development,
improving technological innovation, and replacing the existing stock of
capital, may bring the same pollution reduction, but with a smaller reduction
in the quantity produced, hence a smaller cost. A targeted refund of the tax
revenue can therefore make the transition and adaptation to new prices easier.
If tax revenues are used for such targeted measures, there will be a twofold
incentive for faster technological progress: one from the tax, and the other
from the use of the revenues.

Among possible uses for the tax revenues, there are strong reasons for
financing research and development (R&D). The government can subsidize
private R&D, or fund public research. Indeed, the result of the R&D process
(i.e. knowledge) is a public good.[6] Therefore, the private return of an
innovation is smaller than the social one; the difference between the two
warrants a government intervention by means of a technology policy
(Harayama, 1994). However, with patent systems, as they now exist
everywhere, firms can appropriate the results of the R&D, and these results
become a private good (until the end of the patent). The government should
only subsidize the R&D if there are spillover effects which ensure that
competitors will benefit from some of the R&D results, despite the existence
of a patent (Tirole, 1988). It should also subsidize basic research without
direct commercial benefits.

The government can also subsidize 'clean' investments. This measure
helps replace old, polluting capital with new, non-polluting capital. In 1994,
the French government started to subsidize the scrapping of old cars. This
measure helped modernize the fleet by replacing old polluting cars with
cleaner cars. This measure was temporary, but if it had become permanent it

would have reduced the cost of driving a car, leading to more cars on the road, more congestion and possibly more pollution. As we see from this example, it can be risky to subsidize investment that is not totally clean. Other forms of investments can be more favourable. For example, some governments subsidize solar energy installations to replace oil heating systems. Others subsidize energy-saving devices. Subsidizing the sectors producing technologies for a rational use of energy can even enhance economic growth (Grossman and Helpman, 1991).

9.4   REDUCING OTHER LEVIES: THE ECOLOGICAL TAX REFORM

Finally, the revenues from environmental taxes can be used to reduce other taxes or social security contributions. This idea looks appealing. Indeed, all taxes and social contributions entail an excess burden,[7] which is a net loss for the economy. The reduction of existing taxes decreases this loss. We have seen in Chapter 3 that the Pigouvian tax, by reducing pollution, results in a welfare gain. By lowering other taxes, the revenue of the environmental tax brings about a second gain: this is the 'double dividend' (see later in this chapter).

When the revenues from environmental taxes reduce other taxes, we have an ecological tax reform. The expression 'ecological tax reform' contains two terms:

- 'Tax reform' is defined as a modification of all or part of the tax system. In order to have a tax reform, a certain degree of change has to take place, and the reform must have a clearly defined objective (Le Cacheux, 1996).
- 'Ecological' indicates the direction of the change.

The use of the tax revenues is the key element of the definition. Indeed, if tax revenues pay for additional programs or are refunded to the public, there will be an addition of taxes to the existing tax system, but not a 'reform' of the tax system. For example, if tax revenues are refunded on a lump sum basis, we will not have an ecological tax reform. Only when the introduction of an environmental tax occurs in conjunction with a change in the current tax system, will there be a reform of the tax system in an ecological direction.

We can then define the ecological tax reform as the replacement of all or part of the existing taxes by taxes with the objective of improving the state of the environment. We will also use the term ecological tax reform when the tax revenues pay for a reduction in social security contributions, because taxes and social security contributions have similar economic effects.

The revenues from environmental taxes can be substantial, representing several per cent of the GNP. Reducing other taxes in return enables the 'recycling' of substantial revenues, provided that these taxes are major revenue sources for the government. The main public revenues in OECD member countries are presented in Table 9.1. We then discuss the economic effects of reducing each of these taxes.

Table 9.1 Main public revenues as percentage of GDP, OECD countries*, 1995

Taxes on personal income	10.4
Social security contributions	9.8
Taxes on general consumption	6.6
Taxes on the consumption of specific goods and services	4.7
Taxes on corporate income	3.0

Notes
* Unweighted average.

Source
Revenue statistics, 1965–1996. Paris: OECD, 1997.

Reducing Taxes on the Consumption of Goods and Services

The most common indirect tax in industrialized countries is the VAT (in the United States, most states have a sales tax instead of a VAT). Because of the broad scope of this tax, reducing the VAT benefits households as well as firms, labour as well as capital, rich as well as poor people, workers as well as retired persons, etc. In most countries, the VAT rate is lower for necessities such as food, housing, books, and medical care; these items are also sometimes exempted from the tax.

The revenues from environmental taxes can be used to reduce either the normal rate of the VAT, or the lower rate. From the point of view of equity, it is better to reduce the lower rate which applies to necessities. On the other hand, efficiency considerations call for a reduction in the normal rate, in order to make it equal to, or even below, the lower rate.[8] Yet if economic efficiency is to be considered, income taxes, rather than consumption taxes, should be reduced, because they are probably less efficient than consumption taxes in practice (Bruce, 1998, p. 616).

Other indirect taxes, such as alcohol, tobacco, or gasoline, are more specific. Their objective is not only to raise revenue, but also to reduce consumption by internalizing the external costs to the public health or the environment. For this reason, it is probably not the best choice to reduce them to compensate for the revenues from the internalization of other external costs. On the other hand, Sweden and Norway recently reduced their energy taxes when they introduced a CO_2 tax, as part of a broader reform aimed at reducing the polluting emissions of the overall energy system.

Reducing Personal Income Tax

Like the VAT, personal income tax is one of the main components of current tax systems. Providing abundant revenues, it may be suited to counterbalancing large tax revenues, such as that from a CO_2 tax.

One of the main characteristics of personal income tax is its graduated tax rate schedule. This has two consequences. First, the progressivity of the schedule makes it one of the most distortional taxes. In the highest brackets, marginal tax rates of 50%, or more, are not uncommon; yet the excess burden of a tax is proportional to the square of the marginal tax rate (this is called the 'square rule'). Therefore, high gains are possible, especially if the higher rates of the tax schedule are reduced. Second, because of the progressivity of the schedule, in many countries personal income tax is the main redistributive tax. The poorest people do not pay personal income taxes, and the richest pay most of them. By reducing these taxes, the progressivity of the overall tax system decreases, especially if the higher tax rates are reduced. This is one more example of the usual conflict between efficiency and equity.

Example
When Sweden introduced its CO_2 tax, as part of a broad reform, the tax on labour income was reduced.

Reducing Taxes on Business Income

The next possibility is to reduce taxes on business income, especially in the sectors that will be most affected by the environmental tax. Theoretically, taxes on the economic profit of businesses do not entail distortions (excess burden): firms maximize their profit, with or without tax. However, in practice, taxes on business income imply several distortions, because business income is not exactly the same as economic profit (see for example Stiglitz, 1988; Bruce, 1998). As business income taxes discourage several economic activities, reducing these taxes can bring about efficiency gains. Reducing taxes on the income of polluting firms also allows a targeted redistribution to these businesses, which may increase the political acceptability of a project.

A major drawback of this solution is that only profitable firms will benefit from a refund of tax revenues, while all the polluting firms will have to pay the environmental tax, even if they do not make any profit. There is a fundamental inequality: firms that need compensation the most do not get anything, and their profitable competitors get the whole refund. Therefore, the tax may push some firms which are in trouble towards bankruptcy.

Reducing Social Security Contributions

Another possibility is to reduce social security contributions, such as health, old age, or unemployment insurance contributions. Generally, social security contributions are paid partly by employers, partly by employees, and are proportional to the salary.[9] Like other taxes, social security contributions create an excess burden, because they affect the labour supply. For this reason, reducing social security contributions yields an efficiency gain. However, the main argument for reducing social security contributions is that it lowers the cost of labour in comparison to capital, which may increase employment and reduce unemployment.

Does a reduction in social security contributions effectively reduce unemployment? First, reducing the rate of social security contributions may have only a limited impact on employment. This is because, in many countries, labour demand is rather elastic, while labour supply is comparatively inelastic (especially for men, for whom labour supply is almost completely inelastic to the net wage). Second, even if employment increases, this does not guarantee that unemployment will decrease, because unemployment depends not only on the cost of labour, but on many other factors, such as demography, the education level, or the business cycle. It seems that social security contributions have only a limited impact on the level of unemployment (Flückiger and Suarez-Cordero, 1995).

Another advantage of this solution is that the government can choose between reducing the contributions of employers and those of employees. In this way, the refund can be directed to households or to firms (at least in the short term). For example, the DIW (1994) advocates a reduction in the employers' share of social security contributions.

The major drawback of this solution is that a reduction in social contributions benefits only those who pay them. Unlike a reduction in the VAT, which benefits every household, reducing social security contributions fails to benefit entire categories of citizens such as retired people, students, or the unemployed (who would nevertheless have to pay the tax). Wage earners are the greatest beneficiaries from this solution.

Example
In the United Kingdom, the revenues of the landfill tax reduce national insurance contributions paid by employers. This redistribution method has facilitated acceptance by manufacturers.

We will now look at three issues which arise when an ecological tax reform is considered: the stability of tax revenues, the interaction of the environmental tax with existing taxes, and the existence of a double dividend.

Is the Stability of Tax Revenues a Problem?

One common argument against an ecological tax reform is that, as the objective of the environmental tax is to reduce emissions, the revenues will decrease, or even disappear. What should we think about this argument?

As a general rule, the revenue from an environmental tax will not inevitably disappear. Indeed, the tax revenue may effectively decrease for different reasons, but it may also increase. For example, with economic growth, the production of the polluting goods expands, increasing emissions and therefore tax revenue. Similarly, if for some reason (such as technological progress) the production cost of the polluting goods decreases, this will also increase production, causing more pollution and more tax revenues.

We can compare environmental taxes to alcohol or tobacco taxes, which raise significant revenues in many countries. Besides raising revenues, their objective is the same as that of environmental taxes, that is, to reduce the consumption of tobacco or alcohol. Nevertheless, their revenues do not disappear because of this objective. If alcohol or tobacco taxes consistently raise revenues, why couldn't environmental taxes do the same?

There are two points to be made about environmental taxes (the first also applies to alcohol or tobacco taxes). Most taxes, such as personal income tax or the VAT, are *ad valorem* taxes , i.e. the tax amount due is a percentage of a value (for example, 9% of the sales, or 15% of the income). On the other hand, alcohol, tobacco, gasoline and environmental taxes are 'specific' taxes, i.e. they are set in Euro, US dollar or Yen per unit of the good (for example, 1 Euro per bottle of wine, or \$12 per kilo of NO_x emissions). When inflation is present, the revenues from specific taxes do not increase automatically as do the revenues from *ad valorem* taxes. For this reason, it will be necessary to peg the level of the environmental tax to inflation in order to avoid a stability problem.

There is a second problem with environmental taxes: the existence of an abatement technology may threaten tax revenues. Indeed, an advance in the pollution reduction technology may suddenly decrease polluting emissions, which would cause a substantial reduction in tax revenues. For this reason, the revenues from environmental taxes will be more stable if no abatement technology exists. For example, the revenues of a tax on CO_2 or waste, for which no such technology exists, will be more stable than revenues from a tax on NO_x, SO_2, or noise, for which such technology exists, and can be improved.

The Interaction with Existing Taxes

As soon as tax reform substantially alters the tax system, the environmental tax cannot be viewed in isolation. Different issues arise. For example, income distribution and equity are affected not only by the introduction of environmental taxes, but also by the reduction of other taxes (see next chapter).

Also, when other taxes are considered (in an optimal tax framework), the rate of the optimal environmental tax is no longer equal to the Pigouvian rate. The reason is that, as environmental taxes raise revenues, other taxes can be lowered, causing a reduced 'excess burden' from other taxes. There is now increasing evidence that, given the presence of distortional taxes, optimal environmental tax rates should be (slightly) below the rates suggested by the Pigouvian principle (Goulder, 1995; Bovenberg and Goulder, 1996).

Furthermore, the environmental tax affects the revenues from existing taxes. Indeed, any new tax, especially a 'big' one, will have an impact on the revenues from existing taxes. In order to determine the net impact on public revenues, it will be necessary to consider not only the revenues of the new tax (and the way they are spent), but also the possible reduction in the existing tax revenues. For example, the introduction of a CO_2 tax decreases energy consumption, thereby causing a decrease in the revenues from several existing taxes, such as the energy tax, the VAT on energy, the gasoline tax, and the tax on business income in the energy sector. On the other hand, other tax revenues may increase, such as revenues from taxes on products which are consumed instead of energy.

Is there a Double Dividend?

Finally we come to the issue of the existence of a double dividend. An ecological tax reform (i.e. the introduction of an environmental tax with a simultaneous reduction in other taxes) involves both costs and benefits:

- the cost (C) is the excess burden of the environmental tax, that is, the distortions resulting from the tax;
- one benefit is the improvement in the quality of the environment (EB),
- another benefit is the efficiency gain made possible by the reduction in other distortionary taxes (IB).

The existence of these two benefits explains the expression 'double dividend' of environmental taxes, which was coined by Pearce (1991).

From an economic point of view, environmental taxes (the revenues of which are used to reduce other taxes) should be introduced if benefits are greater than costs, that is, if $EB+IB>C$. Unfortunately, the environmental benefit EB is difficult to estimate. For this reason, increasing attention has been focused on estimating the benefit of reducing other taxes (IB), in the hope that environmental taxes could yield a net gain on the sole basis of tax considerations, even without any environmental benefit.

This led to the 'strong double dividend' hypothesis. According to this hypothesis, the efficiency gain allowed by the reduction of other taxes is large enough to compensate for the cost of the environmental tax ($IB>C$); the environmental tax yields a net gain even without any environmental improvement, simply because it replaces strongly distortionary taxes with other taxes which are less distortionary. However, the majority of studies, theoretical as well as empirical, show that there is no such thing as a strong double dividend.[10] As a result, in order to evaluate the welfare impact of an environmental tax, we cannot forgo an estimation of the environmental benefits.

Next there is the 'weak double dividend' hypothesis, according to which it is more efficient to redistribute the revenues from the environmental tax by reducing other distortionary taxes, than to redistribute them in a lump sum manner; in other words, $IB>0$. This version of the double dividend is hardly disputed nowadays (see Goulder, 1995). Therefore, from the point of view of economic efficiency, a lump sum transfer is not a good solution. However, this conclusion changes when equity considerations are introduced into the analysis; in this case, Proost and Van Regemorter (1995) show that the equity aspects of a lump sum transfer can be more important, in terms of welfare, than the efficiency gains of a tax reduction. There is no more double dividend, even in its weak form.

Finally, some authors suggested that an ecological tax reform would shift part of the tax burden from labour to other factors, thus allowing a reduction in unemployment (see Bovenberg and Van der Ploeg, 1992). In this case, the second dividend is the reduction in unemployment. An increase in the energy tax, for example, decreases the demand for energy and increases the demand for other factors, such as labour. Can one expect some unemployment reduction? For Bovenberg and Van der Ploeg, there is effectively a double dividend due to the lowering of other distortionary taxes, but this double dividend does not affect employment.[11] Yet Assouline et al. (1994) show that the employment numbers can be improved under the following conditions: (1) the tax revenue is refunded by means of a reduction of the labour cost, especially for those earning lower wages, and (2) there are accompanying measures to avoid wage increases following the initial price shock of the tax.

In summary, there is a double dividend to the extent that it is more efficient to reduce other distortionary taxes than to redistribute the tax revenues in a lump sum manner. However, this double dividend does not guarantee an increase in employment. It is also not sufficient to justify an environmental tax without considering its environmental benefits.

NOTES

1. The problems are the following. (1) If people affected by the externalities are compensated, some newcomers may settle down in the polluted zones, in order to get the compensation. (This happened around Chernobyl, where new families came to the irradiated region in order to get damage compensation from the government.) (2) People affected by the externalities will have no incentive to protect themselves. As a result, the total amount of externalities may increase. (3) Information and negotiation costs are high, and pollution is often a public good (or public bad). Therefore, it is difficult to know exactly who has to be compensated, and by how much. (4) Often, victims are already compensated indirectly, by means of lower rents or lower property prices (Baumol and Oates, 1988; Oates, 1993).

2. For example: Meier and Walter (1991), Von Weiszäcker et al. (1992), in the case of Switzerland. Deutsches Institut für Wirtschaftsforschung (1994) in the case of Germany.

3. Note that in a dynamic setting, the anticipation of a future refund may create an incentive for over-polluting, in order to get a bigger refund once the instrument is implemented. Yet the same problem exists with emission permits and regulations, since polluters can also modify their behaviour in order to get more permits or a less restrictive standard in the future.

4. Flückiger and Suarez-Cordero (1995).

5. Manne-Richels, Edmonds-Barns, Jorgenson-Wilcoxen, Nordhaus, Whalley-Wigle, Green-OECD (for Green, see Burniaux et al., 1991).

6. R&D results are non-rival (everybody can benefit from increased knowledge at no additional cost), and non-excludable (even if people do not pay, they benefit from R&D results).

7. The excess burden is a burden over and above the tax amount paid. It appears because households and firms substitute untaxed goods for taxed goods (or activities).

8. This is because necessities often have a lower price elasticity of demand, and the inverse elasticity rule (Ramsey rule) recommends higher tax rates for goods with a lower price elasticity, that is, higher tax rates for necessities than for luxury goods.

9. If contributions are the same for all, i.e. lump sum, their reduction is similar to a lump sum transfer to households.

10. See for example Bovenberg and De Mooij (1994) for theoretical results, or Goulder (1995) for a comparison of empirical studies.

11. Except if the elasticity of substitution between private consumption and leisure is 1. The reason is that the labour supply will decrease and the leisure will increase; leisure (inactivity) is non-polluting, whereas the consumption of some goods (acquired with the help of the labour income) is polluting.

10. Distributional Impact

In this chapter, and in Chapter 11, we compare the different uses of tax revenues. This chapter concentrates on the most important point for acceptability, income distribution, and leaves the other points for Chapter 11.

Usually, the analysis of distributional considerations is limited to the impact of a policy on different income groups – the terms 'distribution' and 'equity' are often mistaken for one another (OECD, 1994). However, because of acceptability considerations, it is necessary to study how the tax affects all the groups in the economy. Thus, if environmental taxes significantly reduce the income or the purchasing power of a particular group (consumers, motorists, farmers, polluting firms, etc.), this group will oppose the measure. And typically, with distributional considerations, a consensus is very difficult to reach.

Because distribution is so important for acceptability, it is tempting for the government to modify it by means of reduced tax rates, exemptions, or a threshold under which no tax is paid. However, these devices for reducing the distributional impact may also reduce the efficiency of the tax. In most cases, it is possible to compensate the affected groups by giving them (part of) the tax revenues. Unlike exemptions or reduced rates, such a compensation does not impair the efficiency of the tax. For this reason, in the face of acceptability problems, it is better to compensate some groups, than to modify the tax itself.

Environmental taxes mainly change the distribution of income between (1) the rich and the poor, (2) factors of production, (3) polluters and non-polluters, (4) producers, consumers and the government, and (5) different generations.

10.1 REDISTRIBUTION BETWEEN THE RICH AND THE POOR

The impact of environmental taxes on different income groups can be broken down into (a) the impact of the tax itself, (b) the impact of the use of the tax revenues, and (c) the impact of a better environmental quality.

Impact of the Environmental Tax

The environmental tax is progressive if the rich pay a higher percentage of their income than the poor; in the opposite case, it is regressive. Therefore, it is necessary to measure the average tax rate for different income groups.

Take an individual i. T_i is the environmental tax amount paid by this individual, Y_i his income, C_i his total consumption, C_i^{poll} his consumption of the polluting good; and t is the tax rate on the polluting good. For this individual, his average tax rate is T_i/Y_i, which is equivalent to $\dfrac{T_i}{C_i}\dfrac{C_i}{Y_i}$. If $T_i =$ $t \cdot C_i^{poll}$, his average tax rate can be written as:

$$\frac{T_i}{Y_i} = t\,\frac{C_i^{poll}}{C_i}\,\frac{C_i}{Y_i}\,.$$

From this expression, two factors influence the progressivity or regressivity of an environmental tax: C_i^{poll}/C_i, which is the ratio of the consumption of the polluting good to total consumption (or composition of the consumption), and C_i/Y_i, which is the average propensity to consume. The tax will be regressive if C_i^{poll}/C_i or C_i/Y_i is smaller when the income is lower. We know that in proportion to their income, rich individuals tend to save more than poor ones, that is, C_i/Y_i tends to decrease when the income rises. However, the composition of the consumption can also influence the result.

According to different studies, environmental taxes, like most environmental programs, are rather regressive: the poor pay a higher share of their income than the rich (Baumol and Oates, 1988). For example, taxes on heating oil have a regressive impact. The exception is gasoline tax, which is progressive for most income categories (Barde, 1992; Smith, 1992).

However, the following factors reduce the regressivity of environmental taxes:

- The regressivity is reduced when indirect effects on the prices of other goods are taken into account. For example, a fuel tax is less regressive when not only the direct effects on fuel consumption, but also the indirect effects, are taken into account (Casler and Rafiqui, 1993).
- The regressivity is reduced when the permanent rather than the current income is considered. It is also reduced by using consumption rather than income as the basis for assessing the regressivity (Pearson, 1992).

- When the burden of environmental taxes is borne by producers, it falls more heavily on capital owners than on wage-earners (see the appendix to this chapter). We know that capital owners generally belong to high-income households.[1] Therefore, when environmental taxes are borne by producers, their burden falls more heavily on high-income households. This again reduces the regressivity.

When all these factors are taken into consideration, it is not certain whether environmental taxes are regressive.

Impact of the Use of the Tax Revenues

What is the impact of the tax revenues on the distribution of income? With a lump sum refund (ecobonus), everybody receives the same amount of money. Therefore, as a percentage of their income, poor individuals receive a higher refund than rich people. This measure is very favourable to low income individuals.

Social security contributions are rather regressive. The reason is that they are generally proportional to labour income, but do not apply to capital income; and those who receive a significant share of their income from capital generally belong to high income households (see above). If social security contributions are regressive, reducing these contributions will be favourable to low income households.

Consumption taxes, such as the VAT, generally place a higher burden on low-income households than on high-income ones. The main reason is that those with a higher income save a greater proportion of their income, and consume a smaller proportion. Therefore, a reduction in the VAT rate will be favourable to low-income households. Note that, in most countries, the VAT is regressive when related to income, but progressive when related to consumption (Mottu, 1994).

Finally, personal income tax is progressive because of its graduated tax rate schedule. However, its progressivity is sometimes exaggerated. Indeed, in many countries the income from certain forms of savings is exempted; also, tax evasion and tax avoidance tend to limit the progressivity of the income tax, but it is difficult to determine by how much. Because of its progressivity, a reduction in income tax will be more favourable to high-income households.

Impact of a Better Environmental Quality

Does a better environmental quality benefit low-income households, or high-income households? To answer this question, we can first look at the distribution of the physical environment across different income groups. It appears that, in urban surroundings, those who benefit most from a better environmental quality are generally low-income households, because they often live in polluted areas. On the other hand, in rural areas, low-income households do not benefit much from a better environment (OECD, 1994, p. 87).

However, from an economic point of view, we can look beyond the physical improvements, and examine the monetary valuation of these physical improvements across different income groups. In other words, we can compare the demand for an improved environment across different income groups. One measure is the following ratio, called the income-elasticity of the willingness-to-pay for the environment:

$$\frac{\% \ change \ in \ the \ willingness\text{-}to\text{-}pay \ for \ the \ environment}{\% \ change \ in \ the \ income}$$

An elasticity greater than 1.0 means that proportionally, the willingness-to-pay increases more than the income; that is, the environment is a luxury good. With this kind of indicator, results diverge. For Baumol and Oates (1988), those on high incomes benefit more from a better environmental quality than those on low incomes, who often have other priorities. For Barde (1992) on the other hand, a better environmental quality mainly benefits the middle class.

As no definitive conclusion seems to emerge, we will limit the following comments to the impact of the tax and of the use of revenues, and bypass the impact of a better environmental quality.

Overall Impact

What is the overall impact of the tax plus the use of tax revenues? In what follows, let us assume that the impact of environmental taxes is regressive. If the overall impact has to be favourable to low-income households, the redistribution has to overcompensate for the regressive impact of the tax. Two types of refund may bring an overall impact favourable to low-income households:

- a lump sum refund (this refund overcompensates for the regressivity of the tax);
- an increase in social benefits (if they are targeted at the poorer households).

The overall impact will be favourable to high-income households with:

- no refund (nothing compensates for the regressivity of the environmental tax);
- a reduction in personal income tax (as this tax is progressive, reducing it benefits mainly the rich; and the poorest, who do not pay the income tax, would not get any benefit from its reduction);
- a reduction in the tax on business income (cutting business taxes increases after-tax earnings; the measure benefits shareholders, who are usually richer than the average);[2]
- a refund to businesses (because it also benefits shareholders; this measure does not compensate for the regressivity of the environmental tax).

With the following options, the overall impact will be undetermined:

- a reduction in the VAT (because both the environmental tax and the VAT are regressive);
- a reduction in social contributions (because the tax as well as the refund are regressive). Note that those who do not pay social contributions, such as retired persons or students, do not get any refund.

Is it better to have an overall impact (of the tax and the use of revenues) which benefits the rich, which benefits the poor, or one which is neutral? Basically, this is a normative choice. Considerations of social justice support an overall impact favourable to the poor. Supporters of a lump sum refund advocate this solution, which kills two birds (environmental policy and social policy) with one stone. However, and precisely because of this dual objective, a lump sum refund may be open to criticism. Indeed, it is better to avoid the pursuit of a social policy objective with an environmental instrument, in order to avoid a detrimental conflict of objectives (see next chapter). Furthermore, acceptability problems can arise from any attempt to change the existing income distribution.

A neutral impact can be sought for one of the following reasons: (1) The current income distribution is considered to be optimal (this is a normative choice). (2) By keeping the current income distribution, the acceptability problems specifically related to a change in income distribution are avoided. A solution that minimizes income redistributions is more capable of bringing about a social consensus.

Finally, we do not see any reason to favour a policy which makes high income people better off, when social inequalities are a growing preoccupation in most countries. This is all the more true when environmental taxes produce abundant revenues, leading to massive wealth transfers. In this case, solutions such as reducing personal income tax or the tax on business income should be avoided.

The reader may have noted that the preceding analysis refers to the concepts of progressivity and regressivity, which reflect the 'ability-to-pay principle'. This principle is not the only principle of tax equity; there is also the 'benefit principle of equity'. Instead of relating the tax payment to income, as does the ability-to-pay principle, the benefit principle of equity relates the tax payment to the benefits received from the government. For example, gasoline taxes are fair, because they are paid by drivers, who benefit from the government spending on roads.

Are environmental taxes fair according to the benefit principle of equity? It can be argued that the polluters (the taxpayers) make a private use of a public good, the environment. By allowing individuals or firms to pollute, society gives them 'something'. If there is no payment, this 'something' is free. With environmental taxes, the benefit principle of equity applies: taxes are paid for the consumption of the environment; this payment corresponds to the use of a public good. Therefore, according to the benefit principle of equity, environmental taxes are fair. Even if they are regressive, they are fair, because they reflect the benefit principle of equity.[3]

10.2   REDISTRIBUTION BETWEEN FACTORS OF PRODUCTION

As noted in the Appendix to this chapter, it can be assumed that capital owners bear a larger share of the burden of environmental taxes than workers. Depending on the use of the tax revenues, we can distinguish two cases:

- As the tax burden is mainly borne by capital owners, any revenue refund which is not specifically directed towards them will have a final result favourable to labour. This will be the case if the tax revenues help reduce the VAT (which does not affect the capital–labour choice). This will also be the case if social security contributions (which are mainly borne by workers) are reduced: the overall impact will be even more favourable to workers.
- If the tax revenues are directed towards capital owners (for example, by means of a reduction in taxes on business income), the result will be undetermined.

Is it desirable to favour one factor of production? From the standpoint of economic efficiency, shifting part of the overall tax burden from labour to capital is justified, if the marginal excess burden of the taxation of capital is smaller than that of labour. This could well be the case, since nowadays, at least in Europe, labour is taxed much more than capital.

On the other hand, the accumulation of capital is one of the main factors explaining economic growth. With measures unfavourable to capital, the result could be a reduction in long-term growth; this can be a good reason not to increase the tax burden on capital owners. Finally, acceptability considerations could lead us to seek a neutral overall impact, which would not cause any transfers between workers and the owners of capital.

10.3   REDISTRIBUTION BETWEEN POLLUTERS AND NON-POLLUTERS

Environmental taxes are imposed on polluters (firms and households). Polluting firms may shift part of their tax burden onto other groups in the economy, such as consumers or factors of production (for factors of production see the appendix to this chapter). In this case, they do not bear the full burden of the environmental tax. For example, if, following a NO_x tax, an energy producer can increase its price, it will be able to shift the tax burden on to consumers.

In the same way, polluting firms do not bear the full burden of taxes on business income, consumption, or social security contributions. If those taxes are reduced in order to use the revenues from the environmental tax, polluting firms will get only part of the reduction, with the rest benefiting the other groups who originally bore part of the tax burden.

For this reason, it is often difficult to draw a definite conclusion about possible transfers between polluters and non-polluters. However, in some cases, the impact is clear:

- If motorists bear the whole burden of a gasoline tax, and its revenues are refunded to the entire population, there will be a net transfer from motorists to non-motorists.
- If polluters can shift part of the tax burden, but get back all the revenues, there will be a net transfer from the rest of society to polluters.

Is a transfer between polluters and non-polluters desirable? In the long term, a transfer from polluting firms to other groups decreases the financial capacity of these firms, causing a reduction in their number, and a corresponding reduction in the pollution. Similarly, a transfer from polluting households (for example, motorists with gas-guzzlers) to other groups decreases their purchasing power, and therefore the pollution.[4] A transfer from polluters to non-polluters is desirable in order to bring about a long-term reduction in pollution; it can also be seen as a fair compensation for the damage suffered by non-polluters.

However, if a tax transfers significant resources from polluters to non-polluters, it may be opposed by the polluters. In order to avoid that, the tax revenues have to return to the polluting sector. However, even if tax revenues do return to the polluting sector, resources may be transferred between different groups of polluters. This is illustrated by the example of the Swedish NO_x tax, which is imposed on large energy plants. The tax revenues are refunded to the businesses, in proportion to their energy production. With this system, the paper industry and the incineration industry are net payers, while the energy production sector and the metallurgy industry are net recipients (Olivecrona, 1995). The Swedish system avoids transfers between polluters and non-polluters, but not between industries. If transfers between industries have to be avoided, a separate fund may be used for each industrial sector. Each sector gets back from its fund the same amount as it paid in taxes. (This system is recommended by Vos, 1993.)

The same considerations apply to households. Even if the whole population pollutes, some groups may pollute more than others. For example, some people own large sport-utility vehicles, consuming much gasoline, while others have compact, fuel-efficient cars. Drivers of big sport-utility vehicles would be affected by a CO_2 tax more than drivers of small cars. If they are refunded the same amount, they may try to oppose the tax. Just as for industries, each household group may be refunded a different amount in order to reduce the opposition. But what are the implications of compensating the polluters?

Should Polluters be Compensated?

The tax revenues can be refunded either to the polluters only, or to the whole of society. This choice will not only affect income distribution, but also the pollution emitted. That is, distributional considerations will have an impact on the pollution emitted.

In order to show this, suppose there are two subgroups in the population: the polluters, who consume a polluting good, and the non-polluters, who don't. (Polluters can be frequent fliers, or motorists, users of garden fertilizers, etc.) Polluters can choose to allocate their revenue (R) between two goods: x_1, which is polluting, and x_2, which is not. Figure 10.1 represents the budget constraint and the indifference curves of the polluters' subgroup. Each indifference curve (U_1, U_2, U_3, U_0) indicates a given level of utility for the polluters.

Point A represents the initial situation, without any government intervention. Individuals maximize their private utility. They will choose the consumption of x_1 and x_2, which allows them to reach the highest possible utility level, given their budget constraint $(R/p_1, R/p_2)$. They can reach utility level U_0, at point A.

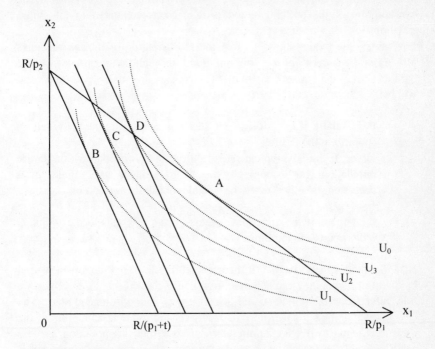

Figure 10.1 The choice of the polluters' subgroup

With an environmental tax on the polluting good x_1, the price of x_1 increases from p_1 to (p_1+t). Therefore, the budget constraint rotates to $(R/(p_1+t), R/p_2)$. We arrive at point B, where consumers maximize their utility again, but this time according to their new budget constraint. Because of the tax, they can only achieve utility U_1. Point B, which is inside of the initial budget constraint, corresponds to the situation without any refund of the tax revenues. We can observe that the consumption of the polluting good x_1 has decreased.

If the tax revenues are refunded to the whole population, the polluters' budget constraint moves to the right. However, the consumption point that maximizes utility will remain inside the initial budget constraint. Indeed, as only polluters pay the tax, but the whole population gets the refund, there is a transfer of income from polluters to the rest of the population; therefore, polluters cannot reach their initial budget constraint. They arrive at point C, which corresponds to utility level U_2.

Only if polluters get back all the tax revenues will they be able to reach their initial budget constraint. This is point D in the figure, with utility level U_3. At point D, the consumption of the polluting good x_1 is lower than at point A. Thus, even if the entire tax revenues are refunded to the polluters, the consumption of the polluting good is reduced as compared to the initial situation.[5]

This simple model shows us that the redistribution of the tax revenues influences the quantity of the polluting good, through the income effect (the parallel shift of the budget constraint). The consumption of the polluting good will be:

- the smallest, if the government does not redistribute the tax revenues (point B in the figure);
- larger, if the government redistributes the tax revenues to the entire population (for example by means of a lump sum refund, or a reduction in other taxes or social contributions) (point C in the figure);
- the largest, if the government redistributes revenues to the polluters only (point D in the figure).

Also, the model shows us that, if the acceptability from polluters is measured by the utility level they can achieve, it will be highest if the tax revenues are fully refunded to the polluters, and lowest if they are not refunded at all. The environmental impact is therefore inversely related to the acceptability of the measure: the more effective a policy measure is at reducing pollution, the less acceptable it is to the polluters, and vice versa. If the acceptability level is low, the government may want to use the tax revenues to compensate the polluters, even if it means that the pollution will be reduced less effectively than it would be with another type of revenue redistribution.

10.4   REDISTRIBUTION BETWEEN PRODUCERS, CONSUMERS AND THE GOVERNMENT

Environmental taxes may also transfer income between producers, consumers, and the government. These transfers may cause political opposition. For example, the American state of Minnesota recently proposed the introduction of a \$50/ton carbon tax, offset by a 25% decrease in the property tax. This tax shift is strongly opposed by industry, because it would transfer resources from industry to residential and commercial property owners.

Consumers and producers share the burden of an environmental tax, and the tax revenues go to the government. If financial transfers are to be avoided, the government will have to give back to each group in the economy exactly what it has paid. Then, the problem is knowing how much each group has paid, i.e. the exact distribution of the tax burden between consumers and producers. This is not always an easy task.

For example, if only consumers bear the environmental tax (that is, the supply of the polluting good is infinitely elastic), a redistribution of the tax revenues to them will not affect the distribution of income between consumers and producers. However, in general consumers share the tax burden with producers. In this case, if the tax revenues are redistributed to the consumers only, there will be a transfer from producers (who bear part of the tax burden) to consumers (who get back all the revenues). This will be the case with:

- a lump sum transfer to households;
- a compensation to the victims of the pollution.

Is it desirable for environmental taxes to cause transfers between different groups in the economy? If the public debt is too large, it may justify a redistribution from consumers and producers to the government. As for transfers to producers or to consumers, there is no apparent reason for them. In any case, acceptability problems imply that such transfers have to be clearly understood, and, if possible, avoided.

10.5 REDISTRIBUTION BETWEEN GENERATIONS

Environmental taxes improve the wellbeing of future generations by decreasing the consumption of non-renewable resources, as well as by decreasing the polluting emissions which accumulate in nature. An improvement in the wellbeing of future generations can also be obtained with the following uses of the tax revenues:

- If the tax revenues reduce the public debt, this will reduce the risks associated with a high debt level. As we have seen, the most likely risk for a country in debt is the risk of future impoverishment.
- The revenues from environmental taxes can pay for environmental policy measures, especially measures aimed at sustainable development. This also benefits future generations.

Is it desirable to favour future generations? In the same way as income is redistributed from high-income to low-income people within a generation, income can also be redistributed between rich and poor generations. But will future generations be richer or poorer than the present generation? Future generations may be better off, because of economic growth and improved productivity. On the other hand, they may also be worse off, because of an irreversible degradation of the environment; they may also be worse off if they inherit a high, unjustifiable debt, or because of the burden of an ageing population. If we think they will be worse off, it makes sense to attempt to improve their welfare.

For economists, intergenerational equity is a normative choice. However, the philosopher Hans Jonas, in his book 'The Imperative of Responsibility' (1990), argues that it is not a choice, but our responsibility to ensure the wellbeing of future generations. Today, modern technology has become a potential threat to nature and also to future generations. For the first time in human history, because of the irreversibility potential of human actions on nature, a new ethic is necessary. As the power of mankind is unprecedented, the traditional ethic inherited from preceding generations is no answer to these threats. Norms such as 'good' and 'evil' are no longer a great help in the face of present challenges and responsibilities. From the moment the power of mankind reaches the ability to put an end to its very existence, the responsibility for the future is part of ethics.

This new collective responsibility for the future of mankind corresponds to the new power given to human beings. The objective is to protect for mankind the integrity of its world against any misuse of power. According to Hans Jonas, we have an obligation to ensure the existence of a future mankind. This responsibility does not only include the obligation to ensure that human beings exist, but also that they have a good life. This means that our responsibility also includes ensuring the welfare of future generations.

APPENDIX. WHO BEARS THE BURDEN OF THE ENVIRONMENTAL TAX?

One of the fundamental concerns with any tax is who eventually bears the burden of it. Indeed, although the tax is paid by the producers of polluting goods, they are able to shift, at least partially, the tax burden to other groups, such as consumers or wage-earners.

This question is interesting in different respects. First, the question of the distribution of the burden of the tax, especially in the short term, is crucial for political acceptability, to the extent that the most affected are also those who will most vigorously oppose the project. Second, if producers cannot shift the tax to consumers, the government may want to lower its ecological ambitions, especially for economic sectors facing strong international competition. Information about the distribution of the tax burden may also be used to introduce compensatory payments. Finally, knowing who will eventually bear the tax provides useful information about the impact of the tax on income distribution: if the tax is shifted to consumers, will poor people pay proportionally more than rich people?

With environmental taxes, producers of polluting goods are generally the statutory taxpayers. They will try to shift part of the tax burden to other economic sectors and to individual consumers; and the share borne by producers eventually results in lower rewards to production factors (labour and capital).

Shifting to Other Economic Sectors

Polluting goods are not always directly used by consumers. Often, polluting goods are intermediate goods, which are used by other sectors in the economy. In this case, the tax may be 'shifted' to other sectors. For example, a tax on oil affects oil producers; but if market conditions allow them to increase their prices in response to the tax, this will have an impact on all the sectors of the economy which use some oil.

Fullerton (1996) shows that the existing environmental taxes in the United States increase the prices in the directly targeted sectors only by a small amount; but they increase the prices of goods in all economic sectors without exception. For example, textiles are not directly targeted by existing environmental taxes. However, the other sectors which are targeted by the taxes (such as the chemical industry, transport, or electricity), increase their prices in response to the tax. This, in turn, indirectly affects textile prices. Overall, in the United States, there is a large shift in the burden of environmental taxes on to the non-taxed sectors.

Shifting to Consumers

Polluting sectors can shift the tax forward to consumers. The distribution of the tax burden between producers and consumers depends on the market structure, that is, on the price elasticity of supply and demand for the products in question. The lower the price elasticity of supply and the higher the price elasticity of demand, the more producers will have to bear this burden. Consumers will bear a greater proportion of the tax burden if the price elasticity of supply is high and that of demand is low. For example, as the market for gasoline is characterized by an inelastic demand, it is mainly consumers who will bear the burden of a gasoline tax.

Such an analysis, which examines only producers and consumers, is valid with the implicit assumption of a perfectly elastic factor supply (see for example Atkinson and Stiglitz, 1980, p. 162). Thus, it will be appropriate to study the effects of a tax on a market that is 'small' in relation to the rest of the economy. However, it is insufficient to study the impact of a more important tax, which will modify the rewards to production factors.

Lower Rewards to Production Factors

When environmental taxes cannot be shifted forward to consumers or other sectors, their burden is eventually borne by production factors. Suppose we have an economy producing two goods, a non-polluting good N, and a polluting good P, the production of which is associated with pollution. The government imposes a tax on P, which increases its price. We suppose that the production of good P is relatively capital-intensive.[6]

Following the tax, the relative price of P increases, leading to a decline in the production of P and an increase in the production of N. This decline in the production of P will make some capital and some labour available, but relatively more capital than labour (because P is a capital-intensive good). Since, in the economy, factors are employed in their totality, relatively large amounts of capital will have to be put to use in the production of N (that is, in the labour-intensive sector); this can only happen with a reduction in the reward to capital. If the capital is easily transferred between sectors, then its relative price will decline in both sectors.

Consequently, we see that with the underlying assumptions, if the production of good P is capital-intensive, the taxation of P will lead to a reduction in the reward to capital in comparison with labour. On the other hand, the relative reward to labour will be reduced if good P is relatively labour-intensive. Therefore, if we want to have an idea of the impact of the tax on factors of production, we have to know if the production of the polluting goods is relatively capital- or labour-intensive.

To answer this question, we classify the different sectors of the Swiss economy according to their capital intensity. We consider the following ratio:

$$\frac{Depreciation\ of\ fixed\ capital}{Personnel\ and\ social\ costs}$$

The more a sector is capital-intensive, the higher the depreciation costs in comparison with personnel costs. Table 10.1 shows that the most polluting or energy-intensive sectors are relatively capital-intensive: the chemical, plastic and metallurgic industries, the energy production sector, the transport sector, and the glass, paper, leather, and cement manufacturing industries are all in the upper part of the table, while none of those sectors is found in the lower part of the table.

Therefore, the table suggests that the production of the polluting goods is relatively intensive in capital. This is not counterintuitive (it is not possible to pollute intensively without capital). In this case, environmental taxes will free up relatively more capital than labour. With the assumptions of the Harberger model, this means that environmental taxes increase the reward to labour and decrease the reward to capital. If the relative reward to capital declines, owners and representatives of the capital will oppose environmental taxes.

Table 10.1 Factor intensity and pollution in Swiss economic sectors

Sector	Ratio of capital to labour costs (%)	Polluting sectors
Energy (private firms)	100.0	x
Energy (public firms)	57.1	x
Real estate	54.0	
Beverage industry	35.0	
Refuse industry	34.4	x
Credit, leasing	29.9	
Navigation, shipping	28.3	
Paper industry	28.3	x
Road transport	26.7	x
Plastic and rubber industry	25.5	x
Non-metallic mineral products industry	24.7	x
Chemical industry	23.4	x
Food industry	22.1	
Airlines	19.9	x
Retail trade	17.5	
Wholesale trade	14.9	
Leather and shoe industry	14.8	x
Metallurgy	14.6	x
Textile industry	14.1	
Watchmaking, jewellery	14.0	
Graphic arts	13.9	
Tobacco industry	13.4	
Wood and furniture industry	13.0	
Catering and lodging	12.5	
Goods repair	11.6	
Health services, veterinary services	11.4	
Electrical, electronic, optical products	11.4	
Research and development	11.2	
Transport intermediaries	11.0	
Commercial services	10.1	

(Continued on next page)

Table 10.1 (Continued)

Sector	Ratio of capital to labour costs (%)	Polluting sectors
Personal services	10.1	
Culture, sports, leisure	10.0	
Other manufacturing	9.5	
Machinery, vehicles construction	8.7	
Clothing industry	8.6	
Construction	6.7	
Teaching	6.5	
Social work	5.5	
Finish work (construction)	4.5	

Source

Own calculations, based on 1993 data from the Swiss Statistical Yearbook (1996).

NOTES

1. See Flückiger and Silber (1995), and Kirchgässner and Savioz (1995), in the case of Switzerland.
2. See for example Fullerton and Rogers (1993, p. 6).
3. Note that every principle of equity is based on value judgements. Equity and fairness are normative concepts.
4. If polluting goods are not inferior goods.
5. As usual, we suppose that the income effect is positive for both goods (they are normal goods).
6. This discussion is based on a model commonly used in analyses of the impact in general equilibrium, the Harberger model (see for example Rosen, 1992, pp. 296–297; Stiglitz, 1988, pp. 567–568). It is a model with two sectors and two production factors. The model starts with the following assumptions: there is perfect competition in the goods markets; businesses maximize their profits; technology is characterized by constant returns of scale; consumers have identical preferences. There are two sectors, one producing a labour-intensive good, the other a capital-intensive one. The total factor quantities are fixed, but factors are perfectly transferable between sectors. For this reason, it is neither a short-term nor a long-term model. As factor suppliers are supposed to maximize their income, factor prices will be equalized between the two sectors.

11. Comparison between the Different Uses

In this last chapter we compare the different uses of the tax revenues, using criteria such as the size of government, the administrative cost, the macroeconomic impact, the number of objectives, and the international impact. We also tackle the question of the earmarking of tax revenues. These criteria, in addition to being recurrent in the debate on environmental taxes, have an impact on the acceptability of environmental taxes.

11.1 THE SIZE OF GOVERNMENT

A recurrent argument against environmental taxes is that they increase the size of government. Indeed, the image of government is often associated with inefficient allocation of resources, a lack of flexibility, and bureaucratic procedures. For example, terms such as bureaucracy or 'big government' are often perceived as pejorative; some people even compare government with a Leviathan[1] whose only goal is to maximize its revenues. Because of this negative image, many people have apprehensions about the government using environmental taxes as a pretext to increase its size. But do environmental taxes really increase the size of government?

We should first recall that the influence of government does not manifest itself only through its size. Economic measures of the size of government do not take into account the impact of regulations, which represent a very significant government intervention in the economy. (For example, most environmental standards do not have any influence on the size of government.) In the same way, tax breaks or tax expenditures increase the influence of government, without increasing its size.

Different indicators may be used to measure the size of government in the economy. Generally, the size of government is measured with reference to public spending:

1. The most common measure of the size of the public sector is the ratio of total government spending as a percentage of GDP. With this definition, the numerator is not part of the denominator: transfers from the

government to the private sector are not part of the GDP. Thus, this is simply a ratio, which measures the size of one thing in terms of another (Manzini, 1992; Bruce, 1998).

2. A definition of the share of government in the economy is final demand (or final consumption) of the government, divided by GDP. Final demand, or final consumption, is defined as the production of government, less the revenue of its sales. This measure relates the goods and services produced by the government to the GDP. It does not include transfers, and is therefore more restrictive than the preceding definition (Stiglitz, 1988; Manzini, 1992).

Although less common, the size of government is sometimes measured on the revenue side:

3. The ratio of taxes and social security contributions as a percentage of GDP, or as a percentage of national income (Manzini, 1992).

When measuring the size of government, there is an important difference between transfer spending (transfers from the government to firms and households) and government consumption (wages for civil servants, interest payments, etc.). With consumption spending, the government controls the use of economic resources; with transfer spending, the government gives this control to the private sector. For this reason, transfer spending may be more easily accepted than consumption spending.

The three measures of the size of government will be affected by the environmental tax, and also by the use of tax revenues:

- If the new tax revenues are added to the other revenues of the government (and reduce its deficit), the size of government is increased according to the revenue side measure (3), but remains constant according to the spending side measures (1, 2).
- With a reduction in other taxes (ecological tax reform), the size of government remains unchanged for all three measures. The reason is that spending is not affected; neither is total government revenue, since new revenues are used to reduce traditional revenues.
- New tax revenues may be refunded as transfers: lump sum transfer, transfers to firms, increase in social benefits, subsidies, etc. In this case, revenues, as well as public spending, increase. The size of government increases for measures 1 and 3. Only measure 2, the share of government, is not influenced by transfer spending and therefore remains unchanged.

- As for environmental policy measures, it is necessary to distinguish between two situations. If the government subsidizes environmental activities, this is similar to the transfers of the preceding case, and the size of government increases according to definitions 1 and 3. On the other hand, if the government itself produces environmental goods and services (for example by operating a waste water treatment plant), then the size of government increases according to all definitions, including definition 2. Note that this last case is the only one in which the real measure of the share of government changes.

When environmental tax revenues reduce other taxes or social contributions, the size of government remains constant, whatever the definition. To the extent that the size of government is a politically sensitive matter, such an ecological tax reform is a good solution. With the other uses, the situation is not so favourable; the size of government increases with some definitions, and remains constant with others.

11.2   THE ADMINISTRATIVE COST

When an environmental tax is introduced, the total administrative cost consists of the administrative cost of the tax, and the administrative cost of the use of revenues.

The Administrative Cost of the Environmental Tax

The administrative cost of the tax depends on the tax base, that is: (*a*) the cost of measurement for each emission source; (*b*) the number of sources; and (*c*) the possible use of existing administrative structures, such as the firms' book-keeping departments, or existing tax structures.

The cost of measurement for each source depends on the available emission measurement technology. Nowadays, technological progress in electronic measurement systems and data-processing make it cheaper to measure individual emissions. As a result, it has become possible to tax emissions where it was impossible some years ago, because of disproportionate administrative costs.[2] For example, today NO_x and SO_2 emissions can be taxed; this would have been impossible previously, because of a lack of cheap and reliable measurement devices.

The administrative cost is low when the environmental costs can be charged in a centralized way, and when the tax can be added to existing taxes or user fees. For example, the administrative cost of an additional tax on water, energy, CO_2 or gasoline is close to zero, since the structures for the levying of the tax already exist. On the other hand, the cost can be high when the measurement of emissions is decentralized. For example, when users have to pay a garbage tax according to the weight of the waste produced, each garbage bag has to be weighed, which is a costly operation. Also, the administrative cost of an environmental tax can be substantially increased if there are complex schemes, such as border adjustments, exemptions or reduced rates, aimed at protecting national industries (see Chapter 8).

The Administrative Cost of the Use of Tax Revenues

The second component of the administrative cost is the cost of the use of revenues. This cost will depend on each specific use of the tax revenues. For example, if the government does not redistribute revenues, this cost is zero. In the case of an ecological tax reform, this cost is negligible. This does not mean that the administrative cost of levying current taxes is negligible (for example, in the United States, the administrative cost of levying the income tax is estimated to be between 5 and 7% of the tax revenue). However, when the rate of current taxes or social contributions is reduced, the administrative cost of levying them is not significantly reduced.

Sometimes the administrative cost may be high, for example, when the compensation scheme is complex and necessitates the creation of new administrative structures. When households or businesses are compensated, if the government simply adapts existing pensions or subsidies, the cost may be low. In other cases, the cost may be higher, for example, if businesses receive money according to the number of employees (because this number is difficult to measure and to control). As for environmental policy measures, they can also imply a high cost, especially if they require the creation of new and complex administrative structures.

11.3   THE MACROECONOMIC IMPACT

Before analysing the macroeconomic impact, it is important to remember that the aim of economic activity is not the maximum production or GNP, but rather the highest possible social welfare (social welfare being a normative concept, based on value judgements). Economic growth does not inevitably increase welfare. The distinction is especially important in the area of the environment, as shown by the numerous attempts to revise the national accounts, in order to take the degradation of the environment into account. Thus, Motta and Thisse (1994) show that environmental taxes can lead to a reduction in economic activity, and at the same time to a welfare increase (because of the pollution reduction). Unfortunately, most studies are limited to the macroeconomic impact of environmental taxes. The few studies which extend the analysis to the impact on welfare do not always integrate the welfare variations resulting from an improvement in the quality of the environment. Therefore, we will have to be satisfied with the impact on GNP.

Environmental taxes affect economic activity in two ways. First, environmental taxes may contribute to stabilizing the business cycle (stabilizing economic activity is one of the three economic functions of the government).[3] Second, when environmental taxes are introduced, they have an impact on the GNP, which can be positive, or negative. Note that macroeconomic considerations are important especially when 'big' taxes are implemented.

Stabilization of Economic Activity

Do environmental taxes help stabilize economic activity, or conversely, do they amplify its natural fluctuations? The answer depends on how the tax revenues, and the implied spending, are affected by the business cycle.

The revenues from environmental taxes depend on the economy: with a strong economy, the production and consumption of polluting goods increases, yielding more tax revenues. As for the use of tax revenues, everything depends on the earmarking of the tax revenues. If the revenue from an environmental tax is earmarked for some specific spending, it cannot be used for anything else; the spending is always equal to the tax revenue. Since the spending is equal to the tax revenue, it will vary according to the state of the economy, giving no stabilizing effect. For example, if, during an economic slowdown, the revenue from an environmental tax goes from $100 million to $80 million, and is earmarked for a specific spending, the spending will also decrease from $100 million to $80 million, which will contribute to depressing the economy. This is one argument against the earmarking of tax revenues (for a further discussion of earmarking, see Section 11.5).

A stabilizing effect will exist only if the spending (made possible by additional tax revenues) is independent of the evolution of the tax revenues. In our example, we will have a stabilization effect, if the spending remains at $100 million, whatever the evolution of the tax revenues.

From this discussion, we can assert that the following uses will help stabilize economic activity:

- spending in the area of the environment (without earmarking of revenues),
- and financial compensation measures (without earmarking of revenues).

In the other cases, we will not have such a clear-cut answer.[4]

Note that the competing instrument, marketable emission permits, adds to the natural fluctuations of the business cycle. When the economy is strong, the demand for permits exceeds supply, leading to an upward pressure on the price, which adds to the overall inflationary pressures existing elsewhere in the economy. Taxes do not present this problem.

Macroeconomic Impact

Studies of the macroeconomic impact of environmental taxes are based on different models; this makes a comparison difficult. However, in some cases similar conclusions emerge from different models, which allows us to draw some general conclusions. Especially interesting are the studies which compare different uses of the tax revenues, using the same model. Table 11.1 presents the expected macroeconomic impact of some environmental taxes, sorted according to how the tax revenues are used.

Even though all the results from Table 11.1 do not point in the same direction, they do suggest the following fact: the macroeconomic impact is not inevitably negative. In some cases, introducing an environmental tax may imply stronger economic growth. The table also shows that the way revenues are used determines the macroeconomic impact of the tax.

In several models, the mechanism functions as follows: the tax increases the general price level, creating the conditions for a negative macroeconomic impact. However, the overall impact depends on the use of tax revenues: if producers get some kind of refund, they will not increase their prices as much as if households get the entire refund and producers get nothing. For this reason, the macroeconomic impact is worse when the tax revenues are refunded to households only. Such a mechanism is explained in detail in Poterba et al. (1986). These authors show that, if salaries are rigid, combining a reduction in direct taxes with an increase in indirect taxes will negatively affect the production level, and this is exactly what happens here: environmental taxes are introduced (increase in indirect taxes), and their revenues are refunded by means of a reduction in the personal income tax or the social contributions of employees (reduction in direct taxes).

These considerations suggest the following: as the negative macroeconomic impact comes from the price hike imposed by producers, *the refunds which directly benefit producers will have a more favourable macroeconomic impact than others*. Thus, in reducing the VAT, business income taxes or employers' social contributions, the results are better than with lump sum transfers, a reduction in the personal income tax, or a reduction in employees' social contributions.

Table 11.1 Macroeconomic impact and the use of tax revenues

Use of revenue	Tax	Study	GNP Impact
No refund	Gasoline	Brinner et al. (1991)	- st, + lt[a]
	CO_2	Jorgenson and Wilcoxen (93)	-
	CO_2/Energy	Welsch and Hoster (1995)	-/+
	CO_2/Energy	Delache (1996)	-
Lump sum refund	Energy	Goulder (1994)	-
	CO_2	Jorgenson et al. (1992)	-
	CO_2	Manne and Richels (1990)	-
	CO_2	Cline (1992)	-
	CO_2	Stephan et al. (1992)	0/-
	CO_2	Whalley and Wigle (1992)	-
	CO_2/Energy	Nicoletti and Oliveira-Martins (1993)	-
	CO_2/Energy	Welsch (1995)	-
	CO_2/Energy	Welsch and Hoster (1995)	+ st, - lt
Reducing VAT	CO_2	Shackleton et al. (1992)	0/+
	CO_2	Barker et al. (1993)	+
	CO_2/Energy	Delache (1996)	0
	CO_2/Energy	Direction de la prévision (1991)	0
Reducing personal income tax	Gasoline	Brinner et al. (1991)	-
	Energy	Goulder (1994)	-
	CO_2	Barker et al. (1993)	+
	CO_2	Karadeloglou (1992)	- st, + lt
	CO_2	Shackleton et al. (1992)	-
	CO_2	Standaert (1992)	-
Reducing business income tax	CO_2	Jorgenson and Wilcoxen (1993)	+
Reducing employers' social contributions	Gasoline	Brinner et al. (1991)	+
	CO_2	Standaert (1992)	-
	CO_2/Energy	Delache (1996)	0/-
	CO_2/Energy	Commission CEE (1994)	+
Reducing employees' social contributions	CO_2	Shackleton et al. (1992)	-
Wage subsidy[b]	CO_2/Energy	Welsch (1995)	+
Increasing public spending	CO_2/Energy	Welsch and Hoster (1995)	-

Notes
a. st = short term, lt = long term.
b. Equivalent to reducing social security contributions from employers and employees.

Some additional remarks:

- In the case without refund of tax revenues, there can be a positive impact in the long term, as in Brinner et al. (1991). The explanation is that, in the long term, additional revenues help reduce the deficit or repay the debt; this in turn lowers interest rates, resulting in more investment. (However, in the short term the impact will be negative.)
- As for the lump sum refund, the macroeconomic impact seems clear: all models come to the same conclusion, a negative impact on the GNP.[5]
- Reducing the VAT rate seems to be a good solution: the impact is zero or positive in all models. Barker (1993) gives another argument for reducing the VAT rather than other taxes. For him, introducing a CO_2 tax brings a high level of uncertainty with it. However, if this indirect tax is offset by the reduction of another indirect tax (for example, in the VAT rate), the uncertainty is smaller than with other solutions.

Overall, even if environmental taxes are not a tool for macroeconomic management, at least potentially adverse macroeconomic consequences can be minimized by choosing the right use for the tax revenues.

11.4 INTERNATIONAL COMPETITION

We already tackled international competition in Chapter 8. However, we did not see how the tax revenues could affect the conditions of competition which have been modified by the unilateral introduction of an environmental tax. We will do that now; for the following analysis, we suppose that there are neither first mover advantage, nor border adjustments.

Examine what happens in an open economy, following the introduction of an environmental tax on a pollutant (P) emitted when a good (X) is produced:

- Because of the tax, the marginal production cost of the polluting firms increases; in addition, many firms will invest in anti-pollution devices. As a result, some firms which did not make a profit will disappear, and others will reduce their production. The production of X decreases.
- However, when tax revenues are refunded, firms get some money back. The tax revenues may be refunded in such a way that the marginal production cost of polluting firms is reduced. This will increase the production of X.

Overall, because of the refund of revenues, X will not decrease as much as it would do without any refund.[6] We can then state that if firms recover tax revenues in a way that reduces their marginal production cost, the tax will have a smaller impact on their production level. This will be the case with a reduction in social security contributions, and with a compensation of polluting sectors. Both measures reduce the marginal cost of polluting firms.

On the other hand, if the refund of tax revenues does not reduce the marginal cost of polluting firms, then the use of revenues will not lessen the reduction in X. This will be the case with the other forms of revenue refund, with which nothing compensates polluting firms for the impact of the environmental tax. For example, if the tax revenues are refunded in a lump sum manner to households, polluting firms get nothing. This will also be the case if the VAT is reduced. The VAT is levied on a destination basis (exports are zero-rated, and imports are taxed at the border), which ensures its neutrality with respect to international trade; therefore, the VAT does not modify the prices of exports. As the VAT is effectively removed from the price of exported goods, exporting firms would not benefit from a reduction in its rate.

Overall, an environmental tax modifies the production costs of polluting firms; as a result, the country reduces its polluting production and specializes in a cleaner production. However, the extent to which this happens depends on the use of revenues: the impact will be smaller with measures that directly reduce production costs of polluting firms than with the other uses of revenues.

Example. Sweden taxes NO_x emissions of large energy production plants. The tax revenues are refunded to the plants according to their energy production; this compensates the plants, at least partially, for the increase in the production cost due to the tax. As a result, border adjustments are not necessary.

11.5 EARMARKING TAX REVENUES AND THE CONFLICT OF OBJECTIVES

The problem of whether or not to earmark tax revenues is linked to a possible conflict of objectives. Earmarking and the conflict of objectives are important issues in the environmental tax debate.

To Earmark or Not to Earmark?

In the case where revenues from the environmental tax pay for additional spending, one solution is to put the revenues into the general fund of the government, and to finance the additional spending with this general fund. Another solution is to earmark the additional revenues for the additional spending. Earmarking means that the revenues can be used only for a certain purpose. Earmarking creates a strict link between the tax revenue and the corresponding spending.[7]

For environmental taxes, Oates (1993) states that 'There seems to be a strong force that leads to the earmarking of such revenues for environmental purposes. This is a force to be resisted!'

Why resist and not earmark revenues? One of the basic rules of budgeting is that revenues should not be earmarked for specific spending. Indeed, nothing guarantees that revenues will correspond to the desired level of spending in a certain area. And even if earmarking is efficient initially, after some time the tax revenues will change, and so will the needs. Therefore, even if today earmarking is a good solution, it may not be so in the future. For example, in France, the earmarking of water tax revenues led to a systematic overinvestment in clean-up facilities, because the tax rates were not adapted to reflect changing investment needs.[8]

Moreover, during the budgeting process earmarking gives a priority to some kinds of spending in comparison to others; as a result, the government loses some of its flexibility (Hansjürgens, 1992). Thus, while today some kinds of spending appear to be a priority, which justifies earmarking, this may not necessarily be the case in the future; but once earmarking is in place, it is not easy to get rid of it in response to changing priorities.

In addition to this lack of flexibility, earmarking causes conflicts of objectives: as revenue and spending are linked, any decision on one has implications for the other, and the situation becomes difficult to manage. For example, revenues from a CO_2 tax may be earmarked for a lump sum transfer to households. As the lump sum transfer is very favourable to the poor, it may become one element of the social policy. In the end, the level of the tax will have to take into account both environmental and social objectives. A reduction in environmental revenues will then be equivalent to a cut in the social budget.

The criticism of this anti-earmarking perspective finds its origin in the public choice theory. According to Buchanan (1963), earmarking revenues allows voters to choose separately the supply of each public good, which increases the efficiency of public choices. With earmarking, the production of public goods reflects voters' preferences. And those who criticize earmarking implicitly suppose that the usual procedure of financing public goods with the general fund works perfectly. But this is far from true.

With general fund financing, decisions about public spending and taxes are made separately. The vote concerns the total budget of the government (Dye and McGuire, 1992). With such a procedure, the opportunity cost of additional spending is not a tax increase (as with earmarking), but rather the reduction of another budgetary expense. By separating spending decisions from financing ones, public choices are not made in an open and efficient manner. Yet, this is exactly what is avoided with earmarking, because earmarking implies a separate choice for each public good produced. With earmarking, citizens are better informed about the cost of public services.

The same happens with environmental taxes. Environmental taxes are more readily accepted when their revenues do not disappear into the general fund, but are earmarked for environmental spending. Indeed, with earmarking, citizens and businesses are sure that the money remains in the chosen area. Note that earmarking is most frequent in countries where governments face the greatest mistrust: in northern European countries, earmarking is uncommon, but in the United States, the revenues from almost all environmental taxes are earmarked (Pearson, 1995).

Another advantage of earmarking is that it may simplify the work of the government. As the revenues from environmental taxes are uncertain, budget management may be simplified, if this uncertainty does not affect the general fund. For example, with a lump sum transfer to households, earmarking completely eliminates any interference with the budget.[9]

Overall, earmarking introduces rigidities and inefficiencies, but allows a clearer reflection of individual preferences, and, hence, a readier acceptance. In practice, earmarking revenues from environmental taxes for environmental spending is common, especially with water charges. Political considerations are always the reason for earmarking (Smith, 1991). However, we may wonder if the easier acceptability is strictly related to earmarking the revenues, and if using the revenues for the environment (without earmarking them) may not be sufficient for a widespread social acceptance. In any case, *if earmarking exists, it should be revised regularly by the government, and if needed, it should be adapted or suppressed.*

The Conflict of Objectives

According to the Tinbergen rule (Tinbergen, 1952), when the government faces multiple objectives, it should have at least one instrument for each objective, otherwise its task is extremely difficult. Moreover, each instrument has to be assigned to the objective it fulfils best.

Like any other instrument, environmental taxes should have only one objective. The natural objective of environmental taxes is reducing pollution. However, besides that, they also raise revenue for the government. This may imply a conflict of objectives.

Indeed, the environmental tax can be managed either by the ministry of the environment, or by the ministry of finance. Yet, in a public choice analysis, the ministry of finance has a tendency to behave as a 'Leviathan' which tries to maximize its tax revenue. Even if it does not maximize the tax revenue, it may want to modify the tax rate in order to get more revenue, to the detriment of environmental considerations. If this is the case, it will impose a different tax rate from the optimal environmental tax, which the ministry of environment would choose by taking environmental considerations into account.[10]

This conflict of objectives will be different, according to whether revenues are earmarked or not:

- If the additional revenues are simply added to the general fund, the tax administration may consider them in the same way as other tax revenues; consequently, it may choose the level of the environmental tax by taking fiscal considerations (and not environmental ones) into account. For example, it may set the level of a CO_2 tax so that the budget deficit is eliminated (fiscal objective), and not so that ecological sustainability is achieved (environmental objective).
- If the additional revenues are earmarked for specific spending, then the conflict will come from the interaction of the tax with the additional spending. For example, if tax revenues are earmarked for social spending (social objective), the tax level may be set in accordance with the financial needs of the social policy, and not with environmental criteria (environmental objective), leading to a conflict of objectives. Even when revenues remain in the area of the environment, the tax level may be set in accordance with the spending needs, and not with environmental costs, causing a possible conflict of interests.

In what follows, we consider the conflict of objectives which exists without earmarking. In fact, this conflict is not of an economic, but of a political nature. Indeed, from an economic point of view, choosing the rate of the environmental tax is a problem of optimal taxation in the presence of externalities. Economists have been able to solve this kind of problem, at least in theory, since the publication of the article by Sandmo (1975). The point is to minimize the excess burden of the whole tax system, taking into account the externalities. In this case, there is only one economic objective, the minimization of the excess burden, given an exogenous level of public spending. The conflict is therefore not economic, but comes from the administrative organization of the government: the division of competencies between separate administrative entities (ministry of finance, ministry of environment).

Sometimes, the conflict of objectives can be diminished by giving the financial responsibility and the environmental responsibility to the same ministry. It can also be lessened with the help of an administrative organization whose task is to reconcile the different interests by coordinating the efforts of the different ministries. Generally, however, the responsibility of the environmental tax will be assigned either to the ministry of finance, or to the ministry of the environment.

For Oates (1993), it is not possible, from an economic point of view, to give preference to one ministry rather than the other. We do not know if the social welfare will be higher if the tax level is chosen by the ministry of finance or by the ministry of the environment. Indeed, it is clear that the tax level chosen by the ministry of finance (the Leviathan which maximizes the tax revenue), will not be optimal from an environmental point of view. Similarly, the tax level chosen by the ministry of the environment (equal to the marginal damage) will not take into account the tax revenues and the interactions with other taxes; therefore it will not be optimal either. As we have two taxes, neither of which is optimal, we do not know which one to choose.

If it is not possible, from an economic standpoint, to give preference to one ministry, *from a policy perspective there is a strong case for placing environmental taxes under the responsibility of the environmental authority* (Oates, 1993). Indeed, environmental taxes are a powerful instrument for environmental protection, and the environmental authority can hardly do without them. On the other hand, the tax authority has a number of other possible tax bases, which are much more productive than environmental taxes. If each instrument has to be assigned to the objective it fulfils best (Tinbergen, 1952), this means that the environmental tax should have an environmental objective, and therefore be assigned to the environmental administration.

Finally, note that environmental taxes are not the only taxes subject to a conflict of objectives. For example, alcohol or tobacco taxes aim both at decreasing the consumption (public health objective), and raising revenues (tax objective). Similarly, personal income tax has three simultaneous objectives: the financing objective (raising revenues), the distributional objective (income tax is one of the main means for the government to correct income inequality), and the macroeconomic stabilization objective (allowing revenues to vary according to the economic situation). These three objectives are not always compatible, yet, if governments have learned to live with the conflict of objectives inherent in traditional taxes, there is no reason why they cannot live with the conflict inherent in environmental taxes.

11.6 OVERALL, HOW TO USE THE TAX REVENUES?

Chapters 9 to 11 have shown the importance of the use of the revenues from environmental taxes. The quantity of pollution emitted depends on it. The distributional, macroeconomic and international impacts cannot be evaluated without knowing what happens to the revenues. Above all, the possibility of adopting and implementing an environmental tax depends on the widespread acceptance of the use of the tax revenues.

The use of the revenues has many ramifications, and no single use has only advantages. Unfortunately, this adds to the overall complexity of environmental taxes. Complexity is a substantial obstacle for the application of an instrument. It can also give rise to mistakes, even to fraud. The implementation of an instrument such as environmental taxes has to be as simple as possible (Barde, 1993). Le Mouël does not contradict this affirmation when he notes that[11]

> This is a time of complexity . . . and with complexity, simplicity is the only possible answer.

Among the possible uses, we have seen that compensating the victims could cause serious efficiency problems, which led us to rule it out. Four basic possibilities remain: the reduction of the deficit or debt, widespread distribution measures, sectorial compensation measures, and environmental policy measures.

Reducing the Deficit and the Debt

Reducing the deficit and/or the debt is possible only for 'small' taxes, which do not raise large revenues. Indeed, if taxes raise large revenues, which are not redistributed, the short-term macroeconomic impact may be very detrimental. This also limits this solution to periods in which the economy is not in recession.

In the long term, this solution allows the government to reduce its debt and therefore to boost growth. However, if the concern is reducing the public debt, the environmental tax may not be the best way to do it. In order to assess it, it will be necessary to compare the overall cost of the environmental tax (including the environmental benefits) to the cost of increasing existing taxes.

From a distributional point of view, a debt reduction favours future generations, but does not compensate the poor nor the polluters for the impact of the environmental tax. There are also political problems with this solution. A conflict may occur between the environmental objective and the debt reduction one. However, the greatest risk is that, after some time, the government may decide to increase spending in order to take advantage of the additional revenues; if this is likely to happen, reducing the deficit is not a feasible solution.

Widespread Distribution Measures

When 'big' taxes are introduced (such as energy or carbon taxes), they raise abundant revenues, which can amount to several percentage points of the GNP. The government must be able to return these abundant revenues into the economy. The following solutions are able to do that: a lump sum transfer, a reduction in taxes, and a reduction in social security contributions.

Lump sum transfer
Compared with reducing other taxes or social contributions, a lump sum transfer has the following advantages:

- A lump sum transfer allows the government to reinject potentially unlimited revenues into the economy.
- This solution is very favourable to the poor, since the lump sum transfer overcompensates for the regressivity of the tax.
- A lump sum transfer is an easy way for the government to refund revenue, because the transfer does not interact with its budget.

A lump sum transfer has the following drawbacks:

- The size of government increases, while it remains constant when other taxes or social security contributions are reduced.
- The reduction in other levies makes a double dividend possible; with a lump sum transfer, there is no double dividend.
- A sizeable lump sum transfer may introduce a conflict between the environmental and the social objectives.
- The lump sum transfer has a negative macroeconomic impact.

It seems that the drawbacks of a lump sum transfer are more important than its advantages. The main advantage, which is the favourable treatment of the poor, can also be attained by reducing other taxes. Now let us examine each tax separately.

Reduction in personal income tax
A reduction in personal income tax benefits those who pay this tax. It can lead to substantial efficiency gains, especially if the highest rates of the tax schedule are lowered. However, a reduction in personal income tax benefits the rich, not the poor. Moreover, as environmental taxes are rather regressive,

compensating for their revenues by reducing the personal income tax implies a transfer from the poor (who pay proportionally more of the environmental tax) to the rich (who get proportionally more of the revenues). A government is supposed to do exactly the opposite. This equity problem can also imply a conflict of objectives, as well as major difficulties related to the acceptability of an environmental tax.

Reduction in business income tax
A reduction in the business income tax only benefits profitable businesses. Firms which are in financial trouble do not profit from this reduction. Therefore, with this solution, some of the least profitable firms may plunge into bankruptcy: they have to pay the environmental tax, but as they are not profitable, they do not get any refund. Another drawback to reducing the business income tax is that it will most likely benefit shareholders, i.e. comparatively high-income people. This does not compensate for the regressivity of the environmental tax.

Reduction in the VAT and in social security contributions
Two solutions remain: reducing the VAT, and reducing social security contributions. Both solutions benefit households and firms simultaneously. In both cases, the expected macroeconomic impact is zero, or slightly positive. In both cases, the administrative cost is close to zero.

The advantages of a reduction in social security contributions are the following:

- While a reduction in the VAT rate does not benefit exporting firms, they benefit from a reduction in their social contributions.
- The contributions of employees and employers can be differentiated.
- Lower social security contributions reduce the cost of labour, hence less unemployment.

Advantages of a reduction in the VAT rate are the following:

- Reducing the VAT benefits all households, while reducing social contributions only benefits workers.
- Like the environmental tax, the VAT is an indirect tax. Replacing an indirect tax with another indirect tax implies less distributional and macroeconomic implications than when an indirect tax replaces social contributions.

Both solutions look appealing. The advantages of reducing the VAT are rather on the distributive side (inclusion of all the population, distributional implications), and the advantages of reducing social contributions are rather on the allocative side (less unemployment, more flexibility, less modification in the comparative advantages). However, in both cases, adverse consequences can be reduced, or even eliminated, with the help of compensatory measures. Thus, exporting firms can be compensated if the VAT is reduced, and non-workers can be compensated if the reduction in social contributions is chosen.

Selective Compensation Measures

A compensation can be necessary to reduce the opposition of the losers, that is, to improve political acceptability. In some cases, all the tax revenues can be refunded to the sector which paid the tax; alternatively, part of the tax revenues can compensate for adverse effects of the tax. When the tax revenues are used for compensation measures, the size of government increases; the macroeconomic effect is somewhat negative.

Increase in social security benefits
An increase in social security benefits may compensate for some of the distributional effects of environmental taxes. It can be directed towards the poor, in order to compensate for the regressive impact of the tax. However, special attention has to be paid to resulting changes in work or consumption behaviour. If the measure is complex, it may imply a high administrative cost.

Compensation of businesses
The compensation of businesses can take different forms. With a compensation proportional to the initial pollution, the effect is similar to that of a grandfathered emission-permits scheme. A compensation related to sales is possible, if the pollution emitted is not directly linked to sales. If a reduction in unemployment is to be sought, a compensation proportional to the number of employees is preferable to a compensation proportional to the payroll. The compensation of some economic sectors improves the rate of acceptability, especially for businesses which are exposed to international competition.

Environmental Policy Measures

When the government uses the tax revenues to finance environmental policy measures, the size of government increases. Despite this fact, this solution is often considered favourably. A tax lower than the Pigouvian can be optimal, if its revenues are used to reduce the pollution in the same area as the tax (see Chapter 5). The advantage is a lower tax, hence a better acceptability.

However, an increase in the size of government may not be welcomed by some groups.

With an optimal Pigouvian tax, spending in the area of the environment can be justified, if it accelerates technological progress. The point is not to use all the tax revenues in this area, but rather to use part of the revenues as accompanying measures. These measures may be favourable to future generations, to the extent that fewer pollutants will accumulate in the environment. If emission reductions can be obtained with technological progress, it will be less necessary to tackle the sensitive issue of demand reduction.

NOTES

1. Brennan and Buchanan (1980).
2. For this reason, the optimal tax system today is not the same as it was 20 years ago (Slemrod, 1990).
3. The other two are economic efficiency and distributional equity.
4. For example, with an ecological tax reform, the tax revenues will vary according to the income-elasticity of each tax. The point is then to know if the income-elasticity of environmental taxes is higher or lower than that of the taxes they replace.
5. Except one, which finds a slightly positive impact in the short term.
6. Overall, X cannot increase, because even if polluting firms recover all the tax dollars they paid, their production cost will still be higher.
7. The literature on environmental taxes often mistakes earmarking for using tax revenues. Earmarking (in French: *affectation*; in German: *Zweckbindung*) comes from the link existing between revenue and expenditure, independent of the use of the revenues.
8. (Pearson, 1995). One exception can also be found in France, where the revenue from traffic fines is earmarked for road safety expenditures. If motorists drive poorly, the government will have more money for this purpose. This is one of the rare examples where tax revenues and financing needs evolve together.
9. However, uncertainty does not disappear, it is only transferred to other groups in the economy: with a lump sum transfer, households will not know how much they are going to receive, and with a spending increase, the beneficiaries will not have a guaranteed payment.
10. With an elastic demand for the polluting product (elasticity < -1) there will be little tax revenue and a great improvement in the environment, while with an inelastic demand ($-1 <$ elasticity < 0) it will be the contrary. The conflict of objectives is all the greater as demand is more elastic. With a high price elasticity, if the revenue objective is more important than the environmental one, there will be a tendency to reduce the rate of the tax below the optimal rate so as to guarantee a certain level of tax revenue. The opposite will be true if the price elasticity is low (Hansjürgens, 1992).
11. (1991). Our translation.

Conclusion

The introduction of this book opened with the idea that, in a market economy, in order for production and consumption decisions to take the environmental impact into account, the prices of goods and services sold had to reflect this environmental impact. We asked ourselves in which way environmental taxes made this possible, what were the implied problems, and how it was possible to solve them. In addition to these questions, we were somewhat surprised by the fact that, despite the unanimously recognized advantages of economic instruments and particularly of environmental taxes, regulatory instruments were still predominant in almost all countries.

At the end of this book, it becomes apparent that the unusual character of environmental taxes is due to the fact that they are a relatively complex instrument. Not only have their technical, economic, scientific and legal aspects to be mastered, but they force governments to compromise constantly with the divergent interests of environmental protection, public finance, and political feasibility. In addition, comprehensive practical experience with them is lacking, because they have not been widely applied until recently. Finally, environmental taxes compete with less complex, more traditional environmental protection instruments.

There is no general recipe or formula for environmental taxes. In each case, the situation has to be analysed thoroughly, taking into account the pollutant under consideration, the economic and environmental impact, the groups in the economy affected, the potential opposition, the regulatory and institutional framework, the cultural factors, etc. Because of this complexity, simple solutions have to be preferred, even if they are not always the most efficient ones. Complex solutions are difficult to implement, and they seldom pass the test of political feasibility. In the implementation of environmental protection instruments, some pragmatism is necessary.

As we saw, complexity characterizes the tax itself. Above all, the objective of the environmental tax has to be clearly specified. It can be one of the following:

- economic efficiency through the internalization of external costs (the textbook Pigouvian tax);

- the achievement of a certain environmental quality objective in a cost-effective manner (the charges and standards approach of Baumol and Oates);
- a shift of production and consumption towards less environmentally damaging goods, when neither a charges and standards approach, nor a Pigouvian tax, are feasible (product charges, taxes on complements and substitutes, equipment taxes, differential taxes);
- the financing of emission reduction activities according to the polluter-pays principle (the user charge), or the financing of incentives for proper disposal (deposit-refund system);
- the levying of tax revenues on potentially damaging goods and activities (revenue-raising environmental taxes).

Most environmental taxes simultaneously improve the environmental quality, raise revenues, and affect production and consumption decisions. However, from an implementation perspective, it is necessary to specify what the main objective of the tax is, in order to define its characteristics, calculate its rate, and compare it to the appropriate alternatives. If the objective is environmental, the tax has to be compared to other environmental protection instruments; if the objective is fiscal, it has to be compared to other taxes. Recall that a unique instrument, such as the tax, is ill-adapted to multiple objectives.

Nowadays, in practice, the most frequent environmental taxes are user charges and product charges; the charges and standards approach is increasingly prevalent; in addition, revenue-raising environmental taxes (like energy taxes) have existed for a long time. However, Pigouvian taxes are rare. Indeed, if they reflect the ideal of economic efficiency, their implementation raises many problems. Numerous technical difficulties, the limits of monetary valuation methods, as well as sustainable development considerations, generally require the adoption of another approach.

Unlike Pigouvian taxes, where an optimal price is set and then the quantity produced is adjusted, with a charges and standards approach a physical quantity is chosen, and then the price (that is, the tax) is set. In this perspective, passing from a Pigouvian tax approach to a charges and standards approach is not a superficial change, but a reversal of logic. While Pigouvian taxes aim to reach an economic optimum, the charges and standards approach aims to achieve an ecological objective. A charges and standards approach is often more feasible than a Pigouvian tax for pollution problems. It is also more appropriate than a Pigouvian tax when ecological constraints, which are an essential factor of sustainable development, are involved. Furthermore, the choice of a particular tax is by no means only technical. While with Pigouvian taxes the optimal quality of the environment is defined by the market (through the consumers' willingness to pay for the environment), with a charges and standards approach, the desired quality of the environment reflects a democratic choice. Not everybody wishes to relegate environmental protection to the market.

Projects of environmental taxes usually face serious acceptability problems. Because of these problems, all existing taxes are compromises between economic efficiency and acceptability. The first issue is the fact that many people, especially ecologists and leftists, do not really trust market mechanisms to solve environmental problems. Such aspects as putting a price on things which were not previously priced, or the reference to an optimal level of pollution, may be detrimental to the acceptance of a tax project. However, the care taken in the preparation and presentation of the project, as well as the introduction of equity considerations, partly address these concerns and improve the probability of acceptance.

In a democracy, the acceptability issue depends on the main players in the process: voters, politicians, civil servants, and interest groups. In a direct democracy, citizens decide the outcome of an environmental tax project; if they vote for the tax, they will have to pay it once it is implemented. In a direct democracy, in order for individuals motivated by self-interest to vote for an environmental tax, it may be necessary to refund them the tax revenues. In a representative democracy, the tax revenues also represent a significant opportunity, for politicians (who otherwise would be reluctant to propose new taxes), as well as for the administration (which is interested in exercising control over the environmental instruments).

In any case, when environmental taxes are introduced, industries are the losers. Indeed, with the tax, they must bear not only the cost of reducing their emissions, but also the tax payment for the remaining emissions. Also, in an increasingly competitive environment, they often cannot afford to pay the tax when their foreign competitors do not. Moreover, businesses are generally opposed to an increase in the size of government, as can result from some environmental taxes. However, much will depend on the use of the tax revenues. Thus, if the revenues are reinjected into the economy through a reduction in other taxes, the size of government does not increase, and firms get back, at least partly, what they have paid; this may also reduce their concerns about a decline in competitiveness.

When trying to implement a tax, the use of the tax revenues has to be studied carefully. Although it is generally considered as a secondary point, a contested use of the tax revenues is often the single most important reason for the rejection of a tax project. When the main objective of the tax is environmental, revenues are rather a source of embarrassment, because they add to the complexity of the tax instrument. The tax also competes with other instruments (regulations, 'grandfathered' emission permits), which do not raise revenues.

On the other hand, tax revenues provide significant opportunities, for example, to correct the negative impact of the tax on equity, to reduce the macroeconomic impact, or to improve acceptability. For efficiency reasons, these aspects should not be corrected through a modification of the tax itself, but rather through an appropriate use of the tax revenues. However, although the tax revenues seem to provide new spending possibilities, these should not become another objective of the tax, or a potentially damaging conflict of objectives appears: the environmental tax can easily be represented as just another tax increase, which makes it extremely difficult to get it adopted in the face of strong opposition.

We have seen that the optimal level of pollution can be reached with a tax set at a low level (much lower than the Pigouvian level), combined with the earmarking of the tax revenue for emission reduction spending. For polluters, the financial impact of this combination is equivalent to that of other instruments (such as grandfathered emission permits, or a tax, the revenues of which are refunded to polluters). This combination leads to the same pollution level as the usual Pigouvian tax, but yields a readier acceptability.

When the tax is set at a level high enough to bring about significant emission reductions, for example at the Pigouvian level, as a rule the revenues should not be earmarked for environmental spending. (Part of the tax revenues may, however, finance complementary environmental policy measures aimed at accelerating technological progress.) One possibility is to use the revenues to compensate the most affected groups in the economy, as is the principle of the Swedish NO_x tax; the refund of the tax revenues to polluters makes the tax instrument acceptable, and does not impair its efficiency. A second acceptable possibility is to refund the tax revenues to the population in a lump sum manner by means of the ecobonus, as is the principle of the Swiss heating oil and VOC taxes; the ecobonus is a simple solution that redistributes income to the poor; however, it is only feasible for 'small' taxes, because it increases the size of government, and may reduce the GNP. A third solution is to use the revenues to reduce the deficit or the debt; however, given the existence of these additional revenues, in the end politicians may prefer to increase spending instead of reducing the deficit.

The last possibility is to use the revenues from environmental taxes to reduce other taxes, that is, to implement an ecological tax reform. For various reasons, an ecological tax reform is the most attractive solution. The size of government does not increase; because of the double dividend (which is a supplementary efficiency gain), it is the most efficient solution; and in some cases, additional advantages can be expected, such as a reduction in unemployment or even higher GNP. When implementing such a reform, it will be necessary to be careful about fiscal issues, such as equity or the stability of revenues. In any case, an ecological tax reform cannot be implemented without a social consensus. For this reason, the possibility of implementing such a reform largely depends on society's perception of the severity of the environmental problem.

There are now approximately one hundred environmental taxes and charges in OECD countries. By solving theoretical problems and experimenting with various types of instruments, substantial progress has been made over the past thirty years. However, we are still a long way from a market system where prices truly reflect the scarcity of environmental goods. In order to get there, the search for efficient and feasible solutions, and the experimentation with new instruments, have to continue. When not enough knowledge is available, it is always possible to introduce a tax at a low level, so as to create incentive mechanisms, and to gather more information about the environmental policy process and the various economic and social responses to the tax. Later, the tax may be adjusted, after increased knowledge and enough experience with the instrument have been gained.

For environmental taxes, the challenges over the next years will be mainly in two areas. The first is the widespread introduction of carbon taxes. Building a consensus on this matter is a formidable task, because, in addition to the theoretical and practical problems that every environmental tax faces, winners and losers have very unequal weights. In contrast to well-defined, organized and powerful losers, the winners of carbon taxes are mainly future generations, which are not yet in existence. Another challenge posed to environmental taxes is in the area of waste management. Here, the challenge will be to implement innovative policies that provide a more direct linkage between production and consumption decisions, and the unavoidable waste production that results from these decisions.

Considerations about the choice, the design, and the implementation of the appropriate instrument are complex, but this complexity should not conceal the underlying, fundamental question of the objective of the environmental policy. Minimizing the cost of a given environmental policy is one objective; achieving economic efficiency through an optimal environmental policy is another; and achieving sustainability is yet another. From the perspective of a wider application of environmental taxes, it will increasingly be necessary to have a concrete and accepted definition of sustainable development. This definition will reflect society's values. With a precisely defined and widely accepted sustainability objective, the debate over the choice and implementation of the appropriate instrument can be constructive. In the end, the choice of an environmental policy is a choice about values.

References

Assouline, M., D. Brécard and P. Zagamé (1994), 'Politique fiscale de l'environnement, emploi et croissance, les conditions d'un double bénéfice'. *Symposium international: Modèles de développement soutenable. Des approches exclusives ou complémentaires de la soutenabilité?* Paris: Université Panthéon-Sorbonne.

Atkinson, A.B. and J.E. Stiglitz (1980), *Lectures on Public Economics*, London, Singapore: McGraw-Hill.

Ayres, R.U. and A.V. Kneese (1969), 'Production, consumption, and externalities', *American Economic Review* **59** (3), 282–97.

Baranzini, A. (1996), 'Second-best Environmental Policy and Nonconvexities. The Asymmetry between Taxes and Tradable Permits', *Cahiers du Département d'économie politique* 96.01, University of Geneva.

Barde, J.-P. (1992), *Economie et politique de l'environnement*, 2nd ed., Paris: Presses Universitaires de France.

Barde, J.-P. (1993), 'Quel instrument choisir, face à un problème d'environnement?', *Actes du colloque Environnement Economie*. Paris: INSEE.

Barde, J.-P. and J. Opschoor (1994), 'Environnement: Du bâton à la carotte', *L'observateur de l'OCDE* **186**, Février–Mars.

Barde, J.-P. and J. Owens (1996), 'L'évolution des écotaxes', *L'Observateur de l'OCDE* **198**, Février–Mars.

Barker, T. (1993), 'The carbon tax: Economic and policy issues', in C. Carraro and D. Siniscalco (eds), *The European Carbon Tax. An Economic Assessment*, Dordrecht: Kluwer Academic Publishers.

Barker, T., S. Baylis and P. Madsen (1993), 'A UK carbon/energy tax: The macroeconomic effects', *Energy Policy* **21** (3).

Baron, R. (1989), *Psychology. The Essential Science*, Boston: Allyn and Bacon.

Baumol, W.J. and W.E. Oates (1972), 'The use of standards and prices for protection of the environment', *Swedish Journal of Economics* **73**, 42–54.

Baumol, W.J. and W.E. Oates (1988), *The Theory of Environmental Policy*, Cambridge: Cambridge University Press.

Binswanger, M. (1993), 'Gibt es eine Entkopplung des Wirtschaftswachstums von Naturverbrauch und Umweltbelastungen? Daten zu ökologischen Auswirkungen wirtschaftlicher Aktivitäten in der Schweiz von 1970 bis 1990', *Diskussionsbeiträge* Nr. 12. Institut für Wirtschaft und Oekologie, Hochschule St. Gallen.

Bird, R.M. (1976), *Charging for Public Services. A New Look at an Old Idea*, Toronto: Association canadienne d'études fiscales.

Bovenberg, A. and H. Goulder (1996), 'Optimal environmental taxation in the presence of other taxes: General-equilibrium analyses', *American Economic Review* **86**, 985–1000.

Bovenberg, A. and R. de Mooij (1994), 'Environmental levies and distortionary taxation', *American Economic Review* **94** (4).

Bovenberg, A. and F. Van der Ploeg (1992), 'Environmental policy, public finance and the labour market in a second-best world', *Centre for Economic Policy Research Discussion Paper* 745, London.

Boyce, J. (1994), 'Inequality as a cause of environmental degradation', *Ecological Economics* **11**, 169–78.

Bregha, F. and J. Moffet (1995), 'The tax for fuel conservation in Ontario', in R. Gale, S. Barg and A. Gillies, *Green Budget Reform. An International Casebook of Leading Practices*, London: Earthscan Publications.

Brennan, G. and J. Buchanan (1980), *The Power to Tax. Analytical Foundations of a Fiscal Constitution*, Cambridge: Cambridge University Press.

Brinner, R., M. Shelby, J. Yanchar, A. Cristofaro (1991), 'Optimizing tax strategies to reduce greenhouse gases without curtailing growth', *The Energy Journal* **12** (4), 1–14.

Brown, G. and R. Johnson (1984), 'Pollution control by effluent charges. It works in the Federal Republic of Germany, why not in the U.S.', *Natural Resources Journal*, October, 929–66.

Bruce, N. (1998), *Public Finance and the American Economy*, Reading MA: Addison-Wesley.

Buchanan, J. (1962), 'Politics, policy and the Pigouvian margins', *Economica* **29**, February, 17–28. Reprinted in R.J. Staaf and F.X. Tannian (1970), *Externalities. Theoretical Dimensions of Political Economy*. New York: Dunellen.

Buchanan, J. (1963), 'The economics of earmarked taxes', *Journal of Political Economy* **71**, 457–69.

Buchanan, J. (1969), 'External diseconomies, corrective taxes, and market structure', *American Economic Review* **59** (March), 174–77.

Buchanan, J. and G. Tullock (1975), 'Polluters' profits and political response: direct controls versus taxes', *American Economic Review* **65**, 139–47.

Bürgenmeier, B. (1991), *Les principes de l'action publique face à la protection de l'environnement*, Séminaire C.E.A.T., Genève.

Bürgenmeier, B. (1994), *La Socio-économie*, Paris: Economica.

Bürgenmeier, B. (1994b), 'The environment: A social or an economic good? The role of values in economic theory and policy recommendations', *Cahiers du Département d'économie politique* 94.13, University of Geneva.

Bürgenmeier, B., Y Harayama, N. Wallart (1997), *Théorie et pratique des taxes environnementales*, Paris: Economica.

Burniaux J., J.P. Martin, G. Nicoletti and J. Oliveira Martins (1991), 'The costs of policies to reduce global emissions of CO_2: Initial simulation results with Green', *OECD Working Papers* no 103, Paris: OECD.

Bütschi, D. and H. Kriesi (1994), 'Dispositions des Suisses à l'égard d'une politique des transports respectueuse de l'environnement', Working Paper (Université de Genève), présenté au congrès de l'Association Suisse de Science Politique, Balstahl.

Carraro, C. and D. Siniscalco (1994), 'Environmental policy reconsidered: the role of technological innovation', *European Economic Review* **38** (April), Papers and Proceedings, 545–54.

Casler, S. and A. Rafiqui (1993), 'Evaluating fuel tax equity: direct and indirect distributional effects', *National Tax Journal* **46** (2), 197–205.

Chichilnisky, G. and G. Heal (1995), 'Markets for tradeable CO_2 emission quotas: principles and practice', *OECD Working Papers* no 153. Paris: OECD.

Cline, W.R. (1992), *The Economics of Global Warming*, Washington: Institute for International Economics.

Coase, R. (1960), 'The problem of social cost', *Journal of Law and Economics* **3**, 1–44.

Coase, R. (1988), *The Firm, the Market and the Law*, Chicago: The University of Chicago Press.

Commission des Communautés européennes (1994), 'Rapport économique annuel pour 1994', *Economie Européenne* **56**.

Crandall, R.W. (1983), *Controlling Industrial Pollution. The Economics and Politics of Clean Air*, Washington DC: The Brooking Institution.

Cropper, M.L. and W.E. Oates (1992), 'Environmental economics: a survey', *Journal of Economic Litterature* **30** (June), 675–740.

De Melo, J., J.-M. Grether and A. Bocquel (1997), 'Commerce, environnement et relations Nord-Sud', in B. Bürgenmeier, Y Harayama, N. Wallart, *Théorie et pratique des taxes environnementales,* Paris: Economica, 237–70.

Delache, X. (1996), 'Implementing ecotaxes in France: some issues', in *Environmental Taxes and Charges. National Experiences and Plans.* Luxembourg: Office for Official Publications of the European Communities.

Delache, X. and S. Gastaldo (1992), 'Les instruments des politiques d'environnement', *Economie et statistique*, **258–9** (Octobre–Novembre), 27–41.

Deutsches Institut für Wirtschaftsforschung (1994), *Wirtschaftliche Auswirkungen einer ökologischen Steuerreform*, Hamburg: Greenpeace.

Diekmann, A. and P. Preisendörfer (1991), 'Umweltbewusstsein, ökonomische Anreize und Umweltverhalten', *Schweizerische Zeitschrift für Soziologie* **17** (2), 207–31.

Direction de la prévision (1991), 'Effets macroéconomiques à moyen terme d'une hausse de la fiscalité sur l'énergie fossile', *Note du Bureau de la politique économique* no. 126.

Dye, R.F. and T.J. McGuire (1992), 'The effect of earmarked revenues on the level and composition of expenditures', *Public Finance Quarterly* **20** (4), 543–55.

Edmonds J. and D. W. Barns (1990), *Factors Affecting the Long-Term Cost of Global Fossil Fuel CO_2 Emissions Reduction*, Washington: Pacific Northwest Laboratory (mimeographed, December).

Erdmann, G. (1993), 'Evolutionary economics as an approach to environmental problems', in H. Giersch (ed.), *Economic Progress and Environmental Concerns*, Berlin: Springer Verlag.

European Foundation for the Improvement of Living and Working Conditions (1996), *Environmental Taxes and Charges. National Experiences and Plans*, Luxembourg: Office for Official Publications of the European Communities.

Factor 10 Club (1994), *Carnoules Declaration*, Friedrich Schmidt-Bleek, Wuppertal Institute.

Faucheux, S. and J.-F. Noël (1995), *Economie des ressources naturelles et de l'environnement*, Paris: Armand Colin.

Faucheux, S., G. Froger and J.-F. Noël (1995), 'What forms of rationality for sustainable development?', *The Journal of Socio-Economics* **24** (1), 169–209.

Flückiger, Y. and J. Silber (1995), 'Income inequality decomposition by income source and the breakdown of inequality differences between two population subgroups', *Swiss Journal of Economics and Statistics* **131** (4/1), 599–615.

Flückiger, Y. and J. Suarez-Cordero (1995), 'Analyse économique des différentes propositions de réforme du financement des assurances sociales', Rapport no. 2 de l'observatoire universitaire de l'emploi, *Publications du LEA no. 7*, Université de Genève.

Freeman III, A.M. (1993), *The Measurement of Environmental and Resource Values. Theory and Methods*, Washington DC: Resources for the Future.

Frey, B. S. (1986), 'Economists favour the price system – Who else does?', *Kyklos* **39** (4), 537–63.

Frey, B. S. (1992), 'Pricing and regulation affect environmental ethics', *Environmental and Resource Economics* **2**, 399–414.

Frey, B.S. and F. Schneider (1996), 'Warum wird die Umweltökonomik kaum angewendet?', Arbeitspapier 9617, Linz: Johannes Kepler Universität.

Fullerton, D. (1996), 'Why have separate environmental taxes?', *Tax Policy and the Economy* **10**, 33–70.

Fullerton, D. and C. Kinnaman (1996), 'Household responses to pricing garbage by the bag', *American Economic Review* **86**, 971–84.

Fullerton, D. and D. Rogers (1993), *Who Bears the Lifetime Tax Burden?* Washington: The Brookings Institution.

Galbraith, J.K. (1975), *Economics and the Public Purpose*, Harmondsworth: Penguin.

Gale, R., S. Barg and A. Gillies (1995), *Green Budget Reform. An International Casebook of Leading Practices*, London: Earthscan Publications.

Golub, A. and E. Strukova (1994), 'Application of a pollution fee system in Russia', in G. Klaassen and F. Forsund, *Economic Instruments for Air Pollution Control*, Dordrecht: Kluwer Academic Publishers.

Goodin, R.E. (1994), 'Selling environmental indulgences', *Kyklos* **47** (4), 573–96.

Goulder, L.H. (1994), 'Energy taxes: Traditional efficiency effects and environmental implications', *Tax Policy and the Economy* **8**, 105–58.

Goulder, L.H. (1995), 'Environmental taxation and the double dividend: A reader's guide', *International Tax and Public Finance* **2**, 157–83.

Gowdy, J.M. and P.R. Olsen (1994), 'Further problems with neoclassical environmental economics', *Environmental Ethics* **16** (Summer), 161–71.

Grosclaude, P. and N. Soguel (1992), 'Coûts externes du trafic routier: Evaluation en milieu urbain', *Revue suisse d'Economie politique et de statistique* **128** (3), 453–69.

Grossman, G.M. and E. Helpman (1991), *Innovation and Growth*, Cambridge: MIT Press.

Hahn, R.W. (1989), 'Economic prescriptions for environmental problems: How the patient followed the doctor's orders', *Journal of Economic Perspectives* **3** (2), 95–114.

Hansjürgens, Bernd (1992), *Umweltabgaben im Steuersystem: Zu den Möglichkeiten einer Einfügung von Umweltabgaben in das Steuer- und Abgabensystem der Bundesrepublik Deutschland*, Schriften zur öffentlichen Verwaltung und öffentlichen Wirtschaft 140. Baden-Baden: Nomos Verlagsgesellschaft.

Harayama, Y. (1994), 'Taxes écologiques et substitution technologique', *Cahiers du Département d'économie politique* 94.14, Université de Genève.

Herber, B. (1983), *Modern Public Finance*, Homewood Illinois: Irwin.

Hueting, R. (1991), 'Correcting national income for environmental losses: Toward a practical solution for theoretical dilemma', in R. Costanza (ed.), *Ecological Economics. The Science and Management of Sustainability*, New York: Columbia University Press.

International Energy Agency (1993), *Taxing Energy. Why and how?* Paris: OCDE.

Jacquard, A. (1991), *Voici le temps du monde fini*, Paris: Seuil.

Jonas, H. (1990), *Le principe responsabilité. Une éthique pour la civilisation technologique*, Paris: Editions du Cerf.

Jorgenson, D. and P. Wilcoxen (1993), 'Reducing US carbon emissions: An econometric general equilibrium assessment', *Resource and Energy Economics* **15** (1).

Jorgenson, D., D. Sleswick, P Wilcoxen (1992), 'Carbon taxes and economic welfare', *Brookings Papers on Economic Activity, Microeconomics* 393–431.

Karadeloglou, P. (1992), 'Energy tax vs carbon tax: A quantitative macroeconomic analysis with the Hermes-Midas models', *European Economy*, Special edn. no 1, Bruxelles.

Katz, M.L. and C. Shapiro (1994), 'Systems competition and network effects', *Journal of Economic Perspectives* **8** (2), 93–115.

Kelman, S. (1981), *What Price Incentives? Economists and the Environment*, Boston: Auburn House Publishing Company.

Kirchgässner, G. and M. Savioz (1995), 'Einheitsrente und Finanzierung über eine Energiesteuer: Mögliche Wege zur Reform der AHV', *Aussenwirtschaft* **4**, 519–42.

Kirman, A.P. (1992), 'Whom or what does the representative individual represent?', *Journal of Economic Perspectives* **6** (2), 117–36.

Le Cacheux, J. (1996), 'Les expériences de réforme fiscale dans les pays de l'OCDE', *Cahiers français* **274** (Janvier–Février).

Le Moigne, J.-L. and M. Orillard (1994), 'Nearly uncontrollable pollution of an agrarian system: A socioeconomic case study', in B. Bürgenmeier (ed.), *Economy, Environment, and Technology*, Armonk, NY: M.E. Sharpe.

Le Mouël, J. (1991), *Critique de l'efficacité*, Paris: Seuil.

Lewis, A. (1982), *The Psychology of Taxation*, Oxford: Martin Robertson.

Maibach, M., R. Iten and S. Mauch (1992), 'Internalisieren der externen Kosten des Verkehrs. Fallbeispiel Agglomeration Zuerich', *Revue suisse d'économie politique et de statistique* **128** (3), 471–93.

Manne, A. and Richels R. (1990), 'CO_2 emission limits: an economic cost analysis for the USA', *The Energy Journal* **11** (2), 51–74.

Manzini, A. (1992), 'La taille du secteur public', in L. Weber (ed.), *Les finances publiques d'un Etat fédératif, la Suisse*. Paris: Economica.

Manzini, A. and M. Zarin-Nejadan (1991), 'The causal relationship between government expenditure and revenue: the case of Switzerland', *Cahiers du Département d'économie politique* 91.03, University of Geneva.

Markandya, A. (1991), 'The value of the environment: A state of the art survey', Paper presented at the International Conference 'Economy and Environment in the 90s', Neuchâtel, 26–27 August 1991.

Marshall, (1890), *Principles of Economics*, 8th edn 1920, London: Macmillan, 1961.

Mattei, A. (1994), 'Estimation de fonctions de demande désagrégées en utilisant les données des budgets des ménages', *Cahiers de recherches économiques* 94.17, Département d'économétrie et d'économie politique, Université de Lausanne.

Meadows et al. (1972), *The Limits to Growth*, Report to the Club of Rome.

Meier, R. (1993), *Umweltgerechte Verkehrsabgaben, Vorschläge für eine Neuorientierung*, Chur/Zürich: Rüegger.

Meier, R. and Walter F. (1991), *Umweltabgaben für die Schweiz*, Chur/Zürich: Rüegger.

Milliman, S. and R. Prince (1989), 'Firm incentives to promote technological change in pollution control', *Journal of Environmental Economics and Management* **17**, 247–65.

Motta, M. and J.-F. Thisse (1994), 'Does environmental dumping lead to delocation?', *European Economic Review* **38** (3/4), Papers and Proceedings, 563–576.

Mottu, E. (1994), *La progressivité des impôts. Théorie et appplications aux impôts directs et à la TVA en Suisse*, Thèse 404 de la Faculté des Sciences économiques et sociales. Université de Genève.

Neuenschwander, R., H. Sommer, S. Suter, and F. Walter (1992), 'Externe Kosten des Agglomerationsverkehrs und Internalisierung', *Revue suisse d'Economie politique et de Statistique* **128** (3), 437–51.

Nicoletti, G. and J. Oliveira-Martins (1993), 'Global effects of the European carbon tax', *The European Carbon Tax. An Economic Assessment*, Dordrecht: Kluwer Academic Publishers.

Nordhaus W.D. (1990), 'An intertemporal general-equilibrium model of economic growth and climate change', in D.O. Wood and Y. Kaya (eds), *Proceedings of the Workshop on Economic/Energy/Environmental Modeling for Climate Policy Analysis*, October 22-23, Cambridge MA: MIT Center for Energy Policy Analysis, 415-33.

Oates, W.E. (1985), 'The environment and the economy: environmental policy at the crossroads', in J. Quigley and D. Rubinfeld (eds), *American Domestic Priorities. An Economic Appraisal*, Berkeley: University of California Press, 311-45.

Oates, W.E. (1990), 'Economics, economists, and environmental policy', *Eastern Economic Journal* **16** (4), 289-96.

Oates, W.E. (1993), 'Pollution charges as a source of public revenues', in H. Giersch (ed.), *Economic Progress and Environmental Concerns*, Berlin: Springer-Verlag.

OCDE (1991), *Politique de l'environnement. Comment appliquer les instruments économiques*, Paris: OCDE.

OCDE (1993), *La fiscalité et l'environnement. Des politiques complémentaires*, Paris: OCDE.

OECD (1989), *Economic Instruments for Environmental Protection*, Paris: OECD.

OECD (1994), *The Distributive Effects of Economic Instruments for Environmental Policy*, Paris: OECD.

Office of Technology Assessment (1994), *Preparing for an Uncertain Climate*, Washington: American Congress.

Olivecrona, C. (1995), 'The nitrogen oxide charge on energy production in Sweden', in R. Gale, S. Barg and A. Gillies, *Green Budget Reform. An International Casebook of Leading Practices*, London: Earthscan Publications, 163-72.

Ossewaarde, M., A. de Savornin Lohman and T. van der Burg (1992), 'L'utilisation de redevances pour la réduction des émissions de gaz à effet de serre: la conception de la redevance', in *Le changement climatique. Concevoir un système pratique de taxe*, Paris, OCDE.

Palmer, A. et al. (1980), *Economic implications of regulating chlorofluorocarbon emissions from nonaerosol applications,* Report R–2524–EPA, Santa Monica CA: Rand Corporation.

Pareto, V. (1896), *Cours d'économie politique*. New edn by G.-H. Bousquet and G. Busino, 1964, Genève: Librairie Droz.

Passet, R. (1979), *L'économique et le vivant*, Paris: Payot.

Passet, R. (1994), 'Le développement durable: D'une remise en cause à l'émergence de la responsabilité intergénérationnelle', *Symposium international: Modèles de développement soutenable. Des approches exclusives ou complémentaires de la soutenabilité?*, 16–18 mars 1994, Paris: AFCET / Université Panthéon-Sorbonne.

Pearce, D. (1988), 'Optimal prices for sustainable development', in D. Collard, D. Pearce, and D. Ulph (eds), *Economics, Growth and Sustainable Environments*. London: Macmillan Press.

Pearce, D. (1991), 'The role of carbon taxes in adjusting to global warming', *The Economic Journal* 101 (July), 938–48.

Pearce, D., A. Markandya and E. Barbier (1989), *Blueprint for a Green Economy*, London: Earthscan Publications.

Pearson, M. (1992), 'Taxe sur le carbone et justice sociale', in *Le changement climatique, concevoir un système pratique de taxe*, Paris: OCDE.

Pearson, M. (1995), 'The political economy of implementing environmental taxes', in L. Bovenberg and S. Cnossen (eds), *Public Economics and the Environment in an Imperfect World*, Boston: Kluwer Academic Publishers.

Pigou, A.C. (1918), *The Economics of Welfare*, London: Macmillan.

Poterba, J. (1991), 'Tax policy to combat global warming: On Designing a Carbon tax' in R. Dornbusch and J. Poterba (eds), *Global Warming. Economic Policy Responses*, Cambridge: MIT Press.

Poterba, J., J Rotemberg and L. Summers (1986), 'A tax-based test for nominal rigidities', *American Economic Review* (September), 659–75.

Potier, M. (1995), 'Quand la Chine fait payer la pollution', *L'observateur de l'OCDE* 192 (Février–Mars), 18–22.

Potier, M. (1996), 'Intégrer l'environnement et l'économie', *L'observateur de l'OCDE* 198 (Février–Mars), 6–10.

Proost, S. and D. Van Regemorter (1995), 'Testing the double dividend hypothesis for a carbon tax in a small open economy', *Public Economics Research Paper* no. 41, Katholieke Universiteit Leuven.

Rosen, H.S. (1992), *Public Finance*, 3rd edn, Homewood/Boston: Irwin.

Sandmo, A. (1975), 'Optimal taxation in the presence of externalities', *Swedish Journal of Economics*, 86–98.

Schmidheiny, S. and Business Council for Sustainable Development (1992), *Changer de cap. Réconcilier le développement de l'entreprise et la protection de l'environnement*, Paris: Dunod.

Shackleton, R., M. Shelby, A. Cristofaro, R. Brinner, J. Yanchar, L. Goulder, D. Jorgenson, P. Wilcoxen and P. Pauly (1992), *The Efficiency Value of Carbon Tax Revenues*, Energy Policy Branch, U.S. Environmental Protection Agency, Stanford energy modeling forum, Report 12.

Slemrod, J. (1990), 'Optimal taxation and optimal tax systems', *Journal of Economic Perspectives* **4** (1), 157–78.

Smith, S. (1991), 'Environmental taxes from the perspective of public finance: possibilies and conflicts with other objectives', *Bulletin de Documentation*, November–December.

Smith, S. (1992), 'Taxation and the environment: a survey', *Fiscal Studies* **13** (4), 21–57.

Solsbery, L. and P. Wiederkehr (1995), 'Energie: actions volontaires contre le CO₂', *L'observateur de l'OCDE* **196** (Octobre–Novembre), 41–45.

Sorensen, P. (1993), 'Pollution taxes and international competitiveness: some selected policy issues', in *Environmental Policies and Industrial Competitiveness*, OECD Documents, Paris: OECD.

Stähelin-Witt, E. (1991), 'Konflikte und Widerstaende', in R.L.Frey et al., *Mit Oekonomie zur Oekologie*, Basel: Helbling und Lichtenhahn.

Standaert, S. (1992), 'The macro-sectoral effects of an EC wide energy tax: simulation experiments for 1993–2005', *European Economy*, Special edn no. 1, Bruxelles.

Statistique globale suisse de l'énergie (1993), Tirage à part, *Bulletin ASE/UCS* **12** (Juin 1994).

Stephan, G., R. Van Nieuwkoop and T. Wiedmer (1992), 'Social incidence and economic costs of carbon limits', *Environmental and Resource Economics* **2**, 569–91.

Stiglitz, J.E. (1988), *Economics of the Public Sector*, 2nd edn, New York: Norton.

Stritt, M.-A. (1997), *Politique environnementale et efficacité économique. Pour l'introduction de certificats négociables en Suisse*, Neuchâtel: Institut de recherches économiques et régionales.

Thogersen, J. (1994), 'Recycling consumer waste: a behavioral science approach to environmental protection policy', in B. Bürgenmeier (ed.), *Economy, Environment, and Technology, a Socio-economic Approach*, New York: M.E. Sharpe.

Tinbergen, J. (1952), *On the Theory of Economic Policy*, Amsterdam: North Holland.

Tirole, J. (1988), *The Theory of Industrial Organization*, Cambridge: MIT Press.

Tobey, J. (1993), 'The impact of domestic environmental policy on international trade', in H. Giersch (ed.), *Economic Progress and Environmental Concerns*, Berlin: Springer-Verlag.

Tuddenham, M. (1995), 'The system of water charges in France', in R. Gale, S. Barg and A. Gillies, *Green Budget Reform. An International Casebook of Leading Practices,* 200–219, London: Earthscan Publications.

Turner, K. (ed.) (1993), *Sustainable Environmental Economics and Management. Principles and Practice*, London/New York: Belhaven Press.

Umwelt- und Prognose-Institut Heidelberg (1988), Oekosteuern als marktwirtschaftliches Instrument im Umweltschutz, *UPI-Bericht* Nr. 9, Heidelberg: UPI.

Van den Doel, H. and B. Van Velthoven (1993), *Democracy and Welfare Economics*, 2nd edn, Cambridge: Cambridge University Press.

Vickrey, W.S. (1972), 'Economic efficiency and pricing', in S. Mushkin (ed.), *Public Prices for Public Products*, Washington: The Urban Institute.

Victor, P.A. (1991), 'Indicators of sustainable development: Some lessons from capital theory', *Ecological Economics* **4** (3), 191–213.

Vivien, F.-D. (1994), *Economie et écologie*, Paris: La Découverte, Collection Repères.

Von Weizsäcker, E.U., J Jesinghaus, P. Mauch and R. Iten (1992), *Oekologische Steuerreform. Europäische Ebene und Fallbeispiel Schweiz*, Chur/Zürich: Rüegger.

Vos, H. (1993), 'L'utilisation des recettes des taxes environnementales', *Actes du Colloque Environnement Economie*. Paris: INSEE.

Wallart, N. (1997), 'Cars and environment in Switzerland: what kind of taxes?', in C. Jeanrenaud (ed.), *Environmental Policy between Regulation and Market*, Basel: Birkhäuser, 69–102.

Wallart, N. and B. Bürgenmeier (1996), 'L'acceptabilité des taxes incitatives en Suisse', *Revue suisse d'Economie politique et de Statistique* **132** (1), 3–30.

WCED (1987), *Our Common Future*, Oxford: Oxford University Press.

Weber, L. (1988), 'De l'intérêt d'un recours accru aux prix publics', *Revue française de finances publiques* **23**, 185–205.

Weber, L. (1991), *L'Etat, acteur économique*, 2nd edn., Paris: Economica.

Weder, R. (1995), 'Lenkungsabgaben und internationale Wettbewerbsfähigkeit: Handels- und standorttheoretische Ueberlegungen', Working Paper, Universität Basel.

Weitzman, M.L. (1974), 'Prices vs quantities', *Review of Economic Studies* **41** (Oct.), 477–91.

Welsch, H. (1995), *Joint vs- Unilateral Carbon/Energy Taxation in a Two-region General Equilibrium model for the European Community*, Working Paper, University of Köln.

Welsch, H. and F. Hoster (1995), 'A general-equilibrium analysis of European carbon/energy taxation: Model structure and macroeconomic results', *Zeitschrift für Wirtschafts- und Sozialwissenschaften*.

Whalley, J. and R. Wigle (1992), 'The international incidence of carbon taxes', in R. Dornbush and J. Poterba (eds), *Global Warming. Economic Policy Responses*, Cambridge: MIT Press.

Wijkander, H. (1985), 'Correcting externalities through taxes on/ subsidies to related goods', *Journal of Public Economics* **28**, 111–25.

Witherspoon, S. (1995), 'Deep fears and free riders: public knowledge, attitudes and behaviour relevant to carbon use and the greenhouse effect in advanced industrial economies', Paper presented at conference: CO_2 – *A challenge for mankind*, Interlaken, 20–21 April 1995.

Wolf, C. (1988), *Markets or Governments. Choosing between Imperfect Alternatives*, Cambridge: MIT Press.

World Bank (1992), 'Development and environment', *World Development Report 1992*. Washington: World Bank.

Zerbe, R.O. and D.D. Dively (1994), *Benefit–Cost Analysis in Theory and Practice*, New York: Harper Collins.

Index

abatement costs 20, 25–33, 35–8, 40, 49–50, 81–3, 124, 126
abatement technology 29, 49, 143, 151–2
acceptability of environmental taxes
  industry opposition to 122–33
  opposition, categories of 93–107
  voting for 109–22
administration (bureaucracy), influence on environmental protection 120–21
administrative cost of environmental taxes 79, 173–4
administrative fees 45
air quality 12, 13, 17, 84, 100, 105, 145
airport noise tax 55
altruism 15–16, 18
American Clean Air Act 100
anthopocentric tradition 96
arbitration 128
asbestos 18
assimilative capacity of environment 69
asymmetric information 22
auctioned emission permits 31, 40, 125, 126, 145
automobile taxation 39, 75, 87, 95, 110–18
  see also gasoline taxes; motorists, taxation

backstop technologies 62
Baumol, W.J. 2, 57–8, 67, 158, 190
benefit principle of equity 160
beverage containers, deposit-refund systems 2, 85
biodiversity 68
border adjustments 131
Brundtland Report 60
bureaucracy
  administrative cost of environmental taxes 79, 173–4
  influence on environmental taxes 120–21

Bürgenmeier, B. 96, 98
business
  compensation of 36–8, 142–4, 187
  cycle, stabilization of 175–6
  income tax 149–50, 159, 161, 176

capital
  impact of environmental taxes on 168–9
  non-substitutability of 64
  owners of 160–61
  substitutability of 62, 67, 68
carbon tax see CO_2 taxes
Carnoules Declaration 71
charges and standards approach
  approach to sustainable development 66–71
  criticism of sustainable development in terms of 60–66
  rationale of 2, 30, 57–60, 101–2
chemical products, user charges on 80
chlorofluorocarbons (CFCs) 18
classification of environmental taxes 45–6
'clean' investments, subsidizing of 146–7
Club of Rome ('Our Common Future') 60
CO_2 emissions 67, 70–71, 84, 146
CO_2 taxes
  existing 59–60, 149
  projected 119, 128, 131, 137, 146, 151–2, 162, 173, 193
Coase, R. 11–12, 16–18, 19, 104
Coase theorem 16–18, 19
combined instruments 31, 38–9, 68, 101–2
command-and-control approach to environmental policy 1, 18–19, 25–8, 38–9

compensation measures
  of business 36–8, 142–4, 187
  lump sum transfers (ecobonus) 86,
    115–17, 140–41, 157, 159, 172,
    176, 178, 185, 192
  of polluters 33–4, 126, 128, 132,
    162–4, 187, 192
competition, impact of environmental
  taxes on 123, 129–32, 133, 178–9,
  191
complexity of environmental problems
  63
concentration limits 18
conflicts of interest, link with
  earmarking of tax revenues 181–3,
  186, 192
consultation with industry 128
consumers, producers and government,
  redistribution of income between
  164–5
consumption spending and taxes 100,
  157, 172
  see also VAT, reduction in
contingent valuation methods 52–3
cost-covering charges (user charges) 45,
  76–84, 190
costs, internalization of external *see*
  external costs, internalization of
covenants (voluntary agreements) 21–2,
  35–8, 40
critical load 65–6
cultural considerations in formulation of
  environmental protection
  instruments 104–6

deep ecologists 96
democratic decision making
  in a direct democracy 58, 107, 109,
    110–18, 120, 133, 191
  in a representative democracy 58, 107,
    119–22, 191
demographic change 68
deposit-refund systems 2, 85
design of environmental protection
  instruments, implications of 99–
  104, 128
direct majority voting 58, 107, 109, 110–
  18, 120, 133, 191
direct taxation (user charges) on
  polluting emissions 81–3

dirty industries, migration of 130, 131,
  145
disposal and recycling taxes 80
distributional impact of environmental
    taxes
  business, compensation of 36–8,
    142–4, 187
  distribution of income *see*
    redistribution of income
  environmental policy measures 187–8
  income tax, reduction of 149–50, 157,
    159, 160, 161, 176
  lump sum transfers 86, 115–17,
    140–41, 157, 159, 172, 176, 178,
    185, 192
  social security benefits, increase in 147,
    187
  social security contributions, reduction
    in 138, 150, 157, 159, 161, 176,
    185, 186–7
  VAT, reduction in 148, 150, 151, 157,
    159, 176, 186–7
  see also ecological tax reform
distributive impact of emission permits
  31, 32–3, 34–5
dose-response valuation method 52
double dividend 147, 152–4, 185

earmarking of tax revenues 81, 179–83,
  192
ecobonus (lump sum transfers) 86,
  115–17, 140–41, 157, 159, 172,
  176, 178, 185, 192
ecocentrism 96
ecological constraints 66–71
ecological economics approach to
  sustainability 65–6
ecological tax reform
  to dematerialize economy 71
  existing taxes, interaction with 152,
    192–3
  goods and services, reduction of taxes
    on 148–9
  income tax, reduction of 149–50, 157,
    159, 160, 161, 176
  size of government, relation to 171–3,
    185, 187, 191
  social security contributions, reduction
    in 138, 150, 157, 159, 161, 176,
    185, 186–7

stability of tax revenues within 151–2
  in Sweden 131
  unemployment, projected impact on
    153–4
ecologists 3, 95, 120, 123, 191
economic activity
  aim of 174–5
  macroeconomic impact of
    environmental taxes on 176–8,
    185, 192
  stabilization of 175–6
economic approach to environmental
  problems *see* environmental
  problems
economic instruments, as tools of
  environmental policy
  compared to command-and-control
    approach 25–8
  emission permits 1–2, 19–20, 29–35,
    37–8, 40, 93, 99, 104, 105, 106,
    119, 176
  negotiation, business and government
    21–2
  property rights 11–12, 17, 19
  subsidies 21, 28–9, 48–9, 75–6, 85–6,
    119, 172
education, role in acceptance of taxation
  94, 95, 104
emission measurement technology 173
emission permits 1–2, 19–20, 37–8, 93,
  99, 104, 105, 119, 176
  auctioned 31, 40, 125, 126, 145
  comparison with taxes as tool of
    environmental protection 29–35
  grandfathered 31, 37, 83, 106, 125–6,
    132–3, 142, 192
emission targets 59–60, 71
employment, creation of 144
  see also unemployment
energy
  consumption 11, 22–3, 76, 147
  production 144, 162, 179
  tax 67, 71, 87, 88, 100, 128, 132, 152,
    173, 185
environment
  assimilative capacity of 69
  awareness of 103–4
  Department (ministry) of 181, 182
  ownership of 97–8
  as a public good 12–14, 17, 39–40, 78

valuation of 51–3, 64–5, 97–100, 191
environmental problems
  alternative instruments 22–3
  command-and-control approach to 1,
    18–19, 25–8, 38–9
  economic instruments approach to *see*
    economic instruments as tools of
    environmental policy
  externalities theory approach to *see*
    externalities
  private solutions to 15–18
  property rights approach to 11–12, 17,
    19
  public good theory approach to 12–14,
    17, 39–40, 78
environmental protection instruments,
  choice of 127, 189–90, 193
environmental tax burden, shifting of
  to consumers 167
  through lower rewards to production
    factors 168–70
  to other economic sectors 167
environmental tax revenues *see* revenues
  from environmental taxes,
  utilization of
equalization of marginal abatement costs
  36–8
equipment taxes 74–5
equity considerations in design of
  instruments 79, 98, 102–3, 160, 186
ethical opposition to environmental taxes
  96–106
exclusion, impossibility of 12, 13
exemptions from taxes 128
externalities
  contingent valuation 52–3
  environmental problems viewed as
    9–11, 39–40
  internalization of 45–55, 89, 111,
    148–9
  market-based valuation of 51–2
  neoclassical approach to, problems
    with 61–3, 69
  network externalities 10

factors of production, redistribution of
  income between 160–61, 168–70
feebate *see* tax differential 86–7
fertilizers 74
final consumption (final demand) 172

final demand (final consumption) 172
finance, ministry of 181–2
financing of environmental protection
    78–9
firms, environmental costs *see* business;
    industry, opposition to
    environmental taxes
fiscal and environmental objectives,
    conflict of interests 181–3, 186, 192
fossil fuel consumption 67
free riding 12, 13, 17, 38, 120
fuel tax 74, 140

garbage disposal 11, 39, 70, 80–81, 100,
    173
gasoline taxes 39, 55, 74–6, 84, 88, 89,
    103, 111–18, 160, 161
  administrative cost of 173
  unleaded/leaded differentiation 86, 87,
    105
GDP, government spending as a
    percentage of 171–2
generations, equity between 53, 61, 89,
    165–6, 193
global warming 3, 66, 67, 119
globalization *see* international
    competition, impact of
    environmental taxes on
government
  debt, reduction of through
    environmental tax revenues 137,
    138–40, 184–5
  failure 109
  intervention 11, 12, 13, 14, 16, 18, 109
  market view of 95, 97, 98
  redistribution of income between
    government, producers and
    consumers 164–5
  size of 138, 171–3, 185, 187, 191
  see also revenues from environmental
    taxes, utilization of
grandfathered emission permits 31, 37,
    83, 106, 125–6, 132–3, 142, 192
greenhouse gases 146
groundwater pollution 74

hedonic pricing method 51
household waste 11, 39, 70, 80–81, 100,
    173
Hueting, R. 69, 70

imperfect information 17
implementation of environmental taxes,
    obstacles to 2, 3–4
impossibility of exclusion 12–13, 78
income redistribution *see* redistribution
    of income
income tax, reduction of
  business levels 149–50, 159, 161, 176
  personal levels 149, 157, 159, 160,
    176
indirect taxes 148–9, 176, 178
  see also VAT, reduction of
industrial effluents 84
industry, opposition to environmental
    taxes
  alternative instruments, comparative
    acceptability of 124–7
  factors influencing 107, 123–4, 191
  lobbying 120
  reduction of 127–9, 131–2
  see also international competition,
    impact of environmental taxes on
information, role in acceptance of
    taxation 95, 104
interest rate, influence on natural
    resource depletion 63
intergenerational equity 53, 61, 89,
    165–6, 193
internalization of costs *see* external
    costs, internalization of
international competition, impact of
    environmental taxes on 123,
    129–32, 133, 178–9, 191
irreversibilities 62–3, 65, 89, 166

Kelman, S. 95, 97
Kyoto Summit (1997) 76, 119

labour
  costs 143, 144, 160–61
  intensity, impact of environmental
    taxes on 168–9
landfill tax 54–5, 71, 80, 150
left-wing political parties, opposition to
    environmental taxes 95, 191
'license to pollute' 3, 98, 99–100, 101–2
London School approach to
    sustainability 64–5, 66
losers resulting from environmental
    protection measures 32, 106–7, 109,

191, 193
low-income households *see*
    redistribution of income
lump sum refunds (ecobonus) 86,
    115–17, 140–41, 157, 159, 172,
    176, 178, 185, 192

MAC (marginal abatement costs) *see*
    marginal abatement costs
macroeconomic impact of environmental
    taxes 176–8, 185, 192
majority voting, *see* direct majority
    voting
Malthus 60, 65
marginal abatement costs (MAC) 25–8,
    30, 36–8, 49–50, 81–3, 124, 126
marginal damage, assessment of 53–4,
    57, 58
marginal external cost (MEC) *see*
    external costs
market failure 109
market mechanisms, relationship to
    environmental protection 96–106,
    191
marketable emission permits *see*
    emission permits
market-based valuation methods 51–2
migration of dirty industries 130, 131,
    145
Mill, John Stuart 60, 65
models of environmental taxes
    alternative taxes 73–89
    charges and standards approach 2, 30,
        57–71, 101–2
    classification of 45–6
    Pigouvian taxes *see* Pigouvian taxes
moral opposition to environmental taxes
    96–106
moral suasion 23
motivation behind environmental
    protection 98, 103–4
motorists, taxation 95, 110, 116–17, 161
multidimensionality of environmental
    problems 63, 89

natural capital 64
nature, rights of 97–8
negative income tax 141
negotiation
    business and government 21–2

externalities problem, negotiated
    solutions to 16–18
neoclassical approach to sustainability
    61–3, 69
network externalities 10
nitrates 65, 71, 144
noise pollution 39, 55, 84, 100
non-rivalry of consumption 12–13, 78
non-substitutability of capital 64
NO_x emissions 20, 59, 105, 106, 132,
    144, 162, 173, 179

Oates, W.E. 2, 57–8, 67, 158, 183, 190
objectives of environmental taxation
    2–4, 9–23, 189–90
oil, user charges on 80
opponents of environmental taxes
    categories of 93–107
    industry 107, 120, 123–33, 191
optimal level of pollution 46, 58, 101,
    192
ownership of environment 97–8, 99–100
    see also property rights
ozone-depletion 39, 59, 62, 131

paper industry 162
Pearce, D. 69, 70, 153
perfectly differentiated regulation 27
performance standards 18
personal income tax 149, 157, 159, 160,
    176
petrol taxes *see* gasoline taxes
philosophical opposition to
    environmental taxes 96–106
phosphates 65
Pigou, Arthur Cecil 2, 9, 10, 47, 104
Pigouvian taxes
    application of 145, 188, 192
    compared with charges and standards
        approach 58–9, 101–2, 190–91
    complicating factors 53–4
    examples of 54–5, 81, 82–3
    external costs, internalization of 2,
        46–54, 75, 77, 86–7, 88–9
plastic bags, tax on 74
political implications of environmental
    taxation 2, 3, 119–20, 139, 140, 142
polluter-pays principle 77, 78, 79, 190
polluters
    and non-polluters, redistribution of

income between 161–4
refund of revenues to 33–4, 128, 132, 162–4, 187, 192
pollution
  complements to polluting goods, taxes on 75–6
  equipment taxes 74–5
  'licence to pollute' 3, 98, 99–100, 101–2
  private cost of 9–10, 11, 46, 48
  product charges 73–4
  user charges 45, 76–84, 190
  see also emission permits
precautionary principle 64, 89
presumption principle 74
prevention expenses valuation method 52
prices, impact of environmental taxes on 30–31
pricing of pollution 98, 100
  see also valuation of environment
private cost of pollution 9–10, 11, 46, 48
producers, consumers and government, redistribution of income between 164–5
product charges (taxes) 45, 73–4, 100, 190
product information 22–3
production factors, rewards to 160–61, 168–70
progressive taxes 156, 157, 158, 159
property rights 11–12, 17, 19
  see also valuation of environment
public choice approach to environmental taxes *see* voting for environmental taxes
public deficit, reduction of through environmental tax revenues 137, 138–40, 184–5
public finance approach *see* revenues from environmental taxes, utilization of
public good, environment viewed as 12–14, 17, 39–40, 78
public revenues *see* revenues from environmental taxes, utilization of
public services, pricing of 78–9
public spending, use of environmental tax revenues for 137, 140
public transport 76

quantity control through emission permits 30–31

R&D 40, 49–51, 146
  see also technological progress
recycling taxes 80
redistribution of income
  between factors of production 160–61
  between generations 53, 61, 89, 165–6, 193
  between polluters and non-polluters 161–4
  between producers, consumers and government 164–5
  between rich and poor 156–60
reduced rate of environmental taxation 128, 132
refunding of environmental tax revenues *see* revenues from environmental taxes, utilization of
refuse disposal 11, 39, 70, 80–81, 100, 173
regressive taxes 156–7, 158, 159, 185–6, 187
regulations *see* command-and-control approach to environmental policy
relocation of polluting industries 130, 131, 145
representative democracy, voting in 58, 107, 119–22, 191
research and development 40, 49–51, 146
  see also technological progress
revenue-raising environmental taxes 81, 87–8, 148–9, 181–3, 190
revenues from environmental taxes, utilization of
  compensation measures *see* compensation measures
  distributional impact 155–70
  ecological tax reform, initiating of 147–54
  government retention of 112–15, 137, 138–40
  lump sum refunds (ecobonus) 86, 115–17, 140–41, 157, 159, 172, 176, 178, 185, 192
  uses, comparison of 171–88
  utilization for environmental policy measures 144–7

Ricardo 60, 65
shifting of environmental tax burden
166-70
'sin taxes' 101
Smith, Adam 65
SO$_2$ emissions 32, 105-6, 129, 173
social cost of pollution 9-10, 11, 48
social pressure 15-16, 18
social security
  benefits, increase of 142, 187
  contributions 138, 150, 157, 159, 161,
    176, 186-7
socially optimal level of pollution
  69-70, 101, 111, 145
subsidies 21, 28-9, 48-9, 75-6, 85-6,
  119, 172
substitutability of capital 62, 67, 68
sustainable development
  charges and standards approach 59,
    66-71, 88
  constraints on 66-7
  ecological economics approach to 65-6
  London School approach 64-5
  neoclassical approach 61-3

tax
  bases of environmental taxes 45
  collection, administrative cost of 79
  combined with regulations 31, 38-9,
    68, 101-2
  comparison with emission permits as
    tool of environmental protection
    29-35
  comparison with subsidies as tool of
    environmental protection 28-9
  credits 119
  differential 86-7
  exemptions 128
  factors influencing acceptability 93-5,
    128-9, 133, 191-2
  revenues 3, 20, 32-4, 81-3, 191 *see
    also* revenues of environmental
    taxes, utilization of
technological progress 10, 40, 61-2, 67,
  68, 146, 173, 188
  see also R&D
technology-based standards 18
toxic effluents 30

tradable emission permits *see* emission
  permits
traffic congestion 39, 75-6, 84, 102
transaction costs 12, 17
transferable emission permits *see*
  emission permits
transport 11, 75-6
  see also automobile taxation; gasoline
    taxes; motorists, taxation
travel cost valuation method 52

uncertainties 62, 65, 89
unemployment 119, 143, 150, 153-4
uniform regulation, application of 26-7
US Office of Technology Assessment
  ('Preparing for an uncertain
  climate') 84
user charges (user fees) 45, 76-84,
  190
utilization of environmental tax revenues
  see revenues from environmental
  taxes, utilization of

valuation of environment 51-3, 64-5,
  97-8, 100, 191
VAT, reduction in rate of 148, 150, 151,
  157, 159, 176, 178, 186-7
virgin materials tax 71
VOC emissions 105, 141
voluntary agreements (covenants) 21-2,
  35-8, 40
vote-seeking 119
voting for environmental taxes 58,
  109-22, 191
  see also acceptability of
    environmental taxes

waste disposal, household 11, 39, 70,
  80-81, 100, 173
water
  charges 104, 145, 173
  pricing 79, 102-3
  quality 12, 74, 105, 128
  waste water 78, 79, 80, 84, 100
willingness-to-pay 46, 158
  see also valuation of environment
World Commission for Environment and
  Development (WCED) 60